Heroes and Scoundrels

THE HISTORY OF COMMUNICATION

Robert W. McChesney and John C. Nerone, editors

A list of books in the series appears at the end of this book.

Heroes and Scoundrels

The Image of the Journalist
in Popular Culture

**MATTHEW C. EHRLICH
AND JOE SALTZMAN**

UNIVERSITY OF ILLINOIS PRESS
Urbana, Chicago, and Springfield

© 2015 by the Board of Trustees
of the University of Illinois
All rights reserved
Manufactured in the United States of America
1 2 3 4 5 C P 5 4 3 2 1
♾ This book is printed on acid-free paper.

Library of Congress Cataloging-in-Publication Data
Ehrlich, Matthew C., 1962–
Heroes and scoundrels : the image of the journalist in popular
culture / Matthew C. Ehrlich and Joe Saltzman.
pages   cm. — (The history of communication)
Includes bibliographical references and index.
ISBN 978-0-252-03902-7 (hardcover : alk. paper) —
ISBN 978-0-252-08065-4 (pbk. : alk. paper) —
ISBN 978-0-252-09699-0 (e-book)
1. Journalists—Professional ethics—United States. 2. Journalists
in motion pictures. 3. Journalists in literature. 4. Popular
culture—United States—History—20th century. 5. Popular
culture—United States—History—21st century. I. Saltzman, Joe,
1939– II. Title.
PN4888.E8E45   2015
305.9'09704—dc23   2014032680

Contents

Acknowledgments

The authors thank Daniel Nasset, Tad Ringo, and the rest of the staff of the University of Illinois Press, as well as John C. Nerone and Robert W. McChesney, the editors of the History of Communication series. Three anonymous readers offered invaluable suggestions regarding the book, as did A. J. Langguth, Jill R. Hughes, and Barbara Saltzman. Steve Hanson and Sandra Garcia-Myers of the Cinematic Arts Library at the University of Southern California and the staff of the Margaret Herrick Library of the Academy of Motion Picture Arts and Sciences assisted in locating images. Joan Marcus and the Manhattan Theatre Club as well as Kevin Thomas Garcia and the Atlantic Theater Company kindly consented to allowing the use of images from the plays *The Columnist* and *CQ/CX.*

Matthew C. Ehrlich thanks his colleagues and students at the Department of Journalism and the College of Media at the University of Illinois for providing an intellectually vital place to investigate and think over the better part of three decades. He sends love and thanks to Mila Jean Ehrlich and Paul Stephen Ehrlich as well as to the rest of his family, and he continues to cherish the memory of his father, George Ehrlich.

Joe Saltzman thanks Barbara Saltzman for her constant love and support both as a wife and editor for the last half century; A. J. Langguth for his friendship and unwavering belief in the Image of the Journalist in Popular Culture (IJPC) project; and Ted Tajima, the high school journalism teacher who believed in him from the start and is responsible for any success he has had in journalism. He also thanks his students and colleagues at USC Annenberg, especially Dean Ernest J. Wilson III, Bruce Missaggia, Geneva

Overholser, Liz Mitchell, and Michael Parks, for providing support for the IJPC, and, most of all, former dean Geoff Cowan and Marty Kaplan, director of the Norman Lear Center at USC Annenberg, for believing in the IJPC from the start. He is grateful to Michael, Sammy, Sarah, and Jennifer Glimpse Saltzman for their constant reminder of the power of love and the value of family, and to David Saltzman for teaching him the meaning of the joy of life and how the laughter that is always inside us can make even the worst moments of life bearable.

Authors' Note

Heroes and Scoundrels: The Image of the Journalist in Popular Culture is not only a book but also a continually updated website and a DVD set that includes excerpts of movies and television shows that are featured in each chapter.

Any reader can visit the Image of the Journalist in Popular Culture website (http://www.ijpc.org), click on "Heroes and Scoundrels," and find all of the supplementary and updated material for each chapter of the book. The IJPC website also has thousands of articles on the subject as well as the IJPC On-line Database, with more than eighty-five thousand entries involving every aspect of popular culture. In addition, the website includes access to the IJPC Archive, the largest repository of research on the image of the journalist in popular culture, including thirty thousand videos; five thousand hours of audiotapes and MP3 files; and more than eighty-five hundred novels, short stories, and plays.

Those purchasing the book will be able to receive a copy of the specially produced DVD set if they join the IJPC at a reduced membership fee. There will also be an opportunity to communicate with the authors on the website about any questions dealing with the image of the journalist in popular culture.

Those with questions may contact Joe Saltzman at saltzman@usc.edu.

Studying the Journalist's Image

Why study the image of the journalist in popular culture? The main reasons are simple: First, journalism itself is supposed to provide us with the stories and information we need in order to govern ourselves. Second, journalists have been ubiquitous characters in popular culture, and those characters are likely to shape people's impressions of the news media at least as much if not more than the actual press does. Third, popular culture is a powerful tool for thinking about what journalism is and should be.

Journalism is "intrinsically tied to democracy," as the introduction to a journalism studies handbook puts it. It "plays a key role in shaping our identities as citizens, making possible the conversations and deliberations between and among citizens and their representatives [that are] so essential to successful self-governance."[1] At least that is what should happen—journalism as it operates in reality may be another matter. By the second decade of the twenty-first century, proclamations of a crisis in the mainstream press had become routine. Critics declared that journalism was "debauched and deteriorating" to the point of having become a "zombie institution,"[2] buffeted by corporate cutbacks, ethics scandals, charges of bias and co-optation, and steady declines in public trust.[3] Regardless, those critics still pointed to the importance of what the press ought to do in theory, even if it did not always do so in practice. Similarly, pollsters who tracked an increase in negative attitudes toward the news media still found steady public support for journalism's watchdog role.[4] The idea of a free press that was genuinely responsive to the needs of the citizenry remained as potent as ever.

Such ideas about the press, whether positive or negative, are shaped by the image of the journalist in popular culture. Few people ever visit a newsroom or any other place where journalists work to report the news of the day. Their notions of what a journalist is and does are more likely to have come from reading about journalists in novels, short stories, and comic books, and from seeing them in movies, television programs, plays, and cartoons. Social scientists who have studied popular culture's depictions of the professions have indicated that those portrayals influence public perceptions of real-world professionals, adding that they "can have a major effect on the perception of, and the clout of, an institution in society."[5] The roots of today's popular image of the journalist can be found in hundreds of novels and silent films dating back more than a century, when a host of characters emerged: the energetic, opportunistic newshound who would do anything for a scoop; the tough, sarcastic female reporter trying desperately to outdo her male competition; the enthusiastic "cub" who wants more than anything else to be a bylined reporter; the big-city newspaper editor committed to getting the story first at any cost; and the ruthless media tycoon using the power of the press for his or her own selfish ends. Those archetypes carried over with relatively little variation into portrayals of radio and television newspeople and later of cyberjournalists. Such images—at once repellent and romantic, villainous and heroic—hint at a complex, contradictory relationship between the press and the public.

As such, developing an understanding of what those images are and how they got that way is important. A parallel can be drawn with popular depictions of other occupations. Movies and television programs about attorneys depict "bad professionals you wouldn't admire or want as your lawyer" at the same time that they reinforce "the ideas that courts work as institutions and that law in general can be trusted both in its articulation and application."[6] Likewise, portrayals of doctors show them as being "egotistical, materialistic, uncaring, and unethical,"[7] while also showing them to be "courageous" and implying that the current medical system works.[8] Depictions of journalists do the same: individual reporters and editors commit dreadful deeds even as the press is portrayed as essential to the proper functioning of a free society. Those portrayals illuminate what have been called "the legitimation myths of liberal journalism"—that is, "those shared values and ideas about how news works which, alongside many other myth systems, bind us together as citizens in a democracy."[9] In brief, studying the image of the journalist in popular culture is a provocative and entertaining way of generating insight into not only journalism but ourselves as well.

Analyzing Journalism's Popular Image

Having addressed the "why" of analyzing the press's portrayal in popular culture, we turn now to the "how." The news media themselves cover popular treatments of journalism with some regularity, especially when a new movie, television series, or film festival about the press debuts. Such occasions inspire lists of favorite journalism movies,[10] or else they prompt disquisitions on how popular culture highlights the sorry contemporary state of the press as compared with its former lofty status, as was the case with the 2012 premiere of the HBO TV series *The Newsroom*.[11] They also can trigger denunciations from journalists who claim that pop culture presents a false (if not defamatory) picture of the news media.[12]

Such critiques are not unique to modern times, particularly when it comes to movies. As far back as the 1930s, professional journalism organizations were pressuring Hollywood to produce portrayals that were more positive than those seen in the likes of *The Front Page*.[13] In later decades, films were denounced for making it seem as though "the newsroom is a giant nursery seething with infantile beings,"[14] as well as for perpetuating notions that "journalists are hard-drinking, foul-mouthed, dim-witted social misfits concerned only with twisting the truth into scandal and otherwise devoid of conscience, respect for basic human dignity or a healthy fear of God."[15] There also for many years have been journalists who have pointed to Hollywood as being symptomatic of the press's fall from grace. For example, James Fallows contrasted 1930s movies that showed reporters "instinctively siding with the Common Man" with more recent films that portrayed them as being "more loathsome than the lawyers, politicians, or business moguls who are the traditional bad guys in films about the white-collar world."[16] At the same time, many other journalists have said that the movies actually helped inspire them to enter the profession. According to one, journalists "love movies about themselves" in that the films make their "ordinary workday world" seem "so exciting [and] so glamorous."[17]

In this book we aim to provide a deeper and more nuanced analysis of the impact of popular culture's portrayals of the press. It is not that what journalists and critics have written is necessarily wrong; it is that it does not go far enough. We will attempt to map the image of the journalist beyond just movies, contextualize it to take into account the environment from which specific popular depictions emerged, and link it to the broader scholarly field of journalism studies.[18]

To "map" the field is to survey more thoroughly the extraordinary amount of material that popular culture has generated about the journalist. As of 2014,

Joe Saltzman's Image of the Journalist in Popular Culture Online Database listed more than eighty-five thousand items, including films, TV, fiction, radio, cartoons, comics, commercials, songs, and more.[19] Many of those areas have received comparatively little scholarly attention. For example, much has been written about movie depictions of journalism, including our own previous books on that subject.[20] Less has been written about television's representations of the press, although TV reaches more people than movies do and may have more influence on popular perceptions. Even less has been written about radio and other media. It brings to mind the challenge posed many years ago by a professor who had amassed a vast archive of historic World War II news broadcasts: "Here are the materials, where are the scholars?"[21] We will not attempt a comprehensive survey here, and we certainly will not ignore Hollywood movies; as one scholar notes, they have the distinction of "crossing national borders and taste hierarchies" and thus can have an especially broad impact.[22] Nonetheless, we will present a wider-ranging map than previous works typically have offered.[23]

We also will put our analysis into context with the aim of moving beyond surface interpretations. Any pop culture product arises from a particular medium produced in a particular time, place, and fashion for a particular audience. It also arises from a cultural tradition involving long-standing popular tastes, hopes, and fears. For example, the final season of the acclaimed U.S. TV series *The Wire* in 2008 dealt with a big-city newspaper and a reporter who made up stories. The reporter's misdeeds won him a Pulitzer Prize, whereas the conscientious editor who shared his suspicions about the reporter with his bosses was demoted. A surface reading would view that as yet another case of popular culture bashing journalism. A more contextualized reading would take into account *The Wire*'s creator (a former reporter who professed his love for journalism even while he denounced current trends in it), as well as *The Wire*'s overall story arc (which was described as focusing on "the decline of the American empire").[24] It also would take into account decades of novels, plays, and movies that have addressed urban newspapers both lovingly and caustically. Although space does not permit a detailed reading for every work we refer to in this book, we will keep in mind both the specific contexts in which particular works were created and experienced as well as the broader context in which works speak to issues and concerns that journalism has always confronted.

Finally, we will link our analysis to other research areas within journalism studies, which has been broadly defined as "the multidisciplinary study of journalism as an arena of professional practice and a subject focus for intellectual and academic inquiry."[25] The field is multidisciplinary in that it is informed by work in areas including sociology, history, language studies, political science, and cultural studies.[26] In particular, a cultural studies perspective encourages scholars to "think with" media artifacts in order "to size up the shape, character, and direction of society itself,"[27] much as popular culture artifacts "can be read as a culture thinking out loud about itself."[28] Here we aim to use those artifacts to think creatively about journalism as a practice and institution, drawing upon related scholarship in such areas as media sociology, media ethics, political economy, visual communication, and gender and ethnic studies, among other fields. We also will draw upon the work of other scholars who have studied the journalist in popular culture.

When we speak about the image of the "journalist," we refer to anyone who performs the journalist's function: to gather and disseminate news, information, and commentary, regardless of the medium. Our focus will be primarily on American examples from approximately 1890 to the present, but we also will look at non-American examples. In terms of our conceptualization of "popular culture," we refer to fictional depictions of the journalist in a wide range of popular media, as the preceding discussion has suggested—from Clark Kent to Mary Richards, Graham Greene to Danielle Steel, *All the President's Men* to *Anchorman*, *Sesame Street* to *The Girl with the Dragon Tattoo*.

Some scholars have argued that hard-and-fast distinctions should not be drawn between journalism and popular culture; one is integral to the other, and there always has been a hazy line between what constitutes journalism and what constitutes fiction.[29] Still, we accept that there is in fact a distinction separating "imagined happenings in the lives of imagined individuals" from "verifiable happenings in the lives of particular [and real] individuals,"[30] just as we take seriously journalism's "reverence for facts, truth, and reality."[31] At the same time, we recognize that the image of the journalist can become so immersed in legend and distortion that it becomes as filled with fiction as a character in a novel or a film. A key benefit of using popular culture to think about journalism is gaining insight into just those sorts of complexities, such as the tension between journalism's "informative, civic, and rational sides" and its "pleasure-inducing, entertaining, or simply affective ones."[32] Pop culture invites a close examination of "the heroic image of the journalist defending the truth against the many dragons of darkness in the modern world" against the flip side of that image: the journalist as a malicious, mendacious agent of the dragons of darkness themselves.[33]

Evolution of the Popular Image of the Journalist

According to media historian Mitchell Stephens, "news" is an intrinsic part of human affairs and has been around in one form or another for thousands of years.[34] From that vantage point one can find depictions of journalist-like characters dating back to ancient times—characters roughly equal to the gossip columnists or publishers or bearers of ill tidings of later eras.[35] The anonymous messengers in Semitic, Greek, and Roman plays, poems, and myths were in effect reporters in the field who brought back vivid eyewitness accounts of what happened, to whom it happened, where it happened, when it happened, how it happened, and sometimes why it happened. At times they paid the price: In the Sophocles play *Women of Trachis*, from 430 BC, a herald related shocking news to the mad hero, who was believed to be involved in a murder plot. The hero bodily seized the herald and dashed his brains upon a rock.[36] Martial (Marcus Valerius Martialis) used the epigram to report on life in Rome in the late first century after Christ. In "The Newsmonger" he tweaked the news purveyors of the day: "You forge a hundred silly lies and state them as reality. . . . And if you grace my board today, remember 'News' is barred from it."[37] Depictions of such characters continued into the following centuries. Playwright Ben Jonson satirized Elizabethan newsmongers in works such as 1625's *The Staple of News,* which in some ways seemed to foreshadow the concerns of our day about monopolistic newsgathering and distribution systems.[38]

If "news" and those who purvey it have existed for eons, "journalism" is said by such historians as Michael Schudson to be a nineteenth-century invention.[39] The novels of that era were often filled with images of odious journalists.[40] Steadfast Dodge, for example, was created by best-selling novelist James Fenimore Cooper in two 1838 works, *Homeward Bound* and *Home as Found.* Dodge was a vulgar, corrupted journalist without decency, who cared only about himself and believed that anyone or anything said in public or in private was fair game for his columns. The 1832 novel *Westward Ho!* by James K. Paulding presented a withering satire of the ignorant, ill-mannered, and unethical editor of a frontier paper. In *My Wife and I* (1871) and *We and Our Neighbors* (1875), Harriet Beecher Stowe wrote about a corrupt press run for profit without regard for the public welfare. Rebecca Harding Davis's 1874 novel, *John Andross,* told of a "poor devil of a newspaper man." It was said of him that if "there's a shameful story to be told of you, he'll write it and charge you so much a line to keep it out of print; if there's a chance for gross flattery of you, he'll print it first, and send you the bill for it as an advertisement next day."[41] Such negative depictions were not limited to America. In France, Honoré de Balzac wrote in his novel *Lost Illusions* (1843) of spiteful, unprincipled literary journalists who would do anything for money; and in Britain, William Makepeace Thackeray's *The Adventures of Philip* (1862) featured the high-handed owner of a periodical who did not care whom he offended with his bad manners and who toadied to the powerful and influential.

Truly modern journalism came into being in the last decade of the nineteenth century. In James Carey's words, it "began with the birth of national magazines, the development of mass urban newspapers, the creation of primitive forms of electronic communication and the domination of news dissemination by the wire services." Modern popular culture simultaneously came into being with the invention of motion pictures, followed in the new century by the invention of radio. According to Carey, those new media along with the mass print media "cut across the structural divisions in society, drawing their audience irrespective of race, ethnicity, occupation, region or social class. This was the first national and first mass audience—open to all."[42] The roles of the reporter, city editor, and other journalistic occupations were fully established, and they regularly appeared as character types in the new mass popular culture, with more heroic portrayals appearing alongside the villainous ones. It is for those reasons that we will focus our study on 1890 to the present.

Novels, many of them written by present or former journalists, depicted the press as it existed at the turn of the twentieth century and in the decades that immediately followed: the age of yellow journalism followed by the age of tabloid or "jazz" journalism. The common literary themes included young reporters arriving at the newspaper hoping to accumulate life experiences they could convert into their own novels. The reporters then endured a multitude of humiliations on the job, including being maltreated by their editors while their romantic relationships suffered. Other themes showed idealistic journalists gradually being worn down by the hideous conditions of the newsroom.[43]

Those poor conditions, and the callousness of the urban journalism of the time, became the subject of Broadway plays after World War I. Examples included Maurine Watkins's *Chicago* (later adapted into the film *Roxie Hart* and then into a Broadway and Hollywood musical), Louis Weitzenkorn's *Five Star Final,* and 1928's *The Front Page,* written by onetime Chicago newspaper reporters Ben Hecht and Charles MacArthur.[44] Hecht had also dabbled in fiction, including his 1921 novel, *Erik Dorn.*[45] Whereas that book was markedly sour regarding journalism, *The Front Page* was, in the words of the authors, a "Valentine" toward the press,[46] even as it showed reporters and editors lying and hurting innocent people. It crystallized many of the stock characters and themes already established by the novels before it—the tyrannical editor and the young reporter in bitter thrall to him, the ignored love interest, and the thrill of scoops and the depths to which the press would stoop in pursuit of them. It also appeared just as talking motion pictures were starting to be made, and it provided a useful template for them.

Although some newspaper novels won popularity and became best sellers, they never attracted the mass audience that the early newspaper films would draw. The newspaper gave the moviemaker an endless flow of story possibilities in an atmosphere that soon became so familiar to movie audiences that journalists could be thrown into a film without the scriptwriter having to worry about motivation or plot. Journalists appeared in movies from the start of the silent era, but with the coming of sound, their image was magnified and put in noisy motion.[47] They were defined by brashness and cunning as creatures of the city who were comfortable with its fast pace, crowds, and opportunities to get ahead. They often acted more like detectives than journalists, and they embodied the myth of the self-reliant individual who pits nerves and resourcefulness against an unfair society.[48]

The 1930s and 1940s were the heyday of the "screwball" comedy newspaper film as epitomized by the likes of *Libeled Lady*, *Nothing Sacred* (written by Ben Hecht), and *His Girl Friday* (a *Front Page* remake). The screwball comedy *It Happened One Night* was directed by Frank Capra, who would repeatedly return to journalism as a theme for works that grew increasingly (some would argue stridently) populist in their themes.[49] Through Capra and others, the press became a backdrop for more ambitious statements in the movies. Orson Welles's *Citizen Kane* in 1941 used the rise and fall of a William Randolph Hearst–like media mogul as part of a broader meditation on ambition and loss. World War II saw the reporter drafted as part of the war effort, with the war correspondent serving as a patriotic and decidedly non-neutral observer of the fight against the enemy in movies such as *Objective, Burma!* and *The Story of G.I. Joe*.

At the same time that journalists were becoming film regulars, they also were becoming regular characters in the comics and on the radio. Superman debuted in comic books just before World War II, with the Clark Kent and Lois Lane characters being inspired by both true-life models and ones in the movies. Significantly, Clark as the mild-mannered reporter was only a disguise for the superhero—he had to abandon the glasses to become "Superman." Superman in turn became a radio star soon after, and the series

Edward G. Robinson and Ona Munson in a publicity photo for the radio series *Big Town*. On the series, Robinson played an intrepid newspaper editor—a classic image of the "hero" journalist. (Courtesy of Cinematic Arts Library, University of Southern California)

established other regular characters such as editor Perry White and young cub journalist Jimmy Olsen.[50] Other radio programs—mostly forgotten today and featuring titles such as *Flashgun Casey, Hot Copy,* and *Night Beat*—depicted journalists as crime busters or other exciting people. One such series, *Big Town,* starred Edward G. Robinson as a heroic editor. Each episode began with a stirring call to duty: "The power and the freedom of the press is a flaming sword; that it may be a faithful servant of all the people, use it justly. Hold it high. Guard it well!"[51] Meanwhile, the comics introduced other journalist heroes such as Brenda Starr, who debuted in the 1940s and whose professional and romantic adventures (like those of Lois Lane) paralleled what had been seen of female journalists in the movies.[52] A couple of decades later, Stan Lee created Spider-Man, whose non-superhero persona resembled Clark Kent in that he was a seemingly mild-mannered news photographer named Peter Parker who managed to draw the ire of a domineering editor who would not have been out of place in *The Front Page.*[53]

In post–World War II cinema, film noir showed journalists as dogged pursuers of the truth in pictures including 1948's *Call Northside 777* and as unadulterated villains in films like *Ace in the Hole* (aka *The Big Carnival*).

Kirk Douglas as an evil news-hound in *Ace in the Hole*—a classic image of the "scoundrel" journalist. (Courtesy of the Academy of Motion Picture Arts and Sciences)

There were earnestly liberal "message pictures," including 1947's *Gentleman's Agreement,* in which a reporter went undercover to expose anti-Semitism, and there were unabashed celebrations of the power of the press (even as that power was threatened from without and within) in such films as *Park Row* and *Deadline, U.S.A.,* both from 1952. Other movies of the 1950s borrowed character types and sometimes whole plots from the prewar films, including romantic comedies such as *Teacher's Pet* and musicals such as *High Society.*

By the age of Vietnam and Watergate, movies more directly addressed the themes of journalists as enmeshed with political and economic power—for example, a television cameraperson coming face-to-face with the tensions and violence of 1968 Chicago in *Medium Cool,* Woodward and Bernstein uncovering the ill deeds of the Nixon administration in *All the President's Men,* a journalist trying to unravel a trail of political assassinations in *The Parallax View,* and a television anchor articulating the nation's rage in *Network.* In the 1980s movies such as *The Year of Living Dangerously, Salvador, Under Fire,* and *The Killing Fields* showed foreign correspondents becoming enmeshed in Third World conflicts.

Television presented a somewhat sunnier view of the journalist. Two of the most popular U.S. series of the 1970s and 1980s, *The Mary Tyler Moore Show* and *Murphy Brown,* presented contrasting female journalists: one a local television news producer who served as a friend and confidant for others in the newsroom, and the other a nationally known television reporter and anchor who would overcome alcoholism to achieve a precarious balance between her career and her role as a single mother.[54]

Over the years, journalists have popped up in a gamut of other popular media, including poems, video games, romance novels, mystery novels, science fiction, the Internet, youth-oriented stories and programs, and niche fiction targeted at ethnic minority and lesbian and gay audiences.[55] They have appeared as an animated bull-and-bear TV news team satirizing international corporate finance in "Hoofy & Boo's News & Views," as the cartoon mouse editor of *The Rodent's Gazette* in the Geronimo Stilton series of children's books, and as world-renowned photojournalist and professional assassin Scarlet Lake in the "third-person espionage action–role playing game" *Alpha Protocol.*[56] They have been regularly featured in the Bollywood films of India and in the popular culture of other industrialized nations.[57] And they remain familiar characters in the twenty-first century in movies, TV shows, plays, and books that shamelessly hearken back to the themes and characters that were established decades ago, even as journalism is said to have moved out of the modern age of mass media and mass audiences into a new and uncertain postmodern era.[58]

Character Types and Themes

Of course, pop culture's depictions of journalists have differed depending on medium, era, and place—once more, context matters. Fictional journalist characters on American radio, for example, largely disappeared as that medium shifted from mass entertainment to news and music. (On the other hand, such characters have continued to appear on British radio via BBC dramatizations of Evelyn Waugh's novel *Scoop* and other literary works.[59]) Furthermore, works focusing on historical episodes in journalism inevitably address the interests of the eras in which they were produced.

However, certain character types and themes have persisted in popular works addressing journalism, even as they also have responded to shifts in cultural zeitgeists, artistic tastes, and estimations of what will sell. The most common characters that have appeared in movies and television as well as in other media include the following, listed in alphabetical order:[60]

> *Anonymous reporters.* One of the most indelible images of the journalist is that of packs of anonymous reporters, played by nondescript actors, who chase after a story and rudely invade the privacy of others. Anonymous reporter characters date back to the earliest days of movies, but they typically

were more likable in those older depictions because they were given witty lines and asked questions that the audience wanted answered. Starting in the 1970s, the portrayals became more intrusive and obnoxious, especially with television reporters and photojournalists armed with cameras and microphones wielded like weapons. They have contributed to an image of overzealous news media.

Columnists and critics. One of the most popular villains in newspaper movies has been the power-hungry gossip columnist who stops at nothing to get that must-read item, and yet who often still redeems himself or herself a bit by acting human and doing the right thing. Such characters commonly were based on the columnists Walter Winchell, Louella Parsons, and Hedda Hopper. Coldblooded, unscrupulous drama critics have also been regular characters. Others include columnists who offer advice on love and lifestyles and those who comment on political and social affairs. Bloggers frequently are depicted in contemporary popular culture and are shown performing roles similar to those of the columnists and critics of the past.

Cub reporters. The young, inexperienced cub reporter is the one journalist with whom everyone in the audience can identify. He or she knows little about journalism and so can ask all the questions that the audience wants to know. When veteran journalists correct the cub, the audience either laughs with knowing derision or learns something along with the cub.

Editors and producers. These journalists are typically gruff and sharp-tongued but often soft under their bluster. They include not only newspaper editors but also television news directors or executive producers. They scream orders at cubs and veterans alike, regularly fire their star reporter (who always comes back for more), and decide what stories to run and where to place them. Journalism movies often feature at least one major argument between the editor or producer and the reporter.

Investigative reporters. The investigative reporter works tirelessly and heroically to aid the public. Such characters are loyal to their news organizations and, most of all, to their colleagues. They are typically threatened by the bad guys, and they show great courage in putting their lives on the line to get the story in the newspaper or on television. Sometimes they pay the ultimate price, especially when they are secondary characters whose deaths can be avenged by the star reporters.

Newsroom families. In popular culture, journalism wreaks havoc on personal relationships. The only friends most journalists have are the people who work with them, and they form extended families centered on the workplace. The families embody the clichés of what it means to be a journalist in the big city: alone, cynical, hardworking, ready to do anything for the paper or news program, and always ready with a wisecrack to keep up spirits even in the worst of times.

Photojournalists. Many news photographers are depicted as courageous characters who take pictures of indescribable horror and barely escape death to bring back those images to the public. Others—especially newsreel shooters in older movies—will do anything to get an exclusive picture of a hot news story, whether it be lying, cheating, or taking advantage of a friend or loved one. Some even fake the picture using miniature models. At times, the fictional tales of photojournalists are grafted onto footage of actual fires, earthquakes, floods, and other disasters.

Publishers and media owners. Whether they are publishers of big-city newspapers or moguls of new media, these men and women are usually depicted as trying to use the media for their own selfish ends. Although there are occasional exceptions in which they are depicted as benevolent journalists trying to offer a good product at a fair price, more often they are either concerned with economic power—willing to do anything to increase ratings or circulation—or else they lust after political power.

Real-life journalists. Real-life reporters and editors from Walter Winchell to Jimmy Breslin have been thrown into journalism movies and television shows to provide authenticity. In recent decades well-known TV journalists have shown up as background to the action or as commentators on the people in the news who happen to be the stars of the movie. In addition, many real journalists have been portrayed by actors.[61]

Sports journalists. Sports reporters and writers are not much different from their "straight news" counterparts, although their venue makes them unique. There are syndicated sports columnists who will do anything to get an exclusive, including using blackmail and payoffs. But the majority of sportswriters simply go out and do their jobs. Some are heroic in that they ferret out corruption in sports, risking public animosity. Most often they are used as realistic dressing for biographies of sports personalities.

Television journalists. Of all the images of the journalist in popular culture, the television journalist is the one most negatively portrayed time and again. Female TV journalists often have been singled out for derision as being without any brains or news experience. Joining them are the male anchors who are shown as being lost without their teleprompters.

Nonetheless, such depictions are counterbalanced at least in part by tough-minded professionals—reporters, anchors or commentators, producers or news executives—who are constantly at odds with those interested only in ratings and profits.

Veteran male journalists. Grizzled male reporters, editors, and TV anchors often appear, and they frequently are heard lamenting the passing of the good old days. Sometimes they serve to remind others in the newsroom of journalism's noblest principles, and other times they wear down their peers with their bitter cynicism.

War and foreign correspondents. The prototypical journalist hero is the war correspondent. World War II Hollywood films sometimes touched on issues of censorship and distorting the truth, but correspondents were firmly behind the war effort, even if it meant blatant flag-waving. More recent depictions have shown the war correspondent struggling with the difficulties of covering non-Western peoples and conflicts, and sometimes the correspondent has been shown to be engaging in ethically questionable behavior. Still, the portrayal of such reporters as leading glamorous, dangerous, and exciting lives has persisted.

Women journalists. In older pop culture depictions, female journalists sometimes were referred to as "sob sisters." That term summed up the dichotomy of the woman reporter character. She was considered an equal by doing a man's job—a career woman drinking and arguing toe-to-toe with any male in the shop, holding her own against everyone and anything—and yet crying long and hard when the man she loved treated her only like a sister or best pal. Such characters, no matter how tough or independent, were continually urged to give up their careers for marriage, children, and a life at home. Female journalist characters in broadcasting and news media have shown more independence, but the resemblances between the early "sob sisters" and the characters of the late twentieth and early twenty-first centuries are striking.

This book will not discuss in detail all of the character types just listed, but many of them will be related to specific issues within journalism studies—for example, the ways in which the cub reporter, the investigative reporter, and the editor exemplify ongoing debates about professionalism in the newsroom. Also noteworthy are the characteristics that journalists in popular culture regularly demonstrate, regardless of their specific character types. They have a round-the-clock obsession with the news, have no significant personal lives to speak of, and have problematic relationships with "civilians" outside the newsroom.

Heroes, Scoundrels, and Myths

The images of the journalist in popular culture have always embodied the basic notions of what a hero and villain are. The hero reflects a culture's innermost hopes and dreams, and the villain its secret fears and nightmares.[62]

Journalist heroes are often self-made persons, independent spirits, or people who are angry about injustice and unfairness. They are unselfish, honorable with a sense of fair play, self-confident, resourceful, and sometimes too witty for their own good. They display tenacity and enterprise in distinguishing themselves by their achievements, not their boasts. The journalist hero is convinced that the ends—the triumph of right over wrong—always justify any means, no matter what the ethical or moral cost may be.

Journalist scoundrels or villains have no scruples. They are braggarts who are vain and conceited. They are usurpers, abusers, snobs, traitors, sneaks, chiselers, narcissists, and parasites who use the news media to serve their own social, economic, political, or personal ends. They care nothing about the public and repeatedly abuse its trust and patronage. They usurp the public's right to know by using information to extort and destroy.

Through the opposing images of the hero and the scoundrel, popular culture reinforces myths about journalism and its place in our culture. "Myth" is not meant to imply something that is false. Instead it refers to a story that "draws upon archetypal figures and forms to offer exemplary models" for people to live by.[63] That is to say, myth presents morality tales, with pop culture being a powerful venue. For example, genre movies such as Westerns and musicals center on characters who represent opposing values. When the good guy vanquishes the bad guy or the romantic protagonists resolve their differences and become one, prevailing cultural values are reinforced: justice prevails, love conquers all.[64] A key role of myth is to smooth over underlying tensions in a culture so that things remain largely the way they are. Nonetheless, those tensions between contrasting values still exist and never can be eliminated entirely.

The film scholar Robert Ray has illustrated that line of reasoning by pointing to what he calls a pair of "competing myths" in classic Hollywood movies: the "official hero" and the "outlaw hero." Official heroes represent a "belief in collective action, and the objective legal process" that takes precedence over "private notions of right and wrong." In contrast, outlaw heroes represent "self-determination and freedom from entanglements." "Outlaws" refer not strictly to those who break the law but also to such figures from literature and myth as Davy Crockett, Huckleberry Finn, and Holden Caulfield, whose shared "distrust of civilization" and "distrust of politics" contrasts with official characters' respect for social order and adult obligations.[65]

The opposition between official and outlaw characters has many parallels to the opposition between heroes and scoundrels in popular depictions of journalism. Professional journalists' "reverence for facts, truth, and reality" and the heroes who embody those values are similar to "official" heroes' commitment toward "sound reasoning and judgment" in serving the greater good.[66] Alongside that, though, has been a persistent fascination with journalists who have challenged or ignored "official" ideals. They represent an outlaw sensibility through living by their own code of conduct and thumbing their noses at polite society and authority.

A key distinction between their being viewed as heroes or scoundrels is the extent to which journalists are portrayed as serving the public interest. They can lie, cheat, distort, bribe, betray, or violate any ethical code as long as they expose corruption, solve a murder, catch a thief, or save an innocent. Such journalists are heroes. If they use the power of the media for their own personal, political, or financial gain, then no matter what they do, no matter how much they struggle with their consciences or try to do the right thing, evil has won out, and they are scoundrels. Either way, the myth of the press acting as a force for public good is reinforced by heroes serving democracy and scoundrels paying the price for their sins. Popular culture offers visions of what the press could and should be, including that of "journalists as defenders of society's right to know, civic virtue and the underdog."[67] That in turn helps journalists "maintain their cultural authority as spokespeople for events in the public domain."[68]

Yet the portrait is always ambiguous. Myth and popular culture can occasionally highlight problems in a culture and challenge the status quo.[69] Contradictions within the myth of a free press serving democracy—for example, concerns about journalism being slanted, ethically compromised, or controlled by entrenched interests—are frequently and sometimes scathingly exposed.

Plan of Procedure

Richard Ness has noted that the "basic pattern" of popular culture's depictions of journalism has centered on "what truth is being sought or suppressed" and "by whom it is controlled"; conflict is "generated by who knows the truth and who is trying to find out about it."[70] That in turn opens the door to broader ruminations about the nature of truth and the utility of journalism in uncovering it, just as those notions also invite closer thinking about a host of other issues that long have interested and sometimes vexed journalism scholars. Rather than presenting a simple chronology of depictions, this book will take a fresh approach by focusing on six thematic areas. They have been chosen because they correspond to specific fields of inquiry within journalism studies that popular culture is particularly helpful in illuminating.

The first field, *history,* is the focus of chapter 1. Some historians have argued that journalism history too often has served only to celebrate the press rather than providing critical insight into its problems.[71] Pop culture regularly depicts journalism's history through simple, linear, dramatic tales that use the past to speak to the present and that adopt partisan viewpoints on historical issues. Again, it both mythologizes and demythologizes the press, at once celebrating and parodying well-known figures and happenings in journalism's past. Fictional tales also can offer valuable historical evidence in their own right.

Professionalism is the subject of chapter 2. Apart from questioning whether journalists are true professionals (or even should be professionals), scholars have been particularly interested in the role of "objectivity" in journalism and in the practice and philosophy behind journalism ethics.[72] In popular culture, so-called objective reporting is shown to be deeply problematic and is often implicitly equated to a lack of passion and commitment. Still, professional values do have a place as ethical dilemmas are brought to dramatic life and journalists who violate the public trust suffer the consequences of their misdeeds.

Chapter 3 looks at *difference.* Journalists have been criticized for seeing themselves as being different from everyone else—as somehow standing above and beyond the rest of the citizenry.[73] At the same time, the struggles of journalists who are not male, white, or heterosexual have been well documented, as have the difficulties of the mainstream press in covering gender, race, and sexual orientation.[74] In the nineteenth century and through most of the twentieth century, journalism was one of the relatively few professions in which a single, divorced, or widowed woman could find work and married women could earn enough money to take care of themselves and their families. Still, in pop culture, journalism has been portrayed as a particularly difficult career choice for women, who are caught between culture's "gendered" expectations of them as being caring and nurturing and the gendered expectations of journalists as being tough and independent—that is, stereotypically masculine. The difficulties of ethnic minority and LGBT (lesbian, gay, bisexual, transgender) journalists also have been depicted, with some of the most interesting portrayals having been produced by minority and/ or gay or lesbian authors or directors.

Power is the focus of chapter 4. Critics have pointed to the circumstances under which the press may violate the trust of the powerless and also how it can serve as an instrument of those who do hold political or economic power.[75] Many popular culture works graphically depict the damage that the press can inflict on individuals, even if they might finally show journalists trying to do the right thing in the end. The negative effects of state control or censorship of the press are often dramatized, with the implication being that privately owned and commercially subsidized news media are right and just. However, pop culture also shows that corporate pressures stemming from private control can themselves lead to censorship or coercion.

If this whole book ponders journalism's popular image, chapter 5 looks at *image* more specifically by focusing on the depiction of photojournalists and television journalists. Critiques of the press often warn of the dangers of manufactured image and spin, as with political events that are orchestrated for the camera. Still, others have pointed to the power of visual images to evoke empathy and emotion and appeal to the imagination, whereas many professionals and educators argue that photojournalism and TV journalism at their best serve journalism's self-proclaimed devotion to truth and social responsibility.[76] Popular culture dramatizes both perspectives on those journalistic professions: they can either help present a picture of the world as it really is, or they can promote lies and fluff over reality and substance.

Chapter 6 looks at *war*. The coverage of war has been considered one of the most important and challenging tasks for the press.[77] Popular culture shows the journalist serving as either a necessary witness and voice of conscience in reporting on global conflict or a sensation seeker and propagandist. Much as in real life, war correspondents in popular culture must answer the questions of whose side they are on and what personal price they are willing to pay in order to report the truth.

Finally, in our conclusion we examine how popular culture has looked at the future of journalism, which itself has been hotly debated by journalism scholars.[78] Speculative fiction points toward a press that perseveres regardless of what else may occur—useful to keep in mind as the press confronts the many challenges of today and the years to come. That is one more reason why we believe that studying the image of the journalist in popular culture is important work. Pop culture's stories illustrate our expectations and our apprehensions regarding the press and its relationship to democracy. The task for scholars is to listen carefully to what those stories say, help decipher them for others, and remember why they matter.

1

History

A growing scholarly literature has highlighted the important role that popular culture plays in shaping the public's thinking about history. Jerome de Groot observes that history "permeates popular culture" and that novels, movies, television shows, and other popular artifacts offer "powerful models and paradigms" for understanding our shared past.[1] "All history lies to us, but at least historical fiction admits it," de Groot asserts, adding that even though readers understand that fiction takes dramatic license, "they also know that all historical representation is subjective. . . . Historical novels are as legitimate a way of thinking about the past as any kind of 'real' history."[2] Other scholars take strong exception to such arguments. They favor a "disciplined method of gathering historical facts and then testing and cross-checking them for validity and reliability," and they reject what they regard as "the obvious mythmaking of popular history" and its distortions of the historical record.[3]

In this chapter we look at the image of journalism's past that is presented by popular culture. After reviewing how pop culture treats history generally, we will focus on two eras of American press history: the early decades of modern journalism from roughly 1890 to 1940 and the so-called age of high modernism from roughly 1945 to 1980.[4] Popular culture employs scrupulous attention to historical detail alongside wholesale invention in shamelessly exalting figures and events that many conventional journalism histories also have celebrated. As such, it reproduces heroic myths about the press's past. Yet pop culture also has presented a less heroic picture at times by casting a skeptical and even mocking eye toward journalism history and by high-lighting more sordid aspects that the conventional histories have sometimes downplayed or overlooked.

History and Popular Culture

Scholars have often pointed to the affinity between history and popular culture. In 1966 Russel B. Nye argued that "history and literature are assuredly branches of the same tree," adding that one could not completely grasp what nineteenth-century New York City was like without the novels of Stephen Crane and Edith Wharton, or what twentieth-century Chicago was like without the works of Theodore Dreiser and Nelson Algren.[5] The following decade Hayden White asserted that historiography at heart represented "a form of fiction-making"—a product of the literary imagination, albeit one based on recorded fact.[6] From that perspective, history cannot be isolated from a culture's master stories or myths. Historians, including Warren Susman and Richard Slotkin, have examined how popular culture exposes the "tension between the mythic beliefs of a people—their visions, their hopes, their dreams—and the ongoing, dynamic demands of their social life," as Susman put it.[7]

Others have focused on how history has been depicted by a particular medium, such as radio, novels, and television shows.[8] Movies have been an especially popular subject.[9] A common argument in such studies is that it is unfair to judge popular culture by the standards to which professional historians are held. Gary Edgerton writes that rather than viewing the professional and popular versions of history as "diametrically opposed traditions (i.e., one more reliable and true, the other unsophisticated and false)," it is better to see them as "two ends of the same continuum." If professional history is "resolutely scientific and empirical," popular history is "artistic and ceremonial." It brings the past to life and sustains collective memory while providing insight into the politics and values of the eras in which it is created.[10]

However, even those who are sympathetic toward popular culture's renderings of the past concede that depictions necessarily simplify and often over-dramatize historical events, focusing on the actions of a few key individuals at the expense of broader and more complex trends. "Motion pictures cannot present comprehensive, definitive studies, and filmmakers understand the foolishness of even trying to cover a topic's length and breadth," writes Robert Brent Toplin in *Reel History: In Defense of Hollywood*.[11] Filmmakers and others working in popular media also understand the commercial imperative of telling a good story that people will pay to see or read, typically one centered on heroes and villains and often featuring a romantic subplot. They thus do two things that many professional historians seek to avoid: they take partisan stances regarding the past, and they engage in "presentism," using the past as a pretext to comment on current issues.[12]

Other historians argue that anyone who writes about history is necessarily speaking to present-day concerns and that taking a clear stance toward them is far preferable to pretending to be neutral and value-free.[13] That is particularly the case with critical or cultural histories of journalism. They reject the premises of "Whig" or "Progressive" press history, which views "the development of the nation and its press in terms of the triumph of the forces of good—freedom, democracy, equality, libertarianism—over the forces of evil—repression, aristocracy, inequality, authoritarianism."[14] One historian has branded it "the story of how white male reporters and editors on metropolitan dailies have championed truth and justice for the people," a story that has lent itself well to inspirational journalism history textbooks even as it has been widely discredited in recent press historiography.[15] In contrast, critical and cultural approaches view history in terms of "challenge and struggle" and "the contradictory character of progress," particularly relating to race, class, and gender.[16] Such approaches also mine history for artifacts that help show how people lived in a specific era and place, including the artifacts produced by popular culture.

Bonnie Brennen has drawn upon the work of cultural theorist Raymond Williams in analyzing early twentieth-century novels with newsroom settings, taking care to "address the specific cultural, economic, and political conditions of [each novel's] production, along with author's intent, and the response to the work." She argues that the novels provide unique insight into the working conditions of actual rank-and-file journalists of that era.[17] Nonetheless, some remain concerned that pop culture obfuscates historical understanding at least as much as it enlightens it. W. Joseph Campbell argues that movies are "powerful agents of media mythmaking" and perpetuate some of the most cherished—if factually false—fables concerning the press's past.[18]

These competing perspectives on popular culture and history can be related to works depicting journalism. According to Campbell, media-fueled myths are "dubious, fanciful, and apocryphal stories about or by the news media that are often retold and widely believed" and that responsible historians should debunk.[19] However, myth can also be viewed as a sacred story that serves to "represent shared values, confirm core beliefs, [and] deny other beliefs."[20] Both understandings of myth apply to popular culture's stories about journalism's past. "Dubious" stories are perpetuated, and yet they "confirm core beliefs" and "offer exemplary models" regarding the press in a manner that is consistent with Whig or Progressive models of journalism history. Simultaneously, popular culture sometimes portrays those myths in an ambivalent and at times pejorative light, in line with a more critical perspective on history.

Early Modern Journalism and Popular Culture

Popular culture has frequently focused on the first decades of modern journalism, beginning in the late nineteenth century and continuing into the years between the two world wars. Modern journalism emerged with a national system of communication and the establishment of the reporter as a distinct occupational type who roamed the city streets looking for news to peddle to the growing working-class and immigrant populations. The era was marked in part by a model of journalism as entertainment, as exemplified first by the yellow journalism of the turn of the century and later by the tabloid "jazz journalism" of the 1920s and 1930s. There were growing concerns about the pernicious influence of entertainment-driven news on a susceptible, gullible public, even as many journalists and press associations promoted more scientific and "objective" models of reporting and sought to establish respectability for journalism as a profession.[21]

The birth of modern journalism is vividly evoked by the 1952 film *Park Row*, written, directed, and produced by Samuel Fuller. It stars a character named Phineas Mitchell, who founds a paper called the *Globe*. "News makes readers, readers make circulation, and circulation makes advertising," he says. "Advertising means I'd print my newspaper without the support of any political machine!" The *Globe* leads a fund drive for the Statue of Liberty's pedestal, prints the story of Steve Brodie's death-defying jump from the Brooklyn Bridge, and introduces the Linotype typesetting machine via inventor Ottmar Mergenthaler. Phineas accomplishes it all despite fierce opposition from Charity Hackett, the female publisher of the rival *Star*, where Phineas used to work. Even though the two share a mutual lust, Phineas calls Charity a "frustrated journalistic fraud," and her paper (without her knowledge) goes after the *Globe* with goons, one of whom Phineas chases down the street and pummels against a statue of Benjamin Franklin. An older member of Phineas's staff dies amid the mayhem, but not before writing his own obituary addressed to Phineas:

Don't let anyone ever tell you what to print. Don't take advantage of your free press. Use it judiciously for your profession and your country. The press is good or evil according to the character of those who direct it. And the *Globe* is a good newspaper. I have put off dying waiting for a new voice that needs to be heard. You are that new voice, Mr. Mitchell.

Somehow it all ends happily: Charity kills the *Star* and joins forces with Phineas at the *Globe,* and the film concludes with the image of the Statue of Liberty (which, the concluding narration asserts, exists thanks to the help of a newspaper).

Park Row displays the common characteristics of popular history, including a simple, linear story and a romantic subplot, while also embodying the Whig or Progressive vision of journalism history. It is "a heroic narrative of newsmongers and muckrakers, of Davids slaying Goliaths,"[22] of a newly responsible press (supported not by the state or political parties but by free enterprise) promoting life, liberty, and the pursuit of happiness, with contemporary papers implicitly carrying on the noble legacy of Phineas Mitchell. Of course, Phineas never actually existed. Still, Samuel Fuller drew on real-life models in creating a character designed "to combine all the great newspaper editors of the period" (that is, the "white male" editors of "metropolitan dailies" who "championed truth and justice for the people").[23] Likewise, Steve Brodie and Ottmar Mergenthaler were real people, and Joseph Pulitzer's *New York World* actually did help raise funds for the Statue of Liberty. Fuller also insisted on being true to historical detail to the point of building a vintage four-story replica of New York's Park Row street.[24] At heart, though, *Park Row* transforms the origins of modern news into celebratory myth.

Fuller said the film represented his "personal gift to American journalism," fueled by nostalgia for his days as a young tabloid reporter.[25] Other celebratory films were driven by institutional rather than personal interests. *A Dispatch from Reuters* (1940) depicts the nineteenth-century development of the Reuters international wire service with a resounding credo: "A censored press is the tool of a corrupt minority. A free press is the symbol of a free people. For truth is freedom. And without truth, there can be only slavery and degradation!" Paul Julius Reuter passionately believes that access to information should be a universal right, and he seeks to better the world through the quick transmission of news. When he is the first to report in Europe that Abraham Lincoln has been assassinated, no one believes the horrific news. Reuter is labeled a "contemptible liar" who has ruined lives by creating panic in the financial markets. Freedom of the press and Reuter's alleged mistake are furiously debated in the House of Commons until a message from the U.S. Embassy confirms that he has been right all the while. "Mr. Reuter, I offer you the apologies of Her Majesty's government," says the prime minister. "By your reliability and your veracity, you have saved the press from another of those countless attempts to take away its freedom!" Reuter's vindication is matched by an exhilarating musical score to present the ultimate image of the journalist as hero.

A Dispatch from Reuters represented one of Hollywood's responses to lobbying efforts from press associations for depictions of journalism as a champion of democracy rather than a servant to money and sleaze.[26] The press associations had reason to worry—the image of journalism that had been presented in the media up until 1940 often had been less than benevolent.

Many poems and novels had addressed the rise of the new entertainment-driven journalism. Media scholar Howard Good argues that the poems can be read "as a shadow history of the press, written not in the dry, factual style of the monographist, but in dread and despair." Such poets as Walt Whitman, Stephen Crane, and T. S. Eliot saw "snappy stories and big, black headlines" as being "distracting and deadening" and as "turning human suffering into hot copy."[27] Novels that appeared between 1890 and 1930—many of which were written by current or former journalists and marketed to mass audiences—also presented a decidedly ambivalent portrayal of the press. According to Good, the novels are notable for their pessimism about the journalist who lingers too long in the trade: "If he fails to get out, he ages prematurely. His spirit slackens and sickens until he becomes a sad and frightening caricature of his younger self. And when his usefulness is gone, he is tossed onto the scrap heap."[28]

For Bonnie Brennen, the newsroom novels that appeared between the two world wars encapsulated the "intellectual ferment and social turmoil" of that era, including "resistance against the exploitative social relationships found in industrialized capitalist society." The novels revealed a seamy underside of journalism not typically dwelled upon by Progressive histories: the "dirty, crowded, noisy, and confused" working conditions that poorly paid journalists of the day endured.[29] The Depression's first years were especially difficult, as related by onetime tabloid reporter Mildred Gilman in her 1931 novel, *Sob Sister*:

> The jails were filled with men who had stolen to keep themselves and their families from starvation. . . . [But] these stories were played down. The editorial slogan was to keep people encouraged. Boost business, never believe in hard times. . . . Newspapers grew thin and anemic from lack of advertising. City staffs were cut ruthlessly. On the *Courier* one afternoon [editor] Joe Baker

Edward G. Robinson as a tabloid editor trapped in the sleazy world of jazz journalism in *Five Star Final.* (Courtesy of the Academy of Motion Picture Arts and Sciences)

fired twenty men, one after another and the latest [female reporter] sob sister. One of the men had worked for the *Courier* twenty-eight years.[30]

Popular culture also targeted the sensationalism of the tabloid journalism that appeared after World War I.[31] Tabloid editor Emile Gauvreau published a confessional of sorts in his novels *Hot News* and *Scandal Monger,* calling himself the "slave" of an age saturated by "bootleg whisky, insane journalism and jazz."[32] *Hot News* was turned into the film *Scandal for Sale* (1932), which appeared alongside others with titles like *Scandal Sheet* (1931). In the movie short *Hot News Margie* (1931), a female journalist goes undercover to try to expose a scandal involving a star quarterback and dies from an inadvertent injury on the football field. She arrives at heaven's gate, only to be sent to hell by the gatekeeper when he learns she is a tabloid reporter.

Five Star Final, which debuted on Broadway in 1930 before becoming a movie the following year, presented an especially grim portrait. It was written by Louis Weitzenkorn, the onetime managing editor of the *New York Graphic,* which critics branded the "*Pornographic.*"[33] *Five Star Final* tells of a tabloid that dredges up a decades-old scandal concerning a young woman who had murdered her boss after he impregnated her and refused to wed her. Now the woman is married and living a respectable life. The paper stops at nothing to get her story—one reporter illegally breaks into an apartment and another poses as a minister. Their irresponsible, lurid reporting finally drives the woman and her husband to suicide. For the newspaper's guilt-stricken editor, Randall (played by Edward G. Robinson), who has been seen repeatedly washing his hands in an attempt to rid himself of tabloid filth, it is the last straw. He shouts out his resignation, condemning the publisher and his minions as "bloodsucking murderers." Randall's secretary, the conscience of the film, proudly walks out of the office with the editor after he quits. The film concludes with the image of the tabloid being splattered with mud and swept into the gutter.

The portrait of the tabloid press that Weitzenkorn presented in *Five Star Final* contrasts sharply with Samuel Fuller's self-described "love affair" with journalism, which he said was forged via stints on the *Graphic* among other papers.[34] Still, it points to a tension between pronounced scorn and deep affection (if not reverence) toward the press among the journalists who applied their talents to popular culture. That tension can be found at the heart of many popular works about journalism.

For example, in the 1926 Broadway play *Chicago,* a woman named Roxie Hart kills her lover and becomes a household name thanks to a cynical press corps hungry for a hot story. "Here I've just been prayin' for a nice, juicy murder—for two weeks now we haven't had nothin' but machine guns and hijackers," one reporter exclaims.[35] In the end, Roxie literally gets away with murder. The play was written by Maurine Watkins, a former *Chicago Tribune* reporter who had specialized in humorously lurid stories about women who killed their husbands or lovers and who, like Roxie, managed to be acquitted of their crimes. *Chicago* is hardly a positive portrayal of journalism, but it also does not condemn either the reporters or Roxie Hart for their actions. As one critic has noted, the play's humor arises from the fact that "everyone, especially the audience, prefers Roxie's fabricated image and absurd explanation [for her crime] to the hard evidence of her lover's corpse."[36] Although Watkins eventually would distance herself from her play—apparently feeling guilty for making celebrities out of murderers—the play itself turns murder and tabloid journalism into boisterous comedy.[37]

Two years after *Chicago, The Front Page* premiered on Broadway. Like Watkins, playwrights Ben Hecht and Charles MacArthur had both been Chicago newspaper reporters. Hecht already had published his own newspaper novel,

Erik Dorn, which branded the press a "scavenger digging for the disgusts and abnormalities of life" and a "yellow journal of lies, idiocies, filth."[38] When he and MacArthur began writing *The Front Page,* they similarly "had in mind a piece of work which would reflect our intellectual disdain of and superiority to the Newspaper."[39] Their completed play in many ways would do just that. It tells of reporter Hildy Johnson, who desperately seeks to escape journalism and his tyrannical editor, Walter Burns, in order to marry and start a public relations career. "Journalists!" sneers Hildy to his fellow reporters:

> Peeking through keyholes! Running after fire engines like a lot of coach dogs! Waking up people in the middle of the night to ask them what they think of Mussolini. Stealing pictures off old ladies of their daughters that get raped in Oak Park. A lot of lousy, daffy, buttinskis, swelling around with holes in their pants, borrowing nickels from office boys! . . . I've been a newspaperman fifteen years. A cross between a bootlegger and a whore.[40]

That is precisely how the journalists behave. A hapless woman whom the reporters have persecuted in the press exclaims to them, "It's a wonder a bolt of lightning don't come through the ceiling and strike you all dead!"[41] When they continue to harass her, she flings herself out a window. Later, Hildy and his editor hide an escaped convict in a desk for the sake of a scoop. *The Front Page* is even harder on municipal government than it is on journalism. One critic sees the play as an "intellectual assault" on Chicago's then mayor and sheriff, in keeping with the pointed social critique of much of the era's popular culture.[42]

For all that, Hecht and MacArthur saw their play as "a romantic and rather doting tale of our old friends—the reporters of Chicago" and themselves as "two reporters in exile."[43] The play's characters were closely based on real-life Chicago models, giving it a docudrama feel despite its outrageously farcical tone.[44] Hildy also represented an exercise in happy nostalgia for the authors: "the lusty, hoodlumesque half drunken caballero that was the newspaperman of our youth."[45] Even with the press's misdeeds in the play, the journalists triumph in the end, uncovering the mayor and sheriff's evil scheme to execute a man whom the governor has pardoned. As for Hildy's efforts to leave journalism, they appear to be thwarted—at least temporarily—by Walter Burns. Certainly the sympathies of the playwrights seemed to be with Hildy's staying put. In contrast with the gloomy depiction of embittered and maltreated journalists that had appeared in many novels of the time, Hecht would declare that a good reporter of his day "was ashamed of being anything else. He scorned offers of double wages in other fields. . . . He dreamed of dying in harness, a casual figure full of anonymous power; and free." Hecht clung to such an image even though he himself had done everything he could to branch out beyond journalism and avoid dying anonymous or poor.[46]

Similar ambivalence appears in one of popular culture's best-known depictions of the press, *Citizen Kane*. The film relates the life of Charles Foster Kane, a would-be contemporary of the likes of Phineas Mitchell, Joseph Pulitzer, and—most notoriously—William Randolph Hearst. As a child, Kane inherits a fortune; as a young man, he decides "it would be fun to run a newspaper." He publishes a "Declaration of Principles" vowing to "tell all the news honestly" and be a "fighting and tireless champion" of the citizenry. Instead, Kane grows ever more reactionary over the years while seeing two marriages fail and much of his media empire disappear. He dies with only the childhood memory of his sled "Rosebud" to keep him company. *Citizen Kane* has been widely seen as a stealth exposé of Hearst (a view perpetuated by later films such as 1999's *RKO 281*). Still, star, director, and cowriter Orson Welles denied that it was based on Hearst, and in fact the film deviates markedly from many details of the media mogul's life.[47] Moreover, the movie vividly depicts Kane's paper's early crusades against corruption and its successful talent raid (celebrated with a raucous party) against a stuffy rival paper. Likely due in part to its having been cowritten by former journalist Herman Mankiewicz, *Citizen Kane* indeed makes it seem that running a paper would be fun.[48]

Popular culture depictions of modern journalism's early decades have continued to the present while responding to the changing times. *The Front Page* has been turned into four movies to date. *Chicago* also has been remade multiple times, including as a Broadway musical and an Oscar-winning film.[49] Perhaps the most unlikely portrayal of modern journalism's early days is *Newsies,* based on an 1899 newsboys' strike against Pulitzer's *New York World* and Hearst's *New York Journal.* Disney's 1992 movie musical about the event was initially unsuccessful, but it subsequently became a cult favorite via home video, and it then became a popular 2012 Broadway musical. *Newsies* highlights an episode that standard press histories had virtually ignored while paying homage to the children and young adults whose labor in selling papers had helped make modern media empires possible.[50] Far from glorifying the likes of Pulitzer the way *Park Row* had done, *Newsies* makes him a villain. Yet it also "draws heavily upon popular mythology" in depicting the newsboy as "a rugged individualist, plucky [and] competitive," whereas the reality was often less rosy and not nearly so amenable to song or dance.[51] *Newsies* thus presents an ambiguous portrayal of journalism history that is typical of popular culture.[52]

"High Modern" Journalism and Popular Culture

If a journalism-as-entertainment model characterized much of the early modern era, a more serious model focusing on social responsibility and public service became the norm in the post–World War II years. Media scholar Daniel Hallin has called it the age of "high modernism" in journalism, "dominated by a culture of professionalism, centered around the norm of 'objective' reporting and rooted in the conviction that the primary function of [the] press was to serve society by providing citizens with accurate, 'unbiased' information about public affairs." That was fueled by a comparatively strong economy that lessened financial pressures on the press and helped encourage professional autonomy. It also reflected a "high level of ideological consensus" in U.S. society, particularly regarding cold war foreign policy. As such, high modernism seemed to many to represent "the final result of the natural evolution of the news media as a social institution"—that is, the culmination of the Progressive perspective on journalism history.[53] For Hallin the shift from the early modern to the high modern periods could be seen in "the change in the journalist's image in popular culture, from the rowdy, corrupt, politically-entangled ambulance-chasers of *The Front Page* to the altruistic professionals of *All the President's Men*."[54] The underpinnings of high modernism finally began to crack during the Vietnam era and the political and economic upheavals of the 1970s.

Works depicting journalism in the post–World War II age present a mixed portrait. Some honor the altruistic public-spiritedness of the journalist, but other popular works question it, satirize it, or depict the formidable forces arrayed against it at specific historical moments. Once more the works reflect the interests of those who created them and the times in which they were produced.

For example, a movie that came out the same year as *Park Row* showed what eventually might have become of Phineas Mitchell's *Globe*. *Deadline, U.S.A.* (1952) was written and directed by Richard Brooks, a former journalist like Samuel Fuller. In the film Ed Hutcheson (played by Humphrey Bogart) edits the *Day* newspaper, which is about to be sold to a sleazy competitor by the ungrateful heirs of the newspaper's founding patriarch. In an effort to stop the sale and expose murderous gangland activity in the city, Hutcheson launches a campaign against a mobster named Rienzi. The campaign succeeds against the mobster, but it fails to save the paper—the final image is of the illuminated "Day" sign at the top of the newspaper building going dark for good.

In many ways *Deadline, U.S.A.* exemplifies the high modern moment in journalism. The staff practices scrupulously neutral reporting, at least at first. "It's not our job to prove [Rienzi is] guilty," Hutcheson says early in the film. "We're not detectives and we're not in the crusading business." It is only after Rienzi's thugs assault a *Day* reporter and the newspaper itself faces extinction that the *Day* goes on the offensive. Hutcheson extols professionalism, saying that journalism is "a performance for public good" and that it "may not be the oldest profession, but it's the best." He also derides the rival paper that seeks to buy the *Day* only to kill it, saying that the rival emphasizes "comics, contests, puzzles" at the expense of real news. When Rienzi phones Hutcheson to try to intimidate him into killing the *Day's* exposé, the editor is unmoved: "People like you have tried it before, with bullets, prisons, censorship. But as long as even one newspaper will print the truth, you're finished!" Hutcheson then holds up the phone to the newspaper printing presses in full roar: "That's the press, baby. The press. And there's nothing you can do about it. Nothing!"

Hutcheson is not perfect; he uses his staff to try to dig up dirt on a man dating his ex-wife. Furthermore, his bravado is not enough to keep his paper from dying, a fate that was true to the historical context in which *Deadline, U.S.A.* was made. Daniel Hallin notes that newspapers "were dying right and left," but those that remained "were for the most part so prosperous in their new, usually monopoly status, that journalists could think of themselves more as public servants or as keepers of the sacred flame of journalism itself than as employees of a profit-making enterprise."[55] So it would be a couple of decades later, in 1972, when the Watergate story first broke and the *Washington Post* launched the investigation that would be immortalized by the film *All the President's Men*.

The 1976 movie has been of particular interest to those who study how popular culture depicts the past. Robert Brent Toplin has said it "represents one of Hollywood's better examples of cinematic history."[56] On the other hand, William Leuchtenburg has criticized the movie for representing "a significant moment in the elevation of the American journalist to mythical status," W. Joseph Campbell has pointed to it as a prime example of a media-driven myth, and Michael Schudson has said it embodies the "central myth of American journalism."[57] Each of those scholars is correct: *All the President's Men* demonstrates great care in being true to the historical record while simultaneously promoting a mythical "Great Person" view of history that once more is in keeping with the Whig or Progressive school.[58]

The film is the story of two young *Washington Post* reporters, Bob Woodward (Robert Redford) and Carl Bernstein (Dustin Hoffman), who under the tutelage of editor Ben Bradlee painstakingly uncover the Watergate scandal—a

Bob Woodward (Robert Redford) and Carl Bernstein (Dustin Hoffman) painstakingly uncover the Watergate scandal in *All the President's Men*.

widespread campaign of political sabotage waged by Richard Nixon's presidential administration. Along the way the journalists confront public denunciations from Nixon's allies and an array of fearful or recalcitrant sources. A mysterious man known only as "Deep Throat" meets Woodward in a parking garage and helps keep the reporters on the right track. Eventually they link the scandal to Nixon's chief of staff, and the movie ends with a series of teletype stories relating the collapse of the Nixon administration culminating with the resignation of Nixon himself.

All the President's Men eschews pop culture convention in dispensing with romantic subplots and instead concentrates on the tedium of investigative reporting.[59] The filmmakers employ long takes and tight close-ups in showing the reporters constantly on the phone and taking copious notes. They visit the Library of Congress to go through hundreds of file slips in a fruitless attempt to find information for the story. Documentary-like detail is added through location filming and a meticulous reconstruction of the *Washington Post* newsroom, with actual trash flown in from the newspaper's offices. The characters and incidents in the film are closely based on Woodward and Bernstein's nonfiction book about their Watergate reporting. That includes Deep Throat, who some critics insisted was a dramatic invention until 2005 when Woodward finally confirmed that the mystery man was FBI official Mark Felt.[60]

Simultaneously, the film gives Woodward and Bernstein's investigation the trappings of myth. It bathes the *Post* newsroom in brilliant white light while often shrouding the rest of the nation's capital (where Nixon's corrupt minions lurk) in darkness. It graphically portrays the David-versus-Goliath odds against the two reporters by showing them as mere specks against the Washington landscape or inside the Library of Congress. It boosts the volume of the journalists' pencils scratching against their notepads (director Alan J. Pakula said he "was fascinated by the idea of words as weapons [and] an enormous power being brought down by tiny little things"[61]). At the very end, cannons being fired to salute Richard Nixon's re-inauguration are gradually drowned out by the news teletypes rattling off the stories of his downfall. One critic charges that those details "enshrined the fallacy of indefatigable newshounds" in the national imagination—newshounds whose dogged reporting seemed to topple the president of the United States.[62]

Robert Brent Toplin, who says that All the President's Men "manages to deliver a bold and informed view of a significant crisis in American political life," also acknowledges that it "gives little notice to the ways in which other journalists, as well as special prosecutors, judges, members of Congress, and even one of the jailed burglars, exposed the Watergate scandal." He says that storytelling imperatives "accent the heroic action of a few people and downplay the role of other individuals and the impact of broad, complex forces."[63] Hollywood's tendencies toward "presentism" and partisanship in historical films also are apparent in All the President Men's foreboding tone toward the federal government. The distrust in political institutions that Vietnam and Watergate engendered gave rise to "conspiracy films" in which evil forces were embedded in vast bureaucracies that were hiding dark and terrible truths.[64] Just before working on the Watergate film, Alan J. Pakula had directed The Parallax View (1974), which featured a reporter who is killed while trying to uncover the conspiracy behind a string of political assassinations. Pakula said the film represented his conviction that the individual was being threatened "in a secret maze by forces of which he has no knowledge."[65] A like sensibility underlay All the President's Men.

The Watergate film celebrates the news media as a bulwark against the "secret maze" of corruption; other conspiracy films do not. Medium Cool (1969) combines documentary footage of the chaos surrounding the 1968 Democratic National Convention with a fictional story of a TV news cameraperson who begins to question his role in desensitizing the public to violence. The film ends with the cameraperson critically injured in an auto accident. Then, as protesters are heard chanting "the whole world is watching," the movie's writer-director, Haskell Wexler, is seen filming the whole scene. Medium Cool is a product of the 1960s critical culture that sharply questioned heroic, Progressive readings of history and so-called objective journalism that seemed only to parrot what those in power said.[66] Its mélange of fact and fiction challenges the conventions of the historical film, being an exemplar of what Robert Rosenstone calls "films of opposition: opposition to mainstream practice, to Hollywood codes of 'realism' and storytelling."[67]

Network (1976) is less radical in its filmmaking approach, but it is even more scathing in its depiction of TV news, with a crazed news anchor howling "I'm mad as hell!" on the air and then being assassinated by his bosses for having "lousy ratings." The picture reflects post-Watergate suspicion regarding big government and big business and the media's complicity in it all. Likewise, *Absence of Malice* (1981) presents what Michael Schudson has described as a vision of "Watergate-in-journalism" by excoriating the press for imperiously putting itself above the public.[68] The movie shows a reporter being used by government officials to try to solve the case of a union leader who has disappeared. Her reporting inadvertently leads to the persecution of an innocent man and the suicide of the man's friend.

More recent works have told stories about major figures of the high modern age in order to serve a variety of ends. *Good Night, and Good Luck* (2005) venerates another journalistic paragon, Edward R. Murrow. The movie recaps Murrow's 1954 telecast denouncing red-baiting senator Joseph McCarthy. Reminiscent of the fictional Ed Hutcheson in *Deadline, U.S.A.,* Murrow unmasks the villain but loses his platform; his TV network decides that his program is too controversial. The film is bookended by excerpts from a speech in which Murrow praises TV's potential while lamenting the trivial purposes for which it is employed: "This instrument can teach, it can illuminate, and yes, it can even inspire. But it can do so only to the extent that humans are determined to use it towards those ends. Otherwise it is merely wires and lights in a box."

Good Night, and Good Luck is another example of documentary combined with fiction. It uses real footage of McCarthy and other historical figures, whereas the rest is filmed in matching monochrome. The movie thus can be seen as a literally black-and-white tutorial in journalistic courage, as the hero stands up for what is right and pays the price for it. It underscores Murrow's status as the "patron saint" of broadcast news.[69] That has irritated some critics, with one saying that "Murrow burns cigarettes like altar incense" and behaves "like a man carrying all the world's sins."[70] Such criticisms are consistent with those who view Murrow less as a saint than as an overrated "glory hog who played it safe, more puffery than paladin," and as someone whose historical importance has been greatly exaggerated given that he did not take on McCarthy until after many other journalists had already done so.[71] However, the film's director, George Clooney, was as interested in addressing the concerns

John Lithgow as the syndicated columnist Joseph Alsop in *The Columnist* (by David Auburn, directed by Daniel Sullivan at MTC's Samuel J. Friedman Theatre, 261 West Forty-seventh Street; copyright 2012, Joan Marcus; used by permission).

of 2005 as he was in sustaining Murrow's legend. Saying he felt that contemporary journalism had "shirked" its responsibilities, Clooney added that he wanted to provide "a reminder of what is possible"—or, as one critic put it, to show that "government needs a vigorous, even oppositional press to find its best nature."[72]

Like *Good Night, and Good Luck,* the 2012 Broadway play *The Columnist* uses the past to offer lessons to the present, but its story is more about the inevitability of change and the dangers of hubris. The play focuses on real-life syndicated columnist Joseph Alsop, who boasts that he had been "going after McCarthy with all guns blazing" when others had not. He also revels in his clout with those in power, especially President John F. Kennedy, who pays a personal visit to Alsop's home. After Kennedy's assassination Alsop grows ever more hawkish on Vietnam, putting him at odds with the new Johnson administration (which Alsop believes is too soft) and with young reporters who are skeptical toward the war, like the *New York Times*'s David Halberstam. The journalist's influence and reputation decline, and he rails against the changing times: "For God's sake, don't expertise and authority mean anything anymore?"[73] *The Columnist*'s portrayal of the close ties between certain prominent journalists and politicians in the high modern era is historically accurate; according to Daniel Hallin, such journalists saw "themselves simultaneously as part of the 'establishment' and as independent."[74] For playwright David Auburn, a key theme was how that position grew increasingly untenable as journalism and society shifted. He said he wanted "to look back at a time . . . when a few guys had the authority over the discourse and impact of policy. And that's changed so much—largely for good, I would say."[75]

Pop culture skepticism toward onetime journalistic icons has extended even to Woodward and Bernstein. Nora Ephron targeted Bernstein in *Heartburn*, her 1983 roman à clef about her troubled marriage to the journalist; it later was turned into a movie with Jack Nicholson in the reporter's role. Woodward became a character in the widely derided film *Wired* (1989), based on his biography of comedian John Belushi. (As Belushi lies dying, he calls Woodward a "vulture" and "fucking bloodsucker," but then pleads, "Breathe for me, Woodward!") Other works downplay Woodward and Bernstein's role in Watergate. Oliver Stone's film *Nixon* (1995) refers to the reporters only in passing, whereas Thomas Mallon's 2012 novel, *Watergate*, views the scandal through the eyes of Nixon associates and loyalists to whom the *Washington Post* and the rest of the press are more of an irritant than a mortal threat. In the movie comedy *Dick* (1999), Watergate is uncovered by two giggling teenage girls with little help from the *Post* reporters, who are played as bumbling buffoons by Will Ferrell and Bruce McCulloch. "People thought that it was more audacious for us to make fun of Woodward and Bernstein than it was to make fun of the president because in some ways they were more sacred figures," said director and cowriter Andrew Fleming.[76]

In the 2006 play and 2008 film *Frost/Nixon*, the hero who finally brings Nixon to account is not an American journalist, but a British TV talk show host, David Frost. The works are based on the 1977 TV interviews featuring Frost and Nixon and representing the former president's first major public comments since his forced resignation. Nixon famously asserted that "when the president does [something illegal], that means it is *not* illegal," but he also admitted that he "let the American people down, and I have to carry that burden with me for the rest of my life."

Playwright and screenwriter Peter Morgan drew liberally upon transcripts of the original telecasts as well as interviews with Frost, and members of his research team, including James Reston Jr. Morgan, noted that he "could just as easily have written the piece—and found substance to support it—to substantiate the idea that Frost didn't get Nixon, that Nixon half threw it, in order for these interviews to sell." Instead—and despite having mixed feelings toward the man himself—Morgan wrote it as "a bouquet to Frost."[77] *Frost/Nixon* shows the host overcoming his own lightweight reputation to break the former president, once more upholding a "Great Person" perspective on history. James Reston Jr. took issue with some of the historical liberties, but he also commended the work for dealing with "such transcendent themes as guilt and innocence, resistance and enlightenment, confession and redemption. These are themes that straight history can rarely crystallize."[78] For his part, Morgan said his "conscience was clear about bringing my own writer's imagination to the piece," especially given that researching and writing it had made him question whether "such a notion as 'history' [could] ever really exist. . . . Never, it seemed to me, had historical record seemed more like a series of other people's fictions."[79]

*   *   *

"Other people's fictions" or not, the historical record relating to journalism remains a rich source of inspiration not only for American popular culture but also for that of other countries.[80] Film, fiction, theater, and television are powerful means through which collective memory is maintained and contested. Our exploration of how U.S. journalism history has been depicted suggests that the press's past is evoked in complex ways.

Pop culture tends to treat journalism history much as it does any other kind of history. As Robert Brent Toplin has written specifically about film, it "simplifies historical evidence and excludes many details," and it "appears in three acts featuring exposition, complication, and resolution."[81] In short, it aims to tell a clear, compelling story, which typically centers on heroes and villains. The heroes get the big scoop and further the cause of press freedom in the face of the villains who try to thwart them. As such, the story is uplifting—in Robert Rosenstone's words, its message "is almost always that things are getting better or have gotten better or both."[82] It aligns with the Progressive or Whig model of press history, which remains alive and well in pop culture despite having fallen out of favor among professional media historians.

Popular culture thus lends itself to the "media-driven myths" of which W. Joseph Campbell writes. If swallowed whole they can promote the kind of distorted historical understanding alluded to by a reporter character at the end of the Western film *The Man Who Shot Liberty Valance* (1962): "When the legend becomes fact, print the legend." Of course, pop culture does not need to adhere to the same criteria as professional historians. Its goal is dramatic veracity, regardless of whatever historical liberties may have been taken along the way. Peter Morgan defended *Frost/Nixon* by saying, "It may not be accurate, but I believe it's truthful."[83] In contrast, the task of the responsible professional historian—and journalist—is to be both accurate and truthful.

Having acknowledged popular culture's limitations in presenting history, we also must acknowledge that it can enhance historical understanding from a critical and cultural perspective. It provides insight into journalism's self-image at different historical moments while simultaneously pointing to contradictions within that self-image.

Pop culture depictions of early modern journalism are awash with nostalgia for the big-city journalist on the thrilling trail of exposing crime and corruption. The nostalgia extends as far back as the original stage production of Hecht and MacArthur's *The Front Page*. A reviewer of that production observed that it represented "the young man's dream of what the fascination of journalism ought to be" and that "such a night in a press room never was, on sea or land." But, he added, "what a gorgeous excitement, what a magnificent riot, what a set of good fellows, what times, what stories, what extraordinary characters, what *bon mots*—Why, of course, what days those good old days WERE!"[84]

In contrast to the likes of Hildy and Walter, who were willing to go to any lengths to get the story, pop culture portrayals of high modern journalism pay tribute to conscientious professionals. Those portrayals are just as full of nostalgia, though. *Good Night, and Good Luck* holds up Murrow as a noble example for today's journalists to emulate so that they may uphold the press's appointed function. Similarly, the opening credits of the debut season of the HBO TV series *The Newsroom* feature high modern icons Murrow, Walter Cronkite, and Chet Huntley, who implicitly are the role models for the show's fictional TV news team. According to Michael Schudson, *All the President's Men*'s depiction of Watergate represents the "central myth" of journalism in that it offers the press "a charter, an inspiration, a reason for being large enough to justify the constitutional protections that journalism enjoys."[85] It is a "myth" in the sense of its offering "exemplary models" for journalists to follow, and yet it also helps to "serve and preserve social order"[86]—in this case, an order in which the press sees itself as an indispensable check on the powers that be.

At the same time, popular culture presents a critical perspective toward the established press mythology, as seen in a number of parodies or critiques of the press's role in Watergate. It also is seen in *The Columnist*'s story about a powerful journalist's arrogance, stubbornness, and inability to adapt. To an extent, such works can be seen as a postmodern critique of high modern values and institutions along with a distrust of the very things that Joseph Alsop reveres in *The Columnist*: "expertise" and "authority." (Tellingly, playwright David Auburn called himself "an obsessive political blog reader," in line with a twenty-first-century model of news that is less reliant on so-called legacy media.[87]) Still, pop culture critiques of the press extend back to the birth of modern journalism—in novels about poor newsroom working conditions; in early talking films about tabloid misdeeds; in plays such as *Chicago* and *The Front Page* that showed journalists more interested in juicy scoops than in public service; and in *Citizen Kane*'s satire of Hearst-style news.

In *Citizen Kane* as well as in works such as *Medium Cool* there also is an implicit critique of history alongside that of journalism. Both movies present a fragmented, nonlinear account of historical personages and happenings, suggesting there is no one clear "truth" about them. Such a perspective is consistent with the idea that history is a collection of competing fictions, or at least that it represents a form of literature that is rooted in imagination and interpretation, as cultural historians argue. The portrayal of journalism's darker side also is consistent with the focus of critical historians on conflict and the disempowered.

More often than not, though, popular culture's tales about the press reproduce the same familiar myths, consistent with an understanding of popular history as being "artistic and ceremonial" in nature.[88] Those are myths not just about journalism, but also about democracy working properly and about good triumphing over evil. Journalism educator Orville Schell has acknowledged as much in responding to criticisms of the mythology surrounding the press's role in Watergate. Schell says that the "almost religious veneration" of Woodward and Bernstein shows that "people did, and still do, feel a deep need to believe that someone can, and will, stand up to [the] prevailing centers of power and propaganda." He adds that it is understandable that in an "age of extreme skepticism, doubt and cynicism . . . people [who] yearn for some hopeful models for human action even polish up, or invent, a few larger than life inspirations."[89]

Popular culture regularly draws upon journalism history to provide such hopeful, inspirational models along with the occasional ammunition to be used against them. Analyzing popular stories enriches the study of press history by "contemplating questions of fact and fiction, or myth and reality" that are key in shaping understandings of the past.[90] It encourages us to view journalism in light of the "transcendent themes" that Reston saw in *Frost/Nixon*—"guilt and innocence, resistance and enlightenment, confession and redemption"[91]—and to ponder the myriad ways that over the years we have venerated and denigrated the Fourth Estate.

2

Professionalism

One of modern journalism's hallmarks was the rise of professionalism. In the face of yellow news and jazz news, journalists sought to promote respectability by putting their occupation on par with professions such as law and medicine. Particularly in the United States, the first decades of the twentieth century saw the development of journalism schools, so-called objective reporting, and professional organizations with ethics codes. By the era of "high modernism" following World War II, "providing citizens with accurate, 'unbiased' information about public affairs" had become the press's chief goal.[1] However, journalistic professionalism started to come under fire by the 1960s and 1970s, with charges that it diminished public life and encouraged passive reporting.[2]

Here we examine how popular culture has portrayed professionalism's key tenets. Our look at recurring types such as the cub reporter, the investigative reporter, and the editor will show that pop culture reinforces many of the critiques of professionalism—hard, cold reality trumps principles taught in school; reportorial objectivity is difficult to achieve; and ethical choices are fraught with unforeseen consequences. On the other hand, good and responsible journalism is consistently celebrated, whereas bad and irresponsible journalism is excoriated.

The Case for and against Professionalism

At the turn of the twentieth century, "American journalists were a rag-tag collection" who were "often radical in their politics and unpredictable in their conduct," according to one account.[3] In 1904 Joseph Pulitzer called for formal college training in journalism that would "create a class distinction between the fit and the unfit" based on "moral and mental superiority" and would promote an "able, disinterested, public-spirited press."[4] Pulitzer endowed the Columbia University Graduate School of Journalism that opened in 1912, and other schools of journalism were founded at the University of Missouri and elsewhere. The growth of journalism education dovetailed with calls among the intelligentsia for more sophisticated models of news. In 1920 Walter Lippmann argued for "professional training in journalism in which the ideal of objective testimony is cardinal," with the new breed of journalists being "not the slick persons who scoop the news, but the patient and fearless men of science who have labored to see what the world really is."[5]

The 1920s also saw the formation of professional organizations like the American Society of Newspaper Editors. They created ethics codes that they hoped would raise journalism's standards. Journalism educators of the day produced multiple studies of press ethics. Such studies, according to one later analysis, "sharply opposed any sort of partisanship, rejected talk of crime, scandal, and sex as repulsive, and sought a 'higher' tone and reputation for their craft."[6] By 1928 the influence of the professionalization of journalism and other media occupations was such that it prompted the consternation of Ben Hecht and Charles MacArthur. In their stage directions to *The Front Page*, the playwrights lamented the gradual disappearance of the "lusty, hoodlumesque, half drunken," and decidedly unprofessional reporter that their character Hildy Johnson personified: "Schools of journalism and the advertising business have nearly extirpated the species."[7] Over the next few decades, objectivity in reporting became the norm, with the journalist seeking to be factually accurate and politically neutral.[8]

By the Vietnam era the premises underlying journalistic professionalism were drawing vigorous criticism,[9] a trend that continued into the following years. It was said that Pulitzer and university leaders had pushed journalism education not so much to elevate the profession but to instill "more order and docility" among unruly news workers.[10] Objective reporting was said to promote not altruistic ends but commercial ends, because reporting that adhered to perceived standards of neutrality and good taste avoided offending significant numbers of people.[11] It was argued that professionalism encouraged the news media to view the public not as fellow citizens but as a passive audience, disempowering the people in that audience until they obtained the tools to produce their own media and leave the mainstream press behind.[12] Finally, it was asserted that professionalism did not help journalists report the news without fear or favor, but instead "reproduced a vision of social reality which refused to examine the basic structures of power and privilege."[13] Journalists were accused of merely quoting what powerful individuals said, the result being that "the most serious biases in the news occur not when journalists abandon their professional standards, but when they cling most closely to the ideal of objectivity."[14]

Twenty-first-century changes in journalism that include the resurgence of openly partisan media have prompted calls for a recommitment to professionalism. Journalists Bill Kovach and Tom Rosenstiel declare the need for what they describe as a journalism of verification, saying, "The discipline of verification is what separates journalism from entertainment, propaganda, fiction, or art." They outline five "intellectual principles of a science of reporting": "never add anything that was not there originally," "never deceive the audience," "be as transparent as possible about your methods and motives," "rely on your own original reporting," and "exercise humility."[15]

It should come as no surprise that popular culture frequently shows journalists violating those principles. Fabrication, deception, obfuscation, plagiarism, and arrogance are all too common. Nonetheless, journalists who in the end uphold the principles of quality journalism tend to be rewarded. The result is that professional ideals are extolled even as the pieties underlying them are often derided.

Cub Reporters and the Education of Journalists

The utility of a journalism school education has always been questioned. American TV journalist Ted Koppel once called it "an absolute and total waste of time," because it was impossible to "replicate true journalism—genuine pressure—in an academic setting."[16] Such an attitude has often been seen in popular culture, where on-the-job training is portrayed as the beginning cub reporter's true education. Journalism school can seem stuffy and effete in comparison. "Professor Standing says that this newspaper is a filthy blot on the escutcheon of American writing," a bespectacled young man intones in the 1933 film *Picture Snatcher* while touring a tabloid's offices with his journalism class. Small wonder that his female fellow student abandons him and the other pupils to go off with James Cagney's ex-convict "picture snatcher," whose job it is to find images of those who are unfortunate enough to make the news.

Still, before it all ends happily, the picture snatcher's new girlfriend grows disillusioned with him, saying he does nothing but "hit old ladies and blow safes and steal pictures from innocent people who are so down in the mouth that they can't fight back." So it is in a host of other films with titles such as *Scandal Sheet* (1939), *Behind the News* (1940), and *Headline Hunters* (1955)—youthful idealism gets a stiff dose of ugly reality as the cub reporter and the audience are taught what journalism is really supposed to be like. In *Behind the News* the cub meets the veteran star reporter who has been his idol, only to discover that the man is a drunken cynic who tries to plant a fake story with the cub in order to get him fired.

Often the naïve cub learns the ropes well enough to get a scoop, as in the Frank Capra silent film *The Power of the Press* (1928). Clem Rogers (Douglas Fairbanks Jr.) graduates from writing comically overwrought weather stories to catching a killer. In *Nancy Drew, Reporter* (1939) the teenage heroine (Bonita Granville) similarly abandons the fluff piece assigned to her in favor of chasing a murder story. Having read in a journalism textbook that "a newspaperman or woman will stop at nothing to get news," she takes that as license to sneak a camera into a jail, break into a house, print fake information, and wiretap a hotel room. "I thought reporters always did things like that," she says when her editor scolds her. "At least they do in the movies."

They also do things like that in newspaper novels, in which cub reporters have been common characters. Howard Good notes that a frequent plotline in early fiction showed "a young, college-educated man entering journalism full of ideals and literary ambition" only to see his stories "either killed or cut beyond recognition." Most often the young man finally comes through with a big exclusive story, but it is only "through bitter experience" that he learns how to succeed in journalism, and even then he might someday find himself "tossed onto the scrap heap—a warning that the newspaper game may be too rough for those who try to play it."[17]

Such works undercut professional pretensions, but others are more benign. The best known cub journalist in popular culture may be Jimmy Olsen, the redheaded supporting character in the many incarnations of Superman stories over the years. According to histories of the comic book superhero, Jimmy apparently started "as an office boy at a very young age before literally growing up at" the *Daily Planet* newspaper. He has had more than his share of misadventures requiring intervention from his friend Superman, particularly in the 1950s George Reeves *Adventures of Superman* TV series, in which Jimmy was mainly a source of comedy. Yet he also has achieved a share of journalistic distinction, as "the cub became a man and went by the first name *James*, eventually becoming one of the senior writers" and photojournalists on the paper and even winning a Pulitzer Prize.[18] In some cases, then, cub reporters can mature into seasoned, principled professionals.

Della Frye (Rachel McAdams, center) and Cal McAffrey (Russell Crowe) confront their editor (Helen Mirren) in the U.S. film version of *State of Play*.

Popular culture also shows academic ideals being reconciled with workplace realities. In the 1958 movie *Teacher's Pet*, gruff tabloid editor Jim Gannon (Clark Gable) poses as a neophyte student in a journalism course taught by Erica Stone (Doris Day). Gannon hates journalism schools, having never graduated from high school himself, and he wants to embarrass Stone in front of her class. Instead she takes him under her wing as her prize student, and Gannon, who is attracted to her, goes along without revealing his true identity. Complications ensue with clashes over journalistic values. Stone says that Gannon's brand of news "went out with Prohibition," adding, "He still considers journalism a trade. It's not a trade. . . . It's a profession. And the basic fundamentals can be taught the same as in medicine." As for Gannon, he dismisses journalism schools as "amateurs teaching amateurs how to be amateurs," and he urges Stone to teach her students what journalism is really like: "Tell them this is a business. A rough, tough, fighting, clawing business!" The two finally compromise in the interests of true love: Stone recruits Gannon to the faculty to share his vast experience with the students, and Gannon instructs his staff to start doing the in-depth and explanatory journalism that Stone espouses.

Another reconciliation between old and new ways occurs in the 2009 film *State of Play*, based on a BBC TV series of the same name.[19] Veteran newspaper reporter Cal McAffrey (Russell Crowe) investigates the death of a congressional aide with help from young Della Frye (Rachel McAdams), who runs the paper's Capitol Hill blog but who also has little reporting experience. McAffrey is dismissive of Frye and her blog at first, telling her he is "just trying to help you get a few facts in the mix the next time you decide to upchuck online." Still, he supports her when the paper's editor tries to take her off the story. In the end McAffrey and Frye prove that a congressman was responsible for his own aide's death, and the two share the byline on the exclusive. "I look at you, I don't see a girl—I just see a reporter," he tells her. "At last!" she replies.

State of Play is notable not only for reproducing the theme of a cub reporter earning her stripes but also for reasserting traditional professional virtues in the face of new media. The newspaper's blog could immediately report the truth about the congressman, but Frye says it should appear in old-fashioned newsprint first.[20] When the congressman belittles McAffrey for his "laughable" sense of self-worth, the reporter eloquently defends the journalism of verification: "In the middle of all this gossip and speculation that permeates people's lives, I still think they know the difference between real news and bullshit. And they're glad that someone cares enough to get things on the record and print the truth."

Investigative Reporters and the Pursuit of Truth

State of Play's director described Cal McAffrey as an "old world journalist, the shining knight who is after the truth."[21] McAffrey thus exemplifies a character who shows up in novel after novel, film after film, comic book after comic book, and TV program after TV program: the investigative reporter who stops at nothing in uncovering a story. These characters (who most often are male) are powerfully ambivalent about professional ideals.[22] They indeed can be "shining knights" when it comes to the pursuit of truth, displaying heroic determination, courage, and self-sacrifice. They also can be deeply flawed individuals whose personal and professional lives are complete messes.

To be sure, some seem to be paragons of virtue. Such is the case with the 1948 film *Call Northside 777*, in which a Chicago reporter (James Stewart) exonerates a man who has been wrongfully convicted of murder. The picture, based upon a true story and shot on location, ends with narration declaring that the onetime prisoner is now free thanks to "the courage of a newspaper and one reporter's refusal to accept defeat." According to studio publicity, Stewart's character represented "the new, modern type of Chicago newspaper reporter. The old, whiskey-bottle-on-hip, Capone-type reporter of 'Front Page' and other newspaper pictures of the 1929 period is definitely 'cut.'"[23] Other films of the immediate post–World War II era employed documentary-like techniques in depicting investigative journalism as a painstaking modern science as opposed to tabloid hijinks.[24] In *The Captive City* (1952) journalist Jim Austin (John Forsythe) exposes mob corruption and is chased out of town by mobsters trying to kill him and his wife. He ends up in Washington testifying before the Kefauver Committee investigating organized crime. In *The Turning Point* (1952) reporter Jerry McKibbon (William Holden) also goes after organized crime and gets the story, but he is eventually killed in the line of duty. "Sometimes, someone has to pay an exorbitant price to uphold the majesty of the law," says another character in the film by way of eulogy.

Investigative journalists who risk their lives have appeared in a host of other works over the years. In both the novel and film versions of *The Pelican Brief*, a reporter and law student are targeted for death as they try to expose a conspiracy that has killed two Supreme Court justices,[25] and in the film *Cloud Atlas* (2012) a reporter barely survives multiple attempts on her life while uncovering a conspiracy involving the safety of a new nuclear reactor. In the "Amos Walker" novel series, reporter Barry Stackpole loses his leg, two fingers, and part of his cranium when a car bomb explodes while he is pursuing a story.[26] In the television series *Scandal* (2012–), journalist Gideon Wallace is stabbed to death with a pair of scissors while trying to expose powerful government officials.[27]

Woodward and Bernstein are likewise threatened in *All the President's Men*, although they survive to break the Watergate story. They are exemplars of careful investigative journalism, relying on their own reporting and publishing only what at least two sources independently confirm. The two reporters "cast hard, merciless light" on the Nixon administration's misdeeds, as one observer described it at the time of the movie's release—so merciless, in fact, that the same observer expressed concern that the film might encourage professional arrogance, with investigative journalists seeing "themselves being without shadows" in casting judgment on others while being above judgment themselves.[28] Such concerns are consistent with the broader critique of professionalism. As media scholar James Carey once ironically put it, "professionals are privileged to live in a morally less ambiguous universe than the rest of us."[29]

Yet Woodward and Bernstein do not elude moral ambiguity in their work. They badger and intentionally mislead people and try to obtain private phone records, drawing remonstration from sources and coworkers.[30] Likewise,

Cal McAffrey in *State of Play* engages in questionable conduct driven by a wrenching conflict of interest. He has been close friends with the congressman, and he simultaneously tries to protect and expose his friend. In the TV movie *The Lives of Jenny Dolan* (1975), a journalist's quest for a story has fatal consequences for the person closest to her. "You killed your husband," the reporter is told. "That's the price of excellence, Jenny. You're good at what you do."

If investigative journalism is ethically murky and sometimes even deadly, those who practice it are also often far from the models of respectability that the original boosters of journalistic professionalism envisioned. Cal McAffrey is disheveled, drives a beat-up old car, and subsides on canned food that he eats alone. Other investigative reporter characters are far worse, being akin to the detective characters in popular culture who also are profoundly flawed. Their only real purpose is to seek and report the truth, which the Society of Professional Journalists says is one of the press's central callings.[31] Once they accomplish that, their ethical shortcuts and personal failings seem less important.

The 1999 film *True Crime* (based upon a 1995 Andrew Klavan novel) is a prime example. Clint Eastwood plays Steve Everett, an alcoholic reporter who is sleeping with his city editor's wife after losing his previous newspaper job for sleeping with the owner's daughter. Everett's own wife, fed up with his adultery, throws him out of the house. He cannot even take his young daughter to the zoo without accidentally injuring her. Yet when he senses that a man on death row may be innocent, he pursues the story aggressively. "I don't care about justice in this world or the next," the reporter tells the prisoner. "But you know what this is? . . . That's my nose. To tell you the pitiful truth, that's all I have in life. And when my nose tells me something stinks, I gotta have faith in it, just like you have your faith in Jesus. When my nose is working well, I know there's truth out there somewhere." Everett finally locates that truth and gets the prisoner reprieved at the last possible moment before his scheduled execution. The reporter has lost his family, yet his nose for news still works. He is appallingly unprofessional in most respects, but a hero nonetheless.

One can find investigative journalists with the same traits in many novels, including Gregory Mcdonald's "Fletch" series (1974–94) centering on reporter Irwin Maurice Fletcher. The character has been retrospectively described as "young, cocky and smart but no white knight. A Southern California newspaperman turned beach bum, he flouted authority wherever he found it. He was a slob (at least early on), whose sartorial taste ran to T-shirts and jeans.

He was a cad, a deadbeat (unpaid alimony), an opportunist and a sometime accumulator of vast ill-gotten wealth."[32] He also was a skilled reporter-sleuth adept at solving crimes, and his exploits sold millions of novels that in turn became a pair of Hollywood films starring Chevy Chase as Fletch.[33]

Fletch is a sardonic take on the investigative reporter; Mikael Blomkvist is far more serious. He is the Swedish journalist protagonist of Stieg Larsson's internationally popular *Millennium* novels as well as the associated movie versions.[34] Blomkvist is irresistible to women, even Lisbeth Salander, the formidable and ferociously independent female hero of the novels. Blomkvist's sister tells Salander that her brother is "completely irresponsible when it comes to relationships" and "screws his way through life."[35] The journalist's work is also complicated. He cuts deals with high-level government sources, plants disinformation by fabricating an entire issue of his news magazine, and (in *The Girl with the Dragon Tattoo*) suppresses the truth about a serial killer. "I've already breached so many rules of professional conduct in this whole dismal mess that the Journalists Association would undoubtedly expel me if they knew about it," he says.[36]

Nevertheless, it all seems justified, even covering up the killer's true identity (the killer is now dead, and reporting the truth would hurt the man's sister, whom he had sexually abused for years). Blomkvist proves the maxim that journalists in popular culture can get away with almost anything if the public interest is ultimately served. One critic calls him "the ultimate muckraker," who "defends the democratic order but also the ordinary citizen threatened by the corrupt forces of wealth, status, and power."[37] Blomkvist's breaches of professional conduct are intended to get at the truth and minimize harm of the innocent: another key principle of ethical reporting, according to the Society of Professional Journalists.[38]

Finally, although Blomkvist is scrupulous in documenting his reporting, he makes no effort to be neutral, much as his creator, Stieg Larsson, eschewed neutrality in his own journalism aimed at exposing right-wing extremism in Sweden.[39] "For Blomkvist the golden rule of journalism was that there were always people who were responsible. The bad guys," wrote Larsson.[40] Investigative journalism commonly tells tales of guilty villains wronging innocent victims, and it has been criticized for focusing too much on individual malfeasance as opposed to systemic failings and for fostering corrosive cynicism.[41] Blomkvist does not escape such criticisms entirely; his own cynicism is such that he refuses to vote and believes that every corporate executive is a "cretin." But his dedication to justice is genuine: "A managing director who plays shell company games should do time. A slum landlord who forces young people to pay through the nose and under the table for a one-room apartment with shared toilet should be hung out to dry."[42] Blomkvist delivers a reproach to journalists who soft-pedal such abuses because they want to seem "objective" or not rock the boat.[43]

Objectivity and Clark Kent

No popular culture character has been more devoted to bringing bad guys to justice than Superman. His alter ego, Clark Kent, is a journalist for the *Daily Planet* (and sometimes for TV news and the Internet as well), and he displays a complex relationship to journalistic professionalism. At times he can be a very good reporter, yet he also highlights the potential problems with objectivity and the murky ethics surrounding journalistic deception.[44]

The first Superman comic book appeared in 1938, and the superhero has appeared in multiple versions through several "reboots" of the comics franchise as well as on radio, TV, film, and stage.[45] As early as March 1940 the Superman radio series was proclaiming him a "tireless fighter for truth and justice" ("the American way" would come later).[46] As such, his work has been consistent with the press's highest principles. Superman became a reporter in the guise of Clark Kent specifically to help him further the cause of truth in the public interest: "If I get news dispatches promptly, I'll be in a better position to help people."[47]

That makes it all the more ironic that in having a dual identity Clark Kent is living a lie. Popular culture has regularly depicted reporters assuming false identities in pursuing stories, but according to the Society of Professional Journalists, deception is allowable only in exceptional cases after there has been a "meaningful, collaborative, and deliberative decision making process," for which Kent typically has no time or inclination.[48] In that, he is little different from journalists who resort to deception out of laziness or as a stunt rather than asking if the story they are pursuing is profoundly important or if there are any alternative ways of getting it.

One might ask why Kent even wants or needs to be a journalist. As of 1938 being close to a news ticker to find out immediately what crises needed remedying made some sense. Seventy years later, in the *Smallville* TV series, Kent still was in the *Daily Planet* newsroom hunched over a police scanner and a computer set to the Metropolis police website. By then, though, he could have just as easily done that from home with no need for a reporting job. He also could have pursued another line of work close to where the action was, perhaps in law enforcement or as a paramedic. Still, to do so would be

Clark Kent in modern guise—a hard-hitting journalist (Dean Cain) loved by Lois Lane (Teri Hatcher) in the 1990s TV series *Lois & Clark: The New Adventures of Superman*.

to sacrifice a unique advantage—a journalist is the perfect disguise precisely because being one seems so inconspicuous and uninvolved. It exemplifies the "professional communicator" who represents "a relatively passive link in a communication chain [recording] the passing scene for audiences." Critics have charged that a key component of that passivity is the code of objectivity whereby reporters quote official sources and do not take sides.[49] "Journalists wear disguises, and one of them is the disguise of objectivity," two journalism professors have written. "This is fiction. All good journalists have agendas."[50] For Superman, in his quest not to call attention to his alter ego, assuming the identity of a "meek" and "mild-mannered" reporter with no apparent agenda is ideal.[51]

It should be noted that Clark Kent has not always been the glasses-falling-down-the-nose wimp epitomized by Christopher Reeve in the first of his Superman movies. Many times Kent has been a skilled and aggressive journalist. In 1946 the Superman radio series portrayed him and his paper successfully taking on a Ku Klux Klan–like group.[52] The 1950s George Reeves TV series often depicted Kent as a "combative, pugnacious," and "tenacious investigative reporter" who was capable even of standing up to a lynch mob.[53] After a major revamping of the Superman comic strip in 1986, one observer declared that Kent "was no longer a fumbling loser; he became a Pulitzer Prize winner who moonlighted as a successful novelist."[54] The Superman TV shows that followed portrayed him much the same way. In a 1994 episode of the series *Lois & Clark,* he was nominated for a prestigious award for writing a retirement home scandal story that his editor, Perry White, praised as being "first-class journalism" with an "emotional wallop."[55] It is when Kent is the least mild-mannered and "objective" and when he does embrace an agenda that he is the most effective reporter.[56]

Editors for Better or Worse

Some investigative reporter characters are lone wolves, again like many detective characters or Western gunslingers. ("Santa Claus rides alone," growls Clint Eastwood at the end of *True Crime* after buying a Christmas present for the daughter from whom he is now separated.) Other reporters work closely with editors. The role of editorial supervision is another source of debate in journalism studies, with professional journalists saying that careful oversight is essential. Kovach and Rosenstiel call for "skeptical editing" that "involves adjudicating a story—in effect, line by line, statement by statement—editing the assertions in the stories as well as the facts. How do we know this? Why should the reader believe this?" In contrast, scholars like W. Lance Bennett assert that standard editorial practices geared toward objectivity blunt any critical edge in mainstream journalism and "give the news its obvious status quo bias."[57]

In popular culture, editors are typically larger-than-life characters who show journalism at its finest and basest. Well beyond promoting news that is uncritical toward the status quo, they sometimes seem to care only about getting salacious scoops by any means necessary, including brutalizing their hapless staff. Other times they perform exactly the style of skeptical editing that professional journalists advocate, and they do it with a wit and swagger that the average editor would be hard-pressed to muster in real life. Either way, the regular battles between editors and reporters indicate that journalism is high-stakes, adrenaline-fueled work, underscoring the press's importance even when professional niceties are overlooked.

The twin images of the editor as responsible and irresponsible first took hold in the public consciousness between 1835 and 1900 as novels capitalized on the celebrity of editors including James Gordon Bennett of the *New York Herald,* Horace Greeley of the *New York Tribune,* and Henry Jarvis Raymond of the *New York Times.*[58] A multitude of related images, including journeyman printers, crusaders, frontier editors, political hacks, and scandalmongers, captivated the public. They ranged from the villainous Steadfast Dodge in

James Fenimore Cooper's novels to the courageous John Harkless in Booth Tarkington's *The Gentleman from Indiana* (1899).[59]

The Front Page provided an influential example of the editor-as-entertaining-monster in the person of Walter Burns. Hecht and MacArthur modeled him on Walter Howey, a Hearst newspaper editor who was said not to "operate his paper by any code of ethics dreamed up at journalism school in an ivory tower full of idealistic professors."[60] The playwrights described Walter Burns as "that product of thoughtless, pointless, nerve-drumming immorality that is the Boss Journalist," and in the play, reporter Hildy Johnson calls him a "paranoi[a]c bastard," a "lousy snake-brain," and a "God damn ungrateful ape." Walter richly seems to deserve those sobriquets. He ignores a woman who has just jumped out a window, hides an escaped convict in a desk ("Get back in there, you God damn turtle!" he yells when the convict briefly emerges for air), tells Hildy not to fret about whether a car crash has killed his mother-in-law-to-be ("That's Fate. What will be, will be!"), and finally tries to break up Hildy's impending marriage by framing him for theft ("The son of a bitch stole my watch!").[61] Despite those misdeeds, Hildy and Walter maintain a close bond that is difficult to break.

Many Walter-like editors have followed in Burns's wake, often serving as comic foils to the protagonists. They appear in works ranging from *Nothing Sacred* (1937), a Ben Hecht–authored film farce in which a newspaper promotes a fake story about a young woman who supposedly has radium poisoning, to *True Crime,* in which the city editor is a cynical vulgarian: "Do you know my opinion of reporters who have hunches? . . . I can't fart loud enough to express my opinion!" A similar character is J. Jonah Jameson, the cigar-chomping editor in most incarnations of the Spider-Man franchise.[62] More often than not, Jameson has been a thorn in the side of Spider-Man and his alter ego, young photojournalist Peter Parker, even though Spider-Man usually gets the last laugh. The editor has been described as "a foolishly stubborn and pompous skinflint who micromanages his employees and resents Spider-Man out of jealousy."[63] ("He doesn't want to be famous? Then I'll make him infamous!" Jameson says of the superhero in the 2002 film *Spider-Man.*)

There are better role models among the editor characters. J. Jonah Jameson's counterpart in the Superman saga is Perry White, who is just as loud and tobacco-addicted as Jameson, but also said to be "a dedicated professional journalist who made sure that the *Daily Planet* lived up to the ideals of journalism, offering fair and objective coverage of the news."[64] In Jack Webb's film *-30-* (1959), a city editor (William Conrad) is gruff toward his staff but passionate about newspapers: "Do you know what people use these for? They roll them up and they swat their puppies for wetting on the rug. . . . They wrap fish in them. . . . But this also happens to be a couple of more things. It's got print on it that tells stories that hundreds of good men all over the world have broken their backs to get. It gives a lot of information to a lot of people who wouldn't have known about these things if we hadn't taken the trouble to tell them. It's the sum total of the work of a lot of guys who don't quit. Yeah, it's a newspaper, that's all . . . It's still the best buy for your money in the world."

Likewise, Lou Grant was a beloved city editor played by Edward Asner on TV's *Lou Grant* (1977–82) after the character had first appeared as the news director of WJM-TV in Minneapolis on *The Mary Tyler Moore Show* (1970–77). In the premiere of *Lou Grant* the city editor fights to expose a police sex scandal even though the paper's police beat reporter worries that it will alienate his longtime sources. When a different reporter writes the first draft of the story, Grant asks for a revision that is less sensationalistic: "You're really mad at these guys, aren't you? . . . I can tell. I shouldn't be able to tell." Eventually, at Grant's urging, the police reporter produces a piece that reveals not only the scandal but also his own initial efforts to cover it up. *Lou Grant* was popular among actual journalists, and the Associated Press Managing Editors granted Asner honorary membership with a tongue-in-cheek thanks for portraying them as the "journalistically aggressive, ethically pure, even-tempered, heart-of-gold romantics we always knew we were."[65]

A scholarly analysis of *Lou Grant* notes that its "idealized depiction of journalism may have been unavoidable given [TV's] demand for appealing characters whom audiences would want to see week after week."[66] However, equally upbeat portrayals also have appeared in movies and novels. *Call Northside 777* features Lee J. Cobb as a wise editor who first calls the reporter's attention to the story and then fully assists with the investigation. In *All the President's Men,* Ben Bradlee (Jason Robards) deletes a whole section of an early Watergate article for not having enough verifiable facts, much to Woodward's and Bernstein's consternation. He also continually demands that the two reporters produce better-sourced stories even as he defends them against critics inside and outside the paper. The editor in the movie *Capricorn One* (1977) scolds his reporter for trying only to "come up with the scoop of the century" as opposed to "checking little things, like facts."[67] Novels have featured numerous small-town editors (often refugees from big-city journalism) who carry on the ideals of the likes of William Allen White,[68] and they also have portrayed hard-hitting woman editors who expose corruption and solve crime.[69]

In Stieg Larsson's novels, Erika Berger is the editor in chief and majority owner of the *Millennium* monthly news magazine that publishes Mikael
Blomkvist's exposés. She works closely with Blomkvist (and is sometimes his
lover) and is called "the queen of investigative journalism," with "a reputation for being the toughest." Berger leaves *Millennium* to be editor in chief at
Sweden's largest daily paper, but she encounters budget constraints, recalcitrant subordinates, and even sexually harassing emails. In spite of it all, she
presses her staff to report the truth. "Your job description as a journalist is
to question and scrutinize critically—never to repeat claims uncritically, no
matter how highly placed the sources in the bureaucracy," she tells one reporter.[70] Under her leadership the paper reports that its own CEO is involved
in a venture that exploits overseas child labor. Then Berger quits the daily
to return to *Millennium,* but not before informing her staff and the world at
large that management was suppressing stories and imposing cuts that were
damaging the paper's journalism.

Berger's adventures point to another regular pop culture theme: editors
frequently find themselves in the middle of ethical conundrums. The ways in
which those dilemmas are resolved teach lessons about what constitutes good
and bad journalism.[71] For example, in the movie *The Paper* (1994) tabloid
metro editor Henry Hackett (Michael Keaton) and managing editor Alicia
Clark (Glenn Close) literally come to blows over whether to publish a story
that Hackett insists will falsely implicate two young men in a murder. (The
two duke it out in front of the newspaper's printing presses; Hackett wants to
stop the press run, whereas Clark argues that it would cost too much money
to do so.) Clark finally comes around after a colleague tells her that for all its
failings the paper never has knowingly published an incorrect story.[72] In the
film *Ace in the Hole* (1951) utterly amoral reporter Chuck Tatum (Kirk Douglas) keeps a man trapped in a cave for the sake of a big, ongoing exclusive. He
pays no attention to the warnings of his conscientious editor, Mr. Boot, who
has hung embroidered signs in the newsroom reading "Tell the Truth." The
trapped man dies in the cave and Tatum is stabbed by the man's wife, with
whom the reporter has been sleeping. Before he succumbs to his wound, the
guilt-stricken Tatum manages to return to the newsroom and confront his
editor one last time: "How'd you like to make yourself a thousand dollars a
day, Mr. Boot? I'm a thousand-dollar-a-day newspaperman. You can have
me for nothing."[73]

The film *Shattered Glass* (2003) is particularly notable for being based
on the true-life case of Stephen Glass, a young reporter who was fired for
fabricating multiple pieces for the *New Republic* magazine. In the movie

Gus Haynes (Clark Johnson, standing, left) battles for journalistic truth and integrity in the final season of *The Wire*.

Glass (Hayden Christensen) is liked and coddled by everyone at the magazine except for editor Chuck Lane (Peter Sarsgaard), whom the staff views as humorless and aloof. Lane discovers that Glass's profile of a purported computer hacker is a fake and only one of a long series of fabrications. He fires the reporter, and when Glass's closest friend on the staff challenges the decision, Lane admonishes her: "We're all going to have to answer for what we let happen here. We're all going to have an apology to make!" The staff responds by presenting Lane with a written apology to the magazine's readers and then breaks into applause for their editor. The filmmakers declared that "the real heroes of *Shattered Glass* are the editors, who, once they uncovered evidence of Glass's transgressions, acted immediately and decisively, defending their honorable profession."[74]

In at least one instance an editor's attempts to defend his profession against blatant transgressions are punished and squelched. The final season of the HBO TV series *The Wire* featured a fictionalized version of the *Baltimore Sun* and a city editor named Gus Haynes (Clark Johnson). HBO described Haynes as "an old-school reporter's editor who loves to chase down stories and burn corrupt politicians" while devoting himself to "getting it right," no matter that he never completed journalism school.[75] On the show Haynes must cope with cutbacks that lead to the departure of experienced reporters. Even more seriously, he begins to realize that one of his newer reporters, Scott Templeton (Thomas McCarthy), is fabricating pieces. Haynes takes his suspicions to the managing editor and executive editor, but they side with Templeton against him, even after he presents damning evidence against the reporter. Templeton ends up winning a Pulitzer Prize for his fake stories, and Haynes is demoted to the copy desk.

The Wire was created by David Simon, a former journalist for the actual *Baltimore Sun*. Simon had earned praise for his richly textured reporting on Baltimore's police and underclass. He left the *Sun* after being angered by what he felt was a growing emphasis on boosting profits and winning prizes at the expense of journalism that exposed the social and economic inequities underlying the city's ills. Simon turned to HBO and *The Wire*, which over five seasons told an intricate story about the complexities and failings of Baltimore's government, labor unions, schools, police, and newspaper.[76]

In brief, Simon was not using his series to execute a simpleminded hatchet job on the press, even though he was harshly critical of what he believed journalism had become. "In place of comprehensive, complex and idiosyncratic coverage," he wrote in a *Washington Post* op-ed piece, "readers of even the most serious newspapers were offered celebrity and scandal, humor and light provocation." But that was only one part of Simon's broader critique of what America had become, and it did not extend to all of journalism—not to what he believed the press once was and what it ideally should be. "I was a newspaperman from my high school paper until I left the *Sun* at age 35," he said. "I loved my newspaper and I loved working for my newspaper." In fact he had wanted to be a reporter from the time his father (himself a journalist) had taken him as a youth to see *The Front Page*.[77]

Gus Haynes represents that same sensibility in *The Wire*, having spent his whole adult life in journalism and being contemptuous of shortcuts and prize obsession in the newsroom. "Our job is to report the news, not to manufacture it!" he angrily tells his supervisors, whom he privately describes as wanting only to "snatch a Pulitzer or two [before] they are up and gone from this place." Even against the apparent slow death of professional journalism that (according to Simon) once promised "to deliver a complex world, to explain that world, challenge and contend with it," there still is at least one old-school editor to rage against the dying of the light.[78]

*　*　*

Professional journalists have always complained about how popular culture depicts them. The attorney for the *New York Times* wrote an editorial attacking the original stage production of *The Front Page*: "Managing editors are not all conscienceless and cruel. The standards of all newspapermen are not those of the gutter."[79] Not long afterward, journalism educator John Drewry remarked that movies made "the reporter more nearly resemble a gangster than even a moderately well-off business or professional man," and the trade publication *American Press* condemned Hollywood for having "created a false and degraded impression of the newspaper business in the minds of millions."[80] Such criticisms have continued to the present day, and they have been valid to a point—popular culture has frequently shown journalists acting disreputably and unprofessionally. Simultaneously, though, it has underscored the long-standing professional ideal of truth-telling in the public interest, and it has conferred a kind of nobility on the journalist that the likes of Pulitzer might have envied.

Journalism does not have all the trappings that other self-described professions have. One does not require a license to practice it, and there is no way of disbarring miscreants.[81] As a result, journalism has hosted characters ranging from scruffy bohemians to pillars of the community, and that diversity has been reflected in popular culture. Both "outlaw" and "official" types of characters appear in pop culture treatments of journalism.[82] "Outlaw" journalists are resolutely independent and shun convention and obligation while taking pride in seeing through sham or pretension. They cannot be swayed, no matter how much wealth or power others may hold. "Official" journalists are upstanding, decent members of society who work for the common good. They embody white-collar ideals of public service and social mobility, bettering society while they further their own careers.

In retrospect the professionalization of journalism can be seen as trying to promote real-life "official" types over "outlaw" types as part of what has been described as a broad "struggle between professional studies versus practical ones, academic studies versus the apprenticeship system, social-science knowledge versus common sense, ethical practitioners versus amoral hacks."[83] The cub reporter who is educated by the school of hard knocks, the investigative reporter who relies on street smarts over book learning, the "amoral hack" editors who terrorize their newsrooms—those are the pop culture staples that have raised the hackles of actual journalists who prefer to see themselves in a more reputable light. It does not help when journalists lie to get their stories or make them up wholesale, when they put their own interests ahead of the people they cover with disastrous consequences, or when they blithely ignore the abuses of their peers. In those cases popular culture seems to support critiques of professionalism by pointing to the gulf between lofty ideals and grimy practice.

At the same time, the "official" ideals of professional journalism are regularly reaffirmed, often by outlaw-like characters. In works such as *Call Northside 777, Lou Grant,* and the *Millennium* trilogy, conscientious editors hold their staffs to the highest professional standards, whereas Jimmy Olsen learns how to be a good journalist under the tutelage of Perry White and others at the *Daily Planet.* In works such as *State of Play, True Crime,* and the Fletch novels, uncouth investigative reporters scrounge for and ultimately find the truth, much as the suaver Mikael Blomkvist does. Street smarts are reconciled with book learning in *Teacher's Pet* to the betterment of all.

As for bad journalism that is not in the public interest, it is routinely stopped or punished, as when Alicia Clark discovers the errors of her ways in *The Paper,* Chuck Tatum pays the ultimate price in *Ace in the Hole,* Stephen Glass is exposed and banished in *Shattered Glass,* and J. Jonah Jameson continually gets his comeuppance at the hands of Spider-Man. To varying degrees such characters show "in dramatic fashion what happens to those who challenge or ignore social beliefs," in this case the journalistic belief in truth-telling.[84] Excoriating those who have violated such beliefs helps journalism engage in "paradigm repair" and "boundary maintenance,"[85] reinforcing norms of professional conduct by delineating what is proper and what is not and serving to "showcase the central virtues of journalism."[86] Even when bad journalists get away with their misdeeds, those transgressions still are spotlighted and criticized, as in *The Wire* and *The Front Page* (in which the reporters are told more than once that they are little better than dirt). And even in *The Wire* there is a faint glimmer of hope that justice and professional virtue might someday prevail: Gus Haynes warns his supervisors that the truth may eventually come out and they will have to return their ill-gotten Pulitzer.

Finally, one of the main targets of scholarly criticism of professionalism—uncritical reliance on official sources—rarely appears in pop culture when journalists are the protagonists. Routine, status quo–affirming reporting is inherently dull and drab. Journalism is at its most dramatic when the reporters are hot on the trail of big scoops while being urged on by their editors.

In sum, popular culture shows a press that has had more than its share of shameful failings and black eyes and yet still is principled and virtuous when it counts the most. Either way, journalism is exciting and important, an image not far removed from journalism's fondest self-conceptions. According to journalism scholar Michael Schudson, many people "look at the press and see Superman when it's really just Clark Kent."[87] Critics of professionalism might respond that that is precisely the problem with mainstream journalism: it is entirely too meek and mild-mannered. In popular culture that is not an issue. There, journalists (even Clark Kent at times) do thrilling and wondrous things, and if those things do not always coincide with the tidy image that professional journalism organizations have promoted over the years, they may be more likely to stir the imagination and stoke the flames.

3

Difference

A common criticism of professionalism is that it implies that journalists are an elite group with a privileged claim to reporting on public affairs. "A journalist is just a heightened case of an informed citizen, not a special class," press critic Jay Rosen has written in a piece targeted at journalists. "The First Amendment doesn't mention your occupation; it refers to everyone's right to publish."[1] Rosen and others argue that journalists who presume otherwise only make the mainstream press more out of touch than it already is.

In this chapter we look at how popular culture portrays journalists as being different from everyone else and how it treats differences among journalists themselves. Rather than being depicted as above-it-all elitists, journalists more often deviate from society's norms altogether. Those who fall outside the white-male-heterosexual realm lead especially problematic personal and professional lives. Stories by female, minority, and gay or lesbian authors provide a unique take on issues of difference that many journalists confront.

Journalists as Outsiders

Whether in real life or in popular culture, "outlaw" journalists separate themselves from the pack. One film director has said that they represent "the journalist as renegade, the journalist as outsider, the journalist who in his anger comments on the fakeries, the falsities of society."[2] H. L. Mencken was a prime example. The columnist was called "the man who hates everything,"[3] which actually seemed to elevate his status among journalists. Ben Hecht admired Mencken for having made "peace early with the fact that God was a fraud" and that "the only good in life was the derision and laughter one could bring to it."[4]

At the same time, Mencken's cynicism attracted criticism, if sometimes indirectly. The play and film *Inherit the Wind* present a thinly veiled portrait of Mencken through the character of E. K. Hornbeck, who covers a thinly veiled version of the 1925 Scopes "monkey" trial. Hornbeck contemptuously calls a famous politician and lawyer who had opposed the teaching of evolution a "Barnum-bunkum Bible-beating bastard." That draws the remonstration of Henry Drummond, the agnostic attorney who has vigorously supported such teaching. "I'm getting damned tired of you, Hornbeck," Drummond says. "You never pushed a noun against a verb except to blow up something."[5] "Blowing up" things that seem fatuous and hypocritical has its allure, as one observer has noted: "In a society deeply suspicious of the discrepancies between public pronouncement and the hidden workings of power, there is something genuinely attractive about the way a cynic expresses a truth."[6] But it also can become wearisome, as Drummond recognizes. He ultimately makes room in his briefcase for both the Bible and Darwin, whereas Hornbeck is left alone with his scorn.[7]

Hunter Thompson was another well-known outlaw journalist, even embracing that exact label. For him the mainstream press was "a babbling joke" and a "filthy piss-ridden little hole" that was "just deep enough for a wino to curl up from the sidewalk and masturbate like a chimp in a zoo-cage."[8] Like Mencken, Thompson was a hero to many journalists. After his death one columnist observed that he would have had "a savage take on [today's] news-free world," which, the columnist said, is dominated by "counterfeit newsmen."[9]

Thompson's image as a fearless truth-teller was complicated by the fact that he was as well known for his substance abuse and outrageous antics as he was for his reporting, an image that was reinforced by popular culture. He was the inspiration for "Uncle Duke" in Garry Trudeau's comic strip *Doonesbury,* a character who has been described as "an epic consumer of drugs and alcohol, and an amoral trickster with a fondness for firearms."[10] On film Bill Murray played the journalist in *Where the Buffalo Roam* (1980), and Johnny Depp impersonated him in *Fear and Loathing in Las Vegas* (1998). The movies can leave the impression that Thompson's chemical intake was the true reason for his success. "I hate to advocate drugs or liquor, violence, insanity to anyone," he tells a college audience in *Where the Buffalo Roam.* "But in my case, it's worked."[11]

Heavy drinking has been a staple almost from the beginning in pop culture's depictions of journalism. One critic calls it "one of the indestructible
clichés" of the genre, although especially in the movies of the 1930s and 1940s
the drinking was usually either ignored or played for laughs.[12] Journalism
scholar Howard Good writes that "the stereotype of the drunken journalist
has some positive aspects—for example, its sardonic, anti-authoritarian humor." More often it puts journalists "beyond the pale of social respectability,"
much as corrosive cynicism does.[13] To restore respectability they must forsake
liquor entirely. In *Come Fill the Cup* (1951)—one of the first movies to show
alcoholism as a serious problem that affected the journalist's work—James
Cagney plays a journalist who is so enslaved by drink that he goes on five-
day benders with no recollection of his actions or whereabouts. He sobers
up, becomes city editor, and fills his staff with other recovering alcoholics.
"When it comes to newspapermen, give me the reformed lush every time,"
he says. "Work takes the place of liquor." In fact, work becomes Cagney's
entire world. At the end of the film, when the publisher offers him a ride
home from the newspaper, he replies, "I am home."

That too is a stereotype: the newsroom as a refuge and fellow journalists as
a surrogate family, with non-journalists viewed as "civilians" who can never
understand what the news business is truly like. In actuality journalism's
pressures and time commitments can take a heavy toll on one's personal life.
One study reports that journalists have found "most media companies unlikely and unwilling to adopt more family-friendly policies."[14] In that regard

The newsroom family
of WJM-TV gathers for a
tearful group farewell
in the series finale of
*The Mary Tyler Moore
Show.*

popular culture has aped reality. It seldom features journalists in marriages that last; the exceptions typically involve a man and a woman who are both working journalists. The only friends most newspeople seem to have are the people who work with them.

No one would mistake the Mary Richards character from the TV series *The Mary Tyler Moore Show* for a drunken James Cagney or an "outlaw" journalist. Richards is a local TV news producer who is as respectable and well-adjusted as a person could possibly be. But she shares with many other pop culture journalists a surpassing devotion to her job and colleagues. In the series finale, Richards—a single woman without children—tearfully salutes her coworkers: "Sometimes I get concerned about being a career woman. I get to thinking my job is too important to me. . . . But last night I thought, What is a family, anyway? They're just people who make you feel less alone and really loved. And that's what you've done for me. Thank you for being my family."

Female Journalists

Mary Richards and other women journalists in pop culture face an ongoing dilemma.[15] That dilemma is how to incorporate what seem to be the "masculine" traits of journalism that are essential for success—being self-reliant, ambitious, and cynical—while still being the woman it seems that society would prefer her to be: caring, maternal, and sympathetic. In a pioneering study of female journalists in popular fiction, Donna Born found that although they often have been portrayed as "competent, independent, courageous, and compassionate," a "consistent stereotype" has been that their professional achievements come at the expense of their personal happiness.[16]

Women worked as journalists as early as colonial times, but they had to contend with cultural attitudes that consigned them to "submission and obedience" while seeing men "destined for deeds of strength and courage."[17] A history of female journalists notes that writing was one of the only nineteenth-century professions that "constituted a respectable pursuit for middle-class women," although they regularly encountered male resistance, rarely held top positions, and typically lasted only a few years on the job.[18] The movie *A Woman Rebels* (1936) puts a positive spin on that era. Katharine Hepburn plays a young woman named Pamela Thistlewaite in Victorian England and lives up to the film's title by rebelling against her privileged but repressive upbringing. After giving birth to a child outside marriage, she transforms the demure *Ladies' Weekly Companion* into a crusading organ for women's rights.

The male publisher is at first furious, but relents after circulation soars.[19] Some novels of the 1800s also featured female journalists, notably Henry James's *The Portrait of a Lady,* with reporter Henrietta Stackpole. The character has been described by scholar Jean Marie Lutes as being "a fair-minded investigator" who is full of "professional confidence" as a journalist.[20]

At least that is how Stackpole is depicted in the original 1881 James novel. When James issued an updated edition in 1908, he portrayed her less flatteringly. According to Lutes, by then "mainstream newspaperwomen had become so visibly identified with manipulative publicity that James recoiled" from the character.[21] Women had begun entering journalism in increasing numbers by the turn of the century, to the consternation of many men. "Male editors assumed that women could only write *as* women *for* and *about* women," one study notes. "Women entered a gendered public sphere, defined largely on men's terms."[22] That relegated many women to "manipulative publicity," or to what were called "sob stories" written by "sob sisters." Journalist Ishbel Ross sardonically described the role of the sob sister (a label that female journalists disliked) as being "to watch for the tear-filled eye, the widow's veil, the quivering lip, the lump in the throat," with the aim of producing stories that would play on the public's emotions.[23]

Early twentieth-century fiction treated women's growing newsroom presence ambivalently. Donna Born writes that female journalists were shown as "strong and capable," and Jean Marie Lutes says their portrayal was positive enough that it was criticized for giving young women "unrealistic, even dangerous ambitions" about journalism careers.[24] However, Bonnie Brennen observes that there also were "misogynist" depictions of women journalists as "scheming, devious, deceitful, and untrustworthy." Women faced the same poor working conditions as men while coping with additional problems and pressures.[25] Journalist Mildred Gilman addressed those in her novel *Sob Sister.* "She was two Jane Rays," Gilman wrote of her reporter protagonist: "a sensible daytime Jane Ray, who worked hard for a living and gained the satisfaction of doing her duty well, and a night-time Jane Ray, filled with romantic longing, lonely, wishing for her lover, for someone who would care for her always." In the end, Ray gives up her job for marriage—a common denouement for women in newsroom novels of the day.[26]

Even as far back as the silent era, the "sob sister" archetype translated well to films (including *The Active Life of Dolly of the Dailies,* a twelve-part serial produced in 1914 by Edison Studios).[27] Movies created the perfect battleground of the sexes: the underrated female reporter could prove that she was as capable as the male, and the male reporter could gloat that no female could possibly keep pace with him. The prototypical woman journalist of 1930s movies was played by fast-talking Glenda Farrell in the "Torchy Blane" series of low-budget films. Howard Good writes that Blane sometimes has been viewed retrospectively as an "exceptionally attractive, exceptionally energetic, exceptionally tough" character. In reality she "resembled the general run" of female reporters in popular culture in that "she sooner or later submitted to male authority and control" as represented by her policeman boyfriend.[28] No matter how strong and independent female reporters were in the movies of the 1930s and 1940s, in the end they were obliged to want what every woman in the audience was told for generations to want: marriage and family.

Torchy Blane did manage throughout the series to avoid surrendering her job. The women journalists in Frank Capra's films fared differently. In *Mr. Deeds Goes to Town* (1936), she is a Pulitzer Prize winner named Babe Bennett (Jean Arthur). Bennett pursues the story of Longfellow Deeds (Gary Cooper), a simple small-town man who has just inherited a fortune. She assumes a false identity to get close to Deeds and writes stories mocking him, only to have pangs of conscience rooted in her growing attraction to him: "He's got goodness. . . . Do you know what that is? No—of course you don't. We've forgotten. We're too busy being smart alecks." Deeds discovers Bennett's true identity and shuns her, and she leaves journalism in shame. Eventually all is forgiven and the two become a couple.[29] In *Meet John Doe* (1941) columnist Ann Mitchell (Barbara Stanwyck) concocts a hoax about "John Doe" (Gary Cooper again), who supposedly will commit suicide to protest social conditions. Again she discovers the strength and decency of the man she is exploiting; again she repents her sins and quits her job to join him. Capra's heroines thus are made to conform to the same conventions as many other female reporter characters by relinquishing their positions as professional "smart alecks" for true love.[30]

A few movies suggested that female journalists could achieve a fruitful balance between home and work. *His Girl Friday* (1940) is a *Front Page* remake that turns the Hildy character into a woman (Rosalind Russell). A supremely confident and talented reporter, Hildy is determined to leave her job and her ex-husband and editor, Walter (Cary Grant), an outlaw journalist who also manages to be thoroughly charming. Walter stops at nothing to thwart Hildy's plans, including heaping multiple indignities upon her hapless fiancé. "You're a newspaperman!" Walter tells her. "That's why I'm quitting," she replies. "I want to go someplace where I can be a woman." In the end Hildy does not quit, and she and Walter reunite. In *Woman of the Year* (1942) celebrated political journalist Tess Harding (Katharine Hepburn) marries down-to-earth sportswriter Sam Craig (Spencer Tracy). Harding is a model of sophistication and

Hildy Johnson (Rosalind Russell) as the dynamic female journalist hero of *His Girl Friday*. (Courtesy of the Academy of Motion Picture Arts and Sciences)

skilled reportage, but her single-minded devotion to work prompts Craig to leave her. Harding tries to win him back by showing herself to be a good wife, only to wreck the kitchen while fixing him breakfast. "I don't want to be married to Tess Harding any more than I want you to be just Mrs. Sam Craig," he exasperatedly tells her. "Why can't you be Tess Harding Craig?" "I think it's a wonderful name," she says as they embrace.[31]

The endings of *His Girl Friday* and *Woman of the Year* have been controversial in that the formidable female protagonists of both films are reduced to tears as they try desperately to avoid losing the men they love.[32] Yet both films show the women retaining their vitality and their careers, and both provide a tantalizing glimpse of gender equality. One critic has praised *His Girl Friday* for showing "a new kind of marriage, one of mutuality, one in which the turn-on is work," and one in which "male and female do not occupy separate spheres" but instead come together "in a unifying, energizing, and eternally engaging profession."[33]

Strong women journalists also appeared in the comics, although they conformed more to type in their romantic travails. Superman creators Jerry Siegel and Joe Shuster infused the journalist character Lois Lane with "courage, independence, and ambition."[34] In a 1940s Superman animated film series, she was even seen piloting her own plane while chasing a story. When George Reeves's Superman TV series premiered in the following decade, Phyllis Coates played Lane as "tough and direct."[35] For all that, one writer asserts that Lane often "seemed intent on proving that she could be just as silly and frivolous as the feminine mystique required."[36] As opposed to uncovering the truth in her role as a journalist, she appeared more concerned with satisfying her amorous curiosity about Superman's secret identity—never realizing, of course, that he was her mild-mannered coworker Clark Kent.

Also prominent in the comics were Jane Arden and Brenda Starr. Arden was a spirited "girl reporter" who exposed criminals while dressed to the nines. She appeared in an internationally syndicated daily newspaper comic strip that ran for forty-one years (1927–68). Arden's Sunday strip was often accompanied with paper-doll dresses that could be cut out and placed on her.[37] Brenda Starr was similarly glamorous and had her own Sunday paper-doll dresses. She was created in 1940 by Dale Messick, one of the few woman cartoonists of the day. When Messick confronted criticism that Starr was "too well dressed or too focused on 'capturing' the handsome Mystery Man to be serious about her job," the cartoonist had a ready retort: "Authenticity is something I always try to avoid."[38]

That tendency toward soap opera in the portrayal of female journalists continued in the following decades. Best sellers by Barbara Taylor Bradford, Jackie Collins, and Danielle Steel prominently featured women journalists. In Bradford's novel *Remember*, Nicky Wells is "a brilliant investigative reporter" on network TV with "a face that was unusually attractive" and "a willowy grace." Notwithstanding, her private life is "a disaster," with her photojournalist friend and sometime lover being convinced that "she lived out her life on various battlegrounds—the battlegrounds of the wars she covered, the battlegrounds of network politics, the battleground of her damaged heart."[39] In Collins's *Hollywood Kids*, magazine reporter Kennedy Chase is a gifted writer with "an intelligent beauty touched with class," yet she is "completely and utterly alone" after the deaths of her husband and father. Chase produces "a powerful piece on violence and obsession" following a string of Hollywood murders, but her romance with a police detective ends badly.[40]

Things likewise are complicated for Danielle Steel's reporter characters, as the cover blurb of *Passion's Promise* indicates: "Smart, beautiful, and very rich, Kezia Saint Martin leads two lives: one as a glamorous socialite jetting among the poshest places in Europe and America; the other, under a false name, as a dedicated journalist committed to justice and her profession. But the two worlds are pulling her apart, leaving her conflicted about her identity and the lies she tells to every man she meets."[41] In Steel's *Message from Nam*, young and beautiful Paxton Andrews goes to report the war in Vietnam after her fiancé is killed there. Her new lover, an army captain, also is killed there, and her lover after that (the army captain's buddy) goes missing in action. "At times it was hard for her to separate herself as woman and journalist," Steel writes of Andrews. Still, the reporter's professional competence is beyond question: "Her mission in life was to inform, to cut through the lies and brambles with a sword of truth, as it were. . . . And the fact that Kissinger, Nixon, and important journalists around the world had great regard for her, pleased her, but to Paxton, it still did not seem of paramount importance. All that mattered to her was that what she wrote 'made a difference.'"[42]

Whatever its merits as historical literature, *Message from Nam* seems to respect its protagonist. The same cannot be said of all such depictions. According to one observer, the woman journalist "often bears the burden of being depicted as an emotionally empty Super Bitch or Super Whore."[43] Women often fall in love with their sources or male reporters and consummate the relationships with no other agenda involved, but many sleep with their sources because they apparently see it as the only way to get the information they need. Indeed, the female journalist who trades sex for stories is ubiquitous in contemporary popular culture.[44] Heather Holloway (Katie Holmes) in the film *Thank You for Smoking* (2005) becomes annoyed when her source is angry that she used "off the record" material. "I presumed anything said while I was inside you was privileged," he tells her. "If you wanted to talk on a plane or at a movie or over dinner, that would have been fine," she replies. "But you wanted to fuck. That's fine by me."

One of the most persistently negative stereotypes concerns a conniving female TV journalist who is seen sleeping her way to the top or else threatening to replace a more competent veteran journalist.[45] Even when the journalists are more principled and conscientious, they regularly have to confront sexist male managers who believe they are only fit to cover fluff pieces. For example, when Kimberly Wells (Jane Fonda) tries to pursue hard news stories for her TV station in the film *The China Syndrome* (1979), her leering news director resists: "Let's face it, you didn't get this job because of your investigative abilities." Nonetheless, Wells still gets an exclusive story involving falsified records and a near meltdown at a nuclear power plant.

In fact, TV news has formed the backdrop for two of popular culture's most positive images of the woman journalist: Mary Richards in *The Mary Tyler Moore Show* and Murphy Brown in the series named after her (1988–98). Richards begins as an insecure cub in the Minneapolis TV newsroom. By the end of the series she has become a self-assured professional who is ready to move on to bigger things, as affirmed by *Mary and Rhoda,* the 2000 TV movie updating her fictional history. Murphy Brown (Candice Bergen) is an old-fashioned reporter with a past reputation for working, drinking, smoking, and loving hard. She gives up alcohol and cigarettes in the first episode, but never lets go of the passion that has made her a role model for thousands of women. Brown has a child outside marriage and survives breast cancer while remaining at the top of her profession, mixing it up with both imaginary and real journalists and politicians.[46]

For researcher Bonnie J. Dow, the depictions of Richards and Brown are ambiguous when it comes to gender roles. Richards was a progressive character by 1970s TV standards: she was "single by choice," she "saw her job as a career rather than a stopgap on the journey toward marriage," and she worked at "a job traditionally assigned to a man." Yet her place in the newsroom family put her in the "implicit roles as wife, mother, and daughter," with her relying on the fatherly advice of news director Lou Grant and tending to the emotional needs of her coworkers. As for Murphy Brown, she provided "a rare and satisfying portrait of a powerful woman" while also implying that "a woman cannot be professionally successful and retain traditional qualities of femininity." Her "traditionally male characteristics" of being "aggressive, competitive, and often insensitive" continually brought her grief.[47]

Dow suggests that Brown's portrayal reflected postfeminist anxieties of the 1980s and 1990s, but it also reflected the conflicted image of the female journalist that has existed all along. To be sure, the image today is not always as negative as it sometimes used to be. Scholar Brian McNair finds it "striking" that in newer movies, "so many of the lead journalistic roles were occupied by women," and "these women were neither the 'sob sisters' nor the 'superbitches' of past celluloid convention."[48] On the other hand, the twenty-first-century pop culture image is little different from that of the past in that workplace success exacts a personal price. That has parallels with real life, in which women journalists often face a "classic double-bind" in being "devalued either as 'proper professionals' or as negligent towards their families—or both."[49] One study of novels about female Washington journalists found that women had made some progress in that they were depicted as having satisfying careers without seeming to be "desperately seeking a man to fulfill their lives." But they had "a more difficult time proving themselves than men in the male-dominated field of journalism," and they often appeared "to get ahead on the basis of looks as well as ability."[50]

Movies like *The Devil Wears Prada* (2006) are similarly ambivalent. The film is set in the world of style or fashion journalism in which many women have risen to leadership positions.[51] As played by Meryl Streep, *Runway* magazine editor Miranda Priestly is an icon of power, glamour, and acerbic wit. Brian McNair has praised the movie for taking a "female-centered and feminist-oriented perspective" in indicating that "style journalism is a valid subject of interest, a fascinating subject, [and] an honorable trade." That is in contrast to the hugely popular *Sex and the City* TV series and movies that also prominently feature a female lifestyle journalist, but seem more oriented toward "finding your man and getting him to buy you things."[52]

In *The Devil Wears Prada*, though, the woman journalist's life outside work is once again bereft. Priestly appears in a bathrobe without makeup to reveal that her husband has asked for a divorce in another of a series of failed marriages for her. She also tearfully says that although the labels the press has pinned on her (including "dragon lady" and "snow queen") do not bother her, they are deeply unfair to her children. Priestly soon regains her regal composure, but the implication is that she has been left alone, whereas the young woman (played by Anne Hathaway) she has been both bullying and mentoring leaves *Runway* for a career in "serious" journalism.

In her recent incarnations Lois Lane also has demonstrated both newfound strength and typical vulnerability. Like Clark Kent, Lane was "rebooted" in the 1980s to become "the comic book version of a modern feminist: a weight-lifting, gun-toting, fist-fighting fashion plate" who had a more equitable relationship with Kent.[53] Movies and TV series followed suit to a degree. Lane in *Superman Returns* (2006) has been described as "unambiguously the equal of Superman in courage and determination."[54] She even has won a Pulitzer Prize for a piece titled "Why the World Doesn't Need Superman." In the TV series *Smallville* (2001–11), about the early days of Clark Kent, Lane is a hard-driving journalist who is capable of beating up men and drinking them under the table. But unalloyed happiness and success remain elusive: in *Superman Returns,* Lane (who has borne Superman's child) ends up renouncing her prizewinning article; in 2013's *Man of Steel,* Lane (Amy Adams) is tough and aggressive, but still falls for Superman and still needs him to rescue her; and in the finale of *Smallville,* she is relegated to chasing after the bomb scare of the moment for the *Daily Planet,* her planned marriage to Clark Kent forever on hold.[55]

Journalists of Color

Until the 1960s, popular culture largely ignored ethnic minority journalists. Again, that paralleled the journalism of reality. According to Juan González and Joseph Torres, in America "key newspapers, magazines and broadcast stations were owned and operated by whites; the content they produced was aimed largely at white readers and listeners," and journalists of color "were systematically excluded" from newsrooms.[56] Journalist characters also did not easily conform to the most pervasive pop culture stereotypes of minorities— "toms, coons, mulattoes, mammies, and bucks," as Donald Bogle branded them in his history of African Americans in movies.[57]

When journalists of color appeared at all, it was in films targeted at minority viewers or that otherwise were not widely seen. *Mystery in Swing* (1940) features an all-black cast in depicting a journalist's investigation of a jazz trumpeter's murder. The film is similar to mainstream movies in portraying a clash between an editor and reporter. ("You let the paper down, which is something I can't excuse," the editor tells the reporter. "Turn in your press badge.")[58] In *The Lawless* (1950) a white journalist takes over a small-town paper but confronts virulent racism. The female editor of the Spanish-language weekly *La Luz* forces him to take a stand, which results in a mob destroying his newspaper offices. He turns to *La Luz* and its editor (whom he now loves) to help him continue publishing. Although the white journalist is the film's nominal hero, the Latina editor is its conscience. The movie also depicts the news media's role in fueling racial hatred, which González and Torres assert was all too common with the real-world press that routinely portrayed "non-white minorities as threats to white society."[59] Still, *The Lawless* reached comparatively small audiences, and its director, Joseph Losey, was blacklisted by Hollywood not long afterward.[60]

With the civil rights movement of the 1960s, popular culture addressed race and the news media more directly, though still only sporadically and in works that fell outside the mainstream. The film *Black Like Me* (1964) related the true-life story of John Howard Griffin, a white man who darkened his skin to pose as an African American in the Deep South and report on his experiences. James Whitmore starred as "John Finley Horton," but his makeup as a black man prompted a critic to comment that "one almost expects him to burst into 'Mammy' à la Jolson."[61] Regardless, Donald Bogle writes that the film "was an earnest attempt to confront and expose racism in America,"[62] including growing African American frustration with the status quo. A young civil rights worker berates Whitmore's character for "sneaking into here all painted up," and tells him that his reports "won't make any difference—that's just words." By the end of the 1960s, frustration had turned into militancy. The 1968 Kerner Commission report asserted that "the 'white press' . . . repeatedly, if unconsciously, reflects the biases, the paternalism, the indifference of white America."[63] In the countercultural film *Medium Cool* a black power activist directly addresses the camera: "You are the exploiters. You're the ones who distort and ridicule and emasculate us."

Such anger did not carry over into mainstream pop cultural portrayals. Hollywood's biggest African American star of the 1960s, Sidney Poitier, appeared as a journalist in *The Bedford Incident* (1965), but his race was not commented upon in the film. Similarly race-neutral depictions continued in the following years. They included *The Mary Tyler Moore Show*, with weather reporter Gordon "Gordy" Howard (John Amos) leaving WJM-TV to become a major network star, and *The Pelican Brief* (1993), with journalist Gray Grantham (Denzel Washington) investigating the assassination of two Supreme Court justices. *The Pelican Brief* was based on a John Grisham novel in which Grantham was white, but the change in ethnicity is barely an issue in the movie. The only exceptions are brief—the reporter's editor half-jokingly tells him, "I thought of dropping you into the ranks of the unemployed, but I know damn well you'd slap me with a discrimination suit." In addition, Grantham shares just a chaste kiss on the cheek with the law student (Julia Roberts) who is conducting the investigation with him, whereas the two characters had a romantic relationship in the original novel.[64]

A few depictions of minority journalists have been less benign. The long-running animated TV comedy *Family Guy* debuted in 1999. It includes a local TV news team with "Black-U-Weather" reporter Ollie Williams, who bellows one-sentence forecasts: "It's gonna rain!" There also is so-called "Asian reporter" Tricia Takanawa, described by the actor who voices the character as "all presentation and no substance."[65] If *Family Guy* is unapologetic parody, *The Year of the Dragon* (1985) is deadly serious in its depiction of horrific drug gang warfare in New York's Chinatown. The film features a Chinese American TV reporter who investigates the violence. In certain respects the reporter epitomizes the "model minority" stereotype of Asian Americans—she has worked her way to a top reporting position with a lavish apartment. Her knowledge of Mandarin and of Chinese culture helps her report on Chinatown, at least to an extent. But the character also reproduces stereotypes of Asian women as exotic objects of desire. She frequently is shown unclothed and enters into a sexual relationship with the white police detective who is her main source for news. She is also made the victim of rape, which comes in retaliation for her investigation of a mob boss.[66]

More nuanced depictions have appeared in other media, with several series of novels featuring journalists of color as major characters.[67] On television Augustus "Gus" Haynes is an African American who works for the *Baltimore*

Racial tensions in the newsroom are exposed in *CQ/CX*, inspired by the Jayson Blair scandal at the *New York Times*. (Photo by Kevin Thomas Garcia, used by permission of the photographer and the Atlantic Theater Company)

Sun in the final season of *The Wire*. He is a dedicated, experienced journalist who has worked his way up from the police beat to earn a reputation as "a reporter's editor." By contrast, white reporter Scott Templeton is a liar who wins a Pulitzer Prize for a fake story. Haynes hates Templeton and constantly tries to expose him while supporting a young, hardworking Latina reporter, Alma Gutierrez, who watches as the corrupt Templeton wins the praise of the white editors.[68]

On the stage, two plays have negatively portrayed their African American protagonists, although they are not wholly negative toward journalists of color. Gabe McKinley's *CQ/CX* (2012) presents a lightly fictionalized account of Jayson Blair, a young African American reporter for the *New York Times* who was fired in 2003 for plagiarizing and fabricating stories. Critics gave the play mixed reviews, with some commenting that it offered little insight into the motives of "Jay Bennett," the character based on Blair. Other minority characters in the production received better notices, including a young Latina reporter who is betrayed by Bennett when he copies her stories and an older African American editor (based on the *Times*'s Gerald Boyd) whose initial defense of Bennett dissolves into bitter recriminations.[69] *The Story* (2003) tells of a journalist named Yvonne who is loosely based on Janet

Cooke, a *Washington Post* reporter who returned a Pulitzer Prize in 1981 after it was learned that she had faked her story about an alleged eight-year-old heroin addict. As Cooke did, Yvonne creates a false resume that impresses the white editors, but not enough to let her work in the coveted Metro section. She joins the Outlook section instead, which is overseen by an African American editor who is determined to counteract the stereotypes of the black community perpetuated by the white media. The editor distrusts Yvonne with good reason: the reporter's scoop about a black female teen's murder of a white schoolteacher is not all that it purports to be.[70]

The Story was written by African American playwright Tracey Scott Wilson and is an example of the complex portrayals produced by many writers and filmmakers of color. Regular themes have included the difficulties that minority reporters experience in white majority newsrooms and the challenges they face to their personal identities. The movie comedy *Livin' Large!* (1991), directed by Michael Schultz, tells the story of African American broadcasting student Dexter Jackson (Terrence "T. C." Carson). He insinuates himself into a televised hostage situation after his idol, a pompous older African American reporter, is killed by the hostage taker. Jackson parlays it into a full-fledged TV news job. He graphically demonstrates to his viewers the disparities in police response times to emergency calls in black versus white neighborhoods. Under pressure from his bosses, though, he begins to report from more of a "white" perspective—and finds himself literally turning more and more white each time he sees himself on the air or in a mirror. His station even tries to marry him to his white co-anchor to boost ratings. Finally, Jackson regains his senses (along with his original complexion).[71]

Novels by authors of color provide a bleak perspective on the trials and at times mortal dangers faced by minority journalists. In the graphic novel *Incognegro,* set in the early twentieth century, a light-skinned African American reporter goes undercover as a white man to expose violence against blacks in the Deep South. He gets his story, but not before his own brother is lynched. Author Mat Johnson, who himself "grew up a black boy who looked white," said he based his novel on Walter White; the future head of the NAACP was once a journalist who posed as white to investigate lynchings.[72]

My Favorite War, a 1996 novel by Jamaican American journalist Christopher John Farley, relates the adventures of a black newspaper reporter. He is politicized through his relationship with an African American woman columnist. "Black life is worth less than white life in the newspapers," the reporter realizes. "A few homeless people freeze to death every winter's night in Washington, but that's not news. But if a two-man passenger plane goes down and the white businessman flying it sprains his neck, it's a story. It's disgusting moral calculus." In the end the reporter is fired by an editor whom he calls "one of those white liberals who like to hire black people so they can tell themselves, prove to themselves, that black people weren't good enough for the job."[73] In the 2003 novel *Special Interest* by Chris Benson (former Washington editor for *Ebony*), reporter Angela McKenzie struggles to please similarly dubious supervisors: "The pressure was murder. The pressure to get it right, and to get it right on time. The pressure to prove something to her editors, show the White boys they didn't have a monopoly on intelligence and talent." She breaks a huge story and reflects on the irony: "Just a day ago, they were ready to fire her. Now she was everybody's hero. White boys."[74]

Kim McLarin wrote the 1998 novel *Taming It Down* after what she recalled as a "soulsucking" tenure at the *New York Times*.[75] Protagonist Hope Robinson, who worries that her editors will see her as "an affirmative action mistake," is assigned by her newspaper to cover a black neighborhood. She fears that the only result will be that "white people were confirmed in their belief that the black part of town was a godless and dangerous place." She is especially conflicted when she is told to investigate allegations of wrongdoing inside an African American church: "I was being asked to choose between my people, who weren't really my people except in some intangible way, and my would-be people—my professional, establishment people, to whom I owed some kind of allegiance, didn't I? Even if I hated them sometimes?"[76]

Amanda Rossie draws upon critical research on race and gender to suggest that characters like Hope Robinson represent "outsiders within"; they are nominally within the white male power structure of the newsroom and yet are simultaneously outside it by not being white or male. (One of Robinson's coworkers calls the paper "a boys' club, a whiteboys' club. . . . All the glamour beats are reserved for the members.")[77] Such conflicts are consistent with those related by actual women journalists of color.[78] Rossie praises Kim McLarin for dramatizing her own experiences in demonstrating the inequities of contemporary journalism.

Increasingly complex depictions of nonwhite female journalists also have appeared in recent Bollywood films from India, although researchers who have studied them argue that they have their limitations. Sukhmani Khorana observes that movies including *Lakshya* (2004), *No One Killed Jessica* (2011), *Peepli (Live)* (2010), and *Page 3* (2005) reflect "the rising ascendancy of the female journalist in the Indian media sphere." The films feature "university-educated middle- or upper-middle-class women with serious journalistic ambitions," but sometimes those ambitions are thwarted.[79] For example, *Page*

3 tells of a young journalist in Mumbai who grows weary of the celebrity news she is forced to cover. The reporter transfers to the crime beat, but her exposé of child sexual exploitation results in her being fired. She returns to celebrity news for a rival paper. Radhika Parameswaran praises the movie for avoiding "simplistic or crude portraits of soft journalism's female reporter," but says it "aligns good journalism" with "patriarchal ideologies of middle class morality, female sexuality, and male superiority."[80] In associating women with "soft" and implicitly nonserious journalism and in portraying them as not achieving fulfillment, *Page 3* reproduces long-standing popular culture stereotypes.[81]

Lesbian and Gay (LGBT) Journalists

Pop culture's portrayals of journalists who are implicitly or explicitly lesbian or gay date back to movies like *Big News* (1929), which features a female newspaper society editor who dresses like a man.[82] The LGBT journalist's stereotypical characteristics were for years a source of derision or buffoonery. Those include various versions of *The Front Page* with the effeminate reporter "Bensinger," an example of what Vito Russo in his book *The Celluloid Closet* called "the use of the 'harmless sissy' image to present homosexuality."[83] Otherwise the LGBT journalist typically was what Russo described as "a sophisticated but deadly sissy" as epitomized by a "bitchy" columnist or critic, such as the murderous Waldo Lydecker played by Clifton Webb in *Laura* (1944).[84]

It was not until the 1990s that LGBT journalists in movies were accepted for their sexual orientations, with those orientations often figuring prominently in the plots. *In & Out* (1997) is especially notable in featuring a gay entertainment reporter played by Tom Selleck, an actor with a long-standing "macho" image. In *Kissing Jessica Stein* (2001) a copy editor, played by Jennifer Westfeldt, has a romantic relationship with another woman, although that relationship eventually ends and it is implied that the copy editor may renew a romance with her male onetime boss. Perhaps the best-known depiction of a gay journalist is Philip Seymour Hoffman's Oscar-winning turn in *Capote* (2005), about Truman Capote's reporting and writing of *In Cold Blood*. The film showed Capote's simultaneous exploitation of and attraction to the convicted murderer Perry Smith—a relationship that the movie *Infamous* (2006), with Toby Jones in the Capote role, portrayed even more graphically.

Hollywood's mixed image of the contemporary LGBT journalist is exemplified by *The Devil Wears Prada*. *Runway* magazine's second in command is

Philip Seymour Hoffman as Truman Capote in *Capote*.

Nigel (Stanley Tucci), a person of substance and dignity who is very good at his work. Yet he is only a supporting character in the familiar role of the gay best friend. Nigel has no apparent romantic relationships, making him non-threatening to heterosexual sensibilities. He does transcend the most offensive portrayals of gays, which persist in many mainstream movies. According to one critic, the gay journalist friends of Drew Barrymore's character in *He's Just Not That Into You* (2009) are "the flameyest, lispingest, 'fiercest' stereotypes imaginable," presenting a veritable "minstrel show of homosexuality."[85]

Richer and more thoughtful depictions have appeared in films targeted at LGBT audiences or those made outside the United States.[86] *The Velvet Goldmine* (1998), directed by the American Todd Haynes but filmed and set in Britain, tells of a gay reporter's attempts to trace a vanished rock star. The movie, which has achieved cult status, has been praised as "an exhilarating queer homage to 1970s glam rock" as well as to *Citizen Kane,* whose structure the film emulates.[87]

Many American TV programs have provided more sensitive images of LGBT journalists than have Hollywood movies. That dates back at least to 1989, when an episode of the sitcom *Night Court* featured a reporter who was more worried about being "outed" as a romance novelist than as a lesbian. Individual episodes of *Queer as Folk, Dirt,* and *Veronica Mars,* as well as regular characters in such series as *Ugly Betty, Frasier, Da Ali G Show,* and *The L Word,* show other LGBT journalists who are not afraid of or embarrassed about their sexuality.[88]

Again, though, it is novels (many written by onetime journalists who themselves are LGBT) that have provided some of the most provocative depictions of LGBT journalists.[89] According to an overview of the genre, detective fiction "presents the positive, negative, and highly personal aspects of lesbian and gay life," with journalists as recurring protagonists.[90] Vicki P. McConnell's "Nyla Wade" mysteries debuted in 1982 and were published by the lesbian-oriented Naiad Press. They center on a lesbian newspaper reporter whom McConnell has described as pursuing "solutions to problems and injustices that would probably intimidate me sufficiently to stop me in my tracks."[91] In *The Burnton Widows,* Wade investigates and solves a series of killings targeting LGBT people in a town called Burnton. "The fact that two lesbians were murdered and one gay boy is missing matters to *our* community, even if we don't belong in Burnton," she tells the local police chief. "We may be pariahs, but we're not expendable. Even pariahs want justice."[92] The villains include seeming paragons of the town. As one analysis of the novel notes, "The main social fabric becomes the harbinger of criminality, the gay community the repository of moral outrage. This is a neat inversion of the lesbian/gay stereotype 'sick pervert.'"[93] As for the "straight" press, it is typically "portrayed as strongly homophobic" in LGBT detective fiction.[94]

In Penny Mickelbury's and Lisa Haddock's books (again published by Naiad), the sexuality of the reporters is complicated by their ethnicity. Mickelbury is an African American journalist who also writes fiction. One of her series of novels focuses on the romantic relationship between black reporter Mimi Patterson and a white female police detective. "Being queer in America, she thought wryly, was one of the few things worse than being Black," Mickelbury writes of Patterson. The reporter is powerfully attuned to matters of race, gender, and class, sometimes to the discomfort of her editors. When Patterson exposes the murderers of African American prostitutes in *Night Songs,* she feels "no pride, no rush of satisfaction." Instead, "it suddenly struck Mimi that they all were Black. Black like her. And she allowed herself to feel fully the pain of knowing that there were people who believed her life had no value because of her race."[95]

Haddock's "Carmen Ramirez" mysteries feature a young Oklahoma newspaper journalist who is lesbian and part Puerto Rican (a background similar to Haddock's). "I was lonely, bored, isolated, and tired of the company of crass heterosexuals," says Ramirez in *Edited Out.* "I didn't have one real friend in the newsroom, somebody who knew me for who I was." She is assigned to edit a series about a lesbian who is alleged to be a murderer. Convinced that it "is a bunch of gay-bashing nonsense," Ramirez proves in the newspaper that the true villains are a white male journalist and a white male minister.[96] The sequel *Final Cut,* though, reveals that she has been outed in the newsroom without her consent. According to Amanda Rossie, Ramirez represents another "outsider within" viewed by her coworkers as "an unruly lesbian who uses her privilege as a newspaper employee to subvert journalism's noble cause and replace it with a gay 'agenda.'"[97] The character at least achieves some fulfillment by the end of the series; Lisa Haddock says that Ramirez has discovered how "important it was to stand up to a system that didn't want to listen and wasn't interested in the truth."[98]

Things end happily both personally and professionally for Mark Manning, the hero of a mystery series by Michael Craft, a onetime *Chicago Tribune* graphic designer. Craft says that when he began the series, he deliberately made Manning an "unwavering and unapologetic" investigative reporter marked by "his respect for reason and his disdain for faith, superstition, or other forms of illogic." Gradually Manning comes out of the closet, enters into a lasting relationship with another man, becomes guardian to a son, and acquires a small-town newspaper. He also becomes less self-certain and self-righteous, to his benefit. "I was a tight-ass," Manning admits at the end of the last novel in the series. "Not only have I learned a valuable lesson regarding my own rigid views, but I've also felt a measure of liberation." He, his life partner, and his paper have "comfortably blended into the existing fabric of the town," consistent with Craft's "assimilationist" view of gay rights. In sum, according to Craft (who himself is gay), the journalist has achieved "self-definition as a happy, complete, mature gay man."[99]

*   *   *

For better or worse, assimilation for most journalists in popular culture is stubbornly elusive, regardless of their gender, race, or sexual orientation. Part of the mythic appeal of those journalists is how different they are from everyone else. They are the heroes who are "unwavering and unapologetic" in exposing wrongdoing, and they are the sardonic outsiders who ruthlessly mock society's pieties and pretensions. However, just as the hero can succumb to arrogance (or to being a "tight-ass"), the outsider can succumb to cynicism or to drink or to permanent separation from the rest of humanity. Popular culture repeatedly dramatizes such fates in depicting journalists as a species apart. Even when the endings otherwise seem to be happy, journalists are often akin to Shane riding off alone at the end of the classic Western film or are consigned to life with the only other people who can truly understand them—fellow journalists.

The struggle of being different is especially acute for journalists who are not male, white, or straight, whether it is in popular culture or in reality. Pop culture's portrayals have improved in some respects: women today are depicted as more than "sob sisters" wanting only marriage, journalists of color appear more often and are not merely tokens, and LGBT journalists are not just "sissies" or "bitchy." Journalism itself also has improved. Women "now appear well-established in a profession" that not long ago "was a male enclave," and they have played "a significant role in redefining news to incorporate issues associated with the quotidian concerns of women as a whole."[100] Journalists (both of color and white) have managed in many cases "to surmount the ignorance, fear, and rampant clichés that uniquely sabotage reporting about race relations and cultural difference," and they have been able to "transform fear and ignorance into curiosity; turn cliché-laden frames into opportunities for surprise and discovery."[101] Over time, "mainstream newspapers, magazines, and broadcast news entities in the United States have moved from a position of condemnation and scorn to one of familiarity and even support for gay people."[102]

Yet just as the old stereotypes still appear with some regularity in popular culture's depictions of journalists, the press still has a long way to go. Seven decades after Ishbel Ross wrote that women "never were thoroughly welcome in the city room and they are not quite welcome now," a study found that women journalists "continue to be marked as 'other,' as 'different' from their male colleagues," while being "still concentrated in sectors considered to be 'soft' news."[103] Four decades after the Kerner Commission report blasted the "'white press,'" a Knight Foundation report asserted that newsrooms "still reflect the culture, economy and politics of a white America" and that the press "tends to oversimplify, to stereotype, to come loaded with the bias (conscious or not) of its creators." At their "extreme," according to the Knight report, certain elements of the news media have implied that gays and lesbians "all want to get married and upset the nuclear family."[104]

Many critics and journalists call for structural reforms of the media industry to promote a much wider range of ownership and control and to "produce diversity that is more than skin-deep," as one critic has put it.[105] They argue for viewing gender roles as being more malleable than traditionally thought, contributing to "collaborative, non-competitive, horizontal work structures that allow for integrating domestic responsibilities."[106] They point

to the need for remaking newsrooms and news coverage to reflect more accurately the changing demographic makeup of society and to help "unpack
the systemic nature of discrimination" and the "linkages between misogyny,
racism and homophobia."[107] And they suggest that journalists see themselves
not as separate from everyone else, but simply, as Jay Rosen puts it, "informed
citizen[s]."[108]

For now, popular culture continues to dramatize the struggles within journalism. That is particularly true of those stories that are produced outside the
mainstream and that present poignant insight into the lives of nonwhite, non-
male, and nonheterosexual journalists. At their best, those stories—like the
best of journalism—"provoke thought, challenge stereotypes, and promote
a greater understanding."[109] Even when it is not at its best, popular culture
vividly demonstrates the glories that can come with being different, as well
as the sometimes terrible costs.

4

Power

Impassioned defenders and critics of journalism have one thing in common: they both assign significant responsibilities to the press. The Society of Professional Journalists (SPJ) Code of Ethics says that journalists should be "vigilant and courageous about holding those with power accountable," and Bill Kovach and Tom Rosenstiel likewise argue in *The Elements of Journalism* that the press "must serve as an independent monitor of power."[1] For his part, media scholar and critic Robert McChesney agrees that "society needs a journalism that is a rigorous watchdog of those in power and who want to be in power" and that "can ferret out truth from lies." Unfortunately, given that "powerful interests tend to wish to dominate the flow of information" and are consistently allowed to do so, contemporary journalism is "a failure."[2]

Once again we will see that popular culture plays it both ways: it depicts the press as afflicting the comfortable and comforting the afflicted, and it also depicts the press as doing the exact opposite. Journalism's complex entanglements with political and economic power are graphically portrayed. Regardless, through a variety of character types, including the anonymous reporter, the columnist, and the publisher/media owner, the notion that the press is a uniquely potent force to do ill or good is consistently underscored.

Minimizing and Maximizing Harm

One of the tenets of the SPJ ethics code stipulates that journalists should "minimize harm." A journalism ethics handbook acknowledges that this principle "all too often clashes head-on with the principle of truthtelling," simply because reporting the truth can hurt people. Nevertheless, "ethical individuals [must] treat others as deserving of respect, not merely as a means to one's own ends, no matter how important we see those ends to be."[3] Such understandings of the journalist's proper role are consistent with a social responsibility model of the news media: the press, as a powerful institution free of direct state control, is morally obligated to regulate itself by reporting the news in a manner that genuinely serves the public interest.[4]

Some otherwise celebratory popular culture works about journalism still show the pain and discomfort that the press can cause through its actions or inactions. In *Deadline, U.S.A.* the newspaper's investigation of a mobster endangers an elderly woman's life after two of her adult children are murdered. In *All the President's Men* Woodward and Bernstein's insistent questioning of a frightened worker for President Nixon's reelection campaign reduces her to tears. "You don't understand the pressure we're under," she tells them. "Please go away, okay?" In *Good Night, and Good Luck* CBS journalist Don Hollenbeck is red-baited by the Hearst press, and when Hollenbeck asks Edward R. Murrow to defend him publicly, Murrow rejects him: "I will not take on McCarthy *and* Hearst—I can't defeat them both." Hollenbeck then kills himself. Similar portrayals appear in other media from other countries: in the 2003 British TV miniseries *State of Play* (which inspired the later American movie version), a newspaper's unwillingness to share evidence with the police indirectly results in the killing of a police officer, whereas the paper's reporting drives another man to suicide; in the British TV series *The Hour* (2011–12), a news program's investigation of government corruption leads to a young woman's murder; and in Stieg Larsson's *Millennium* novels from Sweden, the tabloid newspapers brand protagonist Lisbeth Salander as a murderer and a Satanist.

Each of the works just cited shows the press triumphing in the end by exposing wrongdoing. Once more, popular culture implies that whatever the niceties of ethics codes, journalists can resort to whatever means are necessary to serve the higher end of promoting the public interest.[5] The harm done to certain individuals is outweighed by the press's heroism and courage. (In *Deadline, U.S.A.* the elderly woman brushes off the potential threats against her life, telling the intrepid editor played by Humphrey Bogart, "You're not afraid. Your paper's not afraid. I am not afraid.")[6]

In other works, though, journalists do clear harm to others while serving no one else's ends but their own. For example, a pervasive image in movies and TV shows since the 1970s has been that of seething mobs of anonymous journalists armed with lights, cameras, and microphones. They poke those cameras into people's faces, yell out questions, and recklessly pursue the protagonists played by popular actors who naturally command the audience's sympathy. The film *The Right Stuff* (1983) tells of the seven original U.S. astronauts who became national heroes. One real-life journalist, CBS correspondent Eric Sevareid, plays himself in the movie and reports calmly and professionally on the astronauts. In contrast, unnamed reporters descend like a plague to the accompaniment of locust sound effects. The reporters fire inane queries at the astronauts and their wives at inopportune moments, block traffic, clamber over balconies, punch through screen doors, and in one darkly comic scene, besiege the hapless driver of what they believe to be a diaper delivery service used by an astronaut's family. ("We don't have a diaper service man!" the astronaut's wife exclaims as the diapers go flying.) Such portrayals contrast markedly with the films of earlier decades in which anonymous journalists were depicted much more benignly, and they imply that the news media have become instruments of harassment as opposed to enlightenment.[7]

Columnists also have often been portrayed negatively. They are the pop culture counterparts of the Hearst columnist Jack O'Brian, whose printed attacks on Don Hollenbeck were said to have contributed to the journalist's despondency and eventual suicide.[8] Hollywood films such as *Is My Face Red?* (1932), *Love Is a Racket* (1932), *Okay, America* (1932), and *Broadway Melody of 1936* (1935) both satirized and lionized fast-talking, big-city columnists. In *Blessed Event* (1932), which was based on a Broadway play of the same name, Lee Tracy plays a newspaper advertising flunky named Alvin Roberts. He becomes author of the "Spilling the Dirt" column and soon amasses twenty million readers. Although some label him "a stench in the nostrils of American journalism," Roberts remains defiant. "Did you ever hear of the power of the press?" he asks a hoodlum. "It's what lets birds like me make suckers out of birds like you!" Far from condemning Roberts, the promotional trailer for *Blessed Event* promised moviegoers insight into the columnist's "daring" and "toughness."[9]

Characters like Roberts were based on Walter Winchell, who had become a pop culture icon by the early 1930s.[10] According to biographer Neal Gabler, Winchell was seen as "the people's champion of the thirties and forties, fighting for Roosevelt and courageously against the Nazis." After World War II he morphed into a "cruel, spiteful rumormonger," having "gone from a man who demonstrated the inspiring power of the press to one who demonstrated its terrifying dangers."[11] That Winchell was immortalized in the 1957 movie *Sweet Smell of Success,* which subsequently was turned into a 2002 Broadway musical. The film was coauthored by Ernest Lehman after his unhappy stint as a press agent toady who chased down gossip for Winchell and others in return for plugs for clients.[12] Burt Lancaster plays J. J. Hunsecker, a New York columnist with a nationwide audience and seemingly unlimited power to make or break entertainers and politicians. He spouts empty platitudes on his TV show: "You know and I know that our best secret weapon is D-E-M-O-C-R-A-C-Y!" Behind the scenes, the columnist is a monster who bribes and bullies press agent Sidney Falco (Tony Curtis) into a series of foul deeds that culminate with the savage assault of Hunsecker's sister's boyfriend, whom Hunsecker claims has "wiped his feet on the choice and predilections of sixty million men and women"—that is, his public. As a rival columnist says of Hunsecker, "He's got the scruples of a guinea pig and the morals of a gangster."[13]

Winchell's female counterparts during the 1930s and 1940s were the powerful and feared Hollywood gossip columnists Louella Parsons and Hedda Hopper.[14] The rivalry between the two women was depicted in the 1985 TV movie *Malice in Wonderland* with Elizabeth Taylor as Parsons and Jane Alexander as Hopper. Parsons's professional relationship with William Randolph

The witch columnist Rita Skeeter as portrayed by Miranda Richardson in the Harry Potter movies.

Hearst also figured in the movie *RKO 281,* in which Hearst orders the columnist to circulate photos of stars in compromising situations to try to kill the film *Citizen Kane,* as well as in *The Cat's Meow* (2001), in which Parsons uses damning information about the publisher to blackmail him into giving her a lifetime contract.[15]

Rita Skeeter is Parsons and Hopper's spiritual descendant. She is the witch journalist in J. K. Rowling's Harry Potter books and the associated movie versions, in which she is played by Miranda Richardson. Skeeter's specialty is said to be "writing poison-pen stories which [are] based on false information and misreported interviews," assisted by her ability to transform herself into a beetle whenever she deems it advantageous.[16] Even taking into account her fantastical qualities, Skeeter still implies that journalists "seek scandals and the sensational," "invade people's privacy," "twist the facts," and "are not concerned about the public interest," according to Daxton Stewart's analysis of the character. As such, she lends support to the Project for Excellence in Journalism's observation that contemporary popular culture portrays journalists as "exploitative jackals."[17] More broadly, the negative depiction of columnists suggests that, as Neal Gabler puts it, gossip has "debased" journalism by "infecting reportage of so-called straight news . . . at the expense of objectivity and duller facts," making a mockery of the social responsibility concept of the press.[18]

There also have been editor and reporter characters who are villains, or who at least do villainous things that damage people; for example, Edward G. Robinson's editor in *Five Star Final,* whose tabloid paper pushes a husband and wife to suicide; Broderick Crawford's editor in *Scandal Sheet* (1952), who commits murder and then orders his staff to play up the killing in the paper; Kirk Douglas's newspaper reporter in *Ace in the Hole,* who allows a trapped man to die in a cave for the sake of a scoop; and Dustin Hoffman's TV reporter in *Mad City* (1997), who parlays a hostage situation into a media circus with fatal consequences.[19] In *Absence of Malice* reporter Megan Carter (Sally Field) writes a story revealing that a devoutly Catholic schoolteacher has had an abortion. When the woman subsequently kills herself, her best friend, Michael Gallagher (Paul Newman), physically attacks and berates Carter: "Couldn't you see what it was to her? Couldn't you stop scribbling for a second and put down your goddamn ballpoint pen and just see her?"

Just as popular culture generally rewards journalists who wield their power to serve the greater good, journalists who do not serve the greater good are regularly made to pay the price or repent by trying to do the right thing. In Ray Flynt's novel *Kisses of an Enemy* (2011), a reporter has been fired for making up sources on a story, but acquits himself by exposing corruption in

Washington, D.C. In James Siegel's *Deceit* (2006), a reporter has seemingly ruined his career by fabricating stories. He then risks his life to uncover a conspiracy that involves murder.

The same is true of the movies: the editor in *Five Star Final* quits the paper in disgust and shame, the editor in *Scandal Sheet* is shot dead by the police, the reporter in *Ace in the Hole* is fatally stabbed by the trapped man's wife, the journalist in *Mad City* helplessly screams, "We killed him!" at his fellow reporters after the media circus results in a man's death, and Megan Carter in *Absence of Malice*—after she has been publicly humiliated and apparently fired—apologizes to Michael Gallagher on behalf of her profession: "I know you think what I do for a living is nothing. It really isn't nothing. I just did it badly." When Gallagher tells her that she is probably, in fact, "a hell of a reporter," Carter demurs: "Not yet." Even in depictions of journalists as "exploitative jackals," there still are gleams of hope for redemption for the press and its public service mission.

The Press and Political Power

Absence of Malice has been said to represent the flip side of *All the President's Men,* with the press abusing its power by having grown too aggressive and intrusive.[20] In actuality the movie showed the press as being a tool of government. The newspaper prints a story that a government source intentionally leaks to it, triggering a disastrous series of events. "You don't write the truth," Gallagher tells Carter. "You write what people say, what you overhear. You eavesdrop!" Such a characterization is consistent with the critique of professionalism and objectivity that holds that a great deal of journalism is mere stenography, with reporters parroting what those in power have told them or permitted them to hear.[21] Although routine dependence on official sources is not dramatically compelling by itself and thus is not often depicted by popular culture, fraught professional and personal relationships between journalists and government officials appear regularly, as do efforts to "spin" or bully the press.

A common complication is a female journalist becoming personally involved with a male source in or near government. In the movie *Washington Story* (1952) magazine reporter Alice Kingsley (Patricia Neal) arrives in the U.S. capital to announce, "I'm here to get a sensational series of articles about Washington, and I don't care who I impose on to get them." She targets Congressman Joseph Gresham (Van Johnson), who is nicknamed "No Comment Joe" for his unwillingness to talk to the press. Kingsley suspects Gresham of

Zoe Barnes (Kate Mara) is the morally compromised and ultimately doomed young journalist in the U.S. version of *House of Cards*.

bribery, but it turns out that he is a pillar of rectitude, and she finally writes a piece praising him as a "true patriot." Along the way, they fall in love.[22]

More recent depictions have been less romantic, as once again women reporters exchange sex for stories.[23] A journalist tries to blackmail her former lover—the Speaker of the House—in Mike Lawson's novel *House Justice* (2010). In the TV miniseries *Political Animals* (2012), a newspaper reporter becomes the favored press contact for the U.S. secretary of state, who is planning a White House run against the incumbent president. The reporter simultaneously enters into a sexual liaison with the secretary of state's son, who provides her with information aimed at thwarting his mother's presidential bid. Jamie Malanowski's novel *The Coup* (2007) features a reporter who habitually sleeps with her sources and is exploited by a vice president seeking to force out the president and take his place in the White House.

The same theme appears in the British and American versions of TV's *House of Cards*. In the American version, which premiered on Netflix in 2013, twenty-something reporter Zoe Barnes (Kate Mara) dons a cleavage-baring top and appears unannounced late at night at the home of U.S. Representative Frank Underwood (Kevin Spacey). In short order she starts a sexual relationship with Underwood in return for news exclusives, which apparently is routine in the world of Washington journalism that the series depicts. "We've all done it," an older female political correspondent tells Barnes. "I used to suck, screw, and jerk anything that moved just to get a story."[24]

Likewise, in the original 1990 British version, reporter Mattie Storin (Susannah Harker) begins an affair with Conservative Party whip Francis Urquhart (Ian Richardson). The incestuous nature of the relationship between the young reporter and the older politician is underscored by her calling him "Daddy." Urquhart aspires to become prime minister by any evil means necessary, and he steers Storin into writing stories that damage his political rivals, all the while deftly avoiding any public association with those stories ("I couldn't possibly comment," he frequently tells her). When Storin learns the truth about Urquhart—including that he has committed murder—he unceremoniously hurls her to her death from the top of the Houses of Parliament (just as in the American version of the series the politician finally dispatches the reporter by shoving her in front of a train).[25]

Politically motivated violence against the Fourth Estate has appeared with some regularity in popular culture. The 1939 Hollywood classic *Mr. Smith Goes to Washington* was directed by Frank Capra, who believed that the Washington press corps were a "terrible" bunch of "yes men" who relied on government handouts.[26] In the film, freshman senator Jefferson Smith (James Stewart) discovers that his idol, Senator Joseph Paine (Claude Rains), is beholden to political boss Jim Taylor (Edward Arnold). Taylor is using Paine's influence to push through a graft-ridden dam project. To avoid exposure the political boss manipulates the press into writing stories that make it look as though Smith is the one guilty of graft, thus turning "Taylor-made" public opinion against the young senator. Smith's loyal and loving aide Clarissa Saunders (Jean Arthur) is appalled—"Freedom of the press!" she snorts— and she arranges for a children's handmade newspaper in Smith's hometown to print the truth. Taylor promptly dispatches thugs to beat up the children and run them off the road. Eventually it all ends happily, but with little help from journalists (although Smith is able to invoke the memory of his late father—a principled small-town newspaper editor who was martyred on the job—in order to shame Paine into confessing the truth about the crooked dam deal).[27]

Conspiracy-minded films and TV shows in the 1970s commonly depicted government machinations against the press.[28] In *The Parallax View* Warren Beatty plays scruffy reporter Joe Frady. He begins investigating a series of political assassinations after his former girlfriend and fellow journalist dies under mysterious circumstances (she had told Frady that she feared she was being targeted for elimination after she witnessed one of the assassinations). Frady's skeptical editor also is murdered, and finally Frady himself—immediately after witnessing a senator being shot to death—is shot and killed as well. In the movie's closing scene a Warren Commission–type group holds a media briefing to declare that it was actually Frady who assassinated the senator, that "there is no evidence of a conspiracy," and that "there will be no questions" allowed from the press.[29]

In the years that have followed, government efforts to thwart and muzzle journalists have continually appeared in films,[30] television,[31] comic and graphic books,[32] science fiction,[33] and novels.[34] Popular culture also has shown sophisticated public relations efforts to deflect attention from government wrongdoing, including homicide. In the TV series *Scandal,* which debuted in 2012, a former chief of staff to the vice president murders a reporter who has been digging up dirt about the presidential administration; the administration's crisis management team covers up the deed. In the film *Wag the Dog* (1997) spin doctor Conrad Brean (Robert De Niro) concocts an entire overseas war (complete with computer-generated imagery) to redirect the press's attention away from a presidential sex scandal. When an egotistical Hollywood producer threatens to expose the scheme so that he can claim professional credit for it, Brean has him liquidated. Scholar Berrin Beasley has written that the movie "capitalizes on the myriad ways in which journalists can be used to advance specific political or business agendas at the expense of the public's right to know."[35]

And yet alongside those portrayals of journalists as sleazy opportunists, hapless victims, and brainless stooges are images of journalists as courageous professionals who stand up to government pressure. They guard the confidentiality of sources who trust them enough to give them valuable information that uncovers corruption, even if that means the journalists refuse to obey court orders. In a 1974 episode of *The Mary Tyler Moore Show* ("Will Mary Richards Go to Jail?"), news producer Richards refuses to reveal a news source and consequently is sent to jail. In subsequent years, similar episodes have been featured by a host of other TV series ranging from courtroom dramas to family-oriented shows and situation comedies.[36]

Novels and films also have depicted journalists shielding confidential sources.[37] In the TV movie *Word of Honor* (1981), reporter Mike McNeill (Karl Malden) of the *Daily Tribune* (billed as "The Paper with a Heart") is a small-town reporter whose unwillingness to unmask such a source sparks a national controversy that almost ruins his life. His publisher and family do not support his stand, and police confiscate his notes and incarcerate him.

The dilemma is finally resolved when McNeill's source agrees to testify. Things end less happily in the film *Nothing but the Truth* (2008), in which journalist Rachel Armstrong (Kate Beckinsale) blows a CIA agent's cover and will not divulge who gave her the story. She goes to prison (where she is savagely beaten by a fellow inmate), loses her husband, and costs her newspaper a fortune. After she is finally released, the federal prosecutor has her arrested for obstruction of justice, and she promptly returns to jail. The movie was partly inspired by *New York Times* reporter Judith Miller, who went to jail in 2005 rather than reveal who gave her information in connection with the outing of CIA operative Valerie Plame. Miller also was the center of controversy for her reporting prior to the second Iraq War. Her stories, which relied on unnamed sources, supported false claims that Iraq possessed weapons of mass destruction.[38]

Because of cases such as Miller's, the use of anonymous sources has come under sharp criticism. Although acknowledging that using such sources is sometimes necessary, researcher Matt Carlson argues that its "gratuitous application" has led to its being a "vehicle for spreading misinformation or opinions without reprisal,"[39] much as the politician ("I couldn't possibly comment!") manipulates the reporter into publishing misinformation in both the British and American TV versions of *House of Cards*.[40] Still, more often than not, pop culture confers nobility upon the practice. As Lou Grant tells Mary Richards in convincing her to go to jail to protect her source: "It's a reporter's job to inform the people. But if a reporter could be forced to reveal his confidential sources of information, he can't do that job, because his sources will dry up. And pretty soon there won't be any information worth printing. The whole concept of freedom of the press will be destroyed—and with it democracy as you and I know it and cherish it."[41]

Such lofty pronouncements about journalism's appointed mission have appeared frequently over the years. "The power and the freedom of the press is a flaming sword," proclaimed the opening of the classic radio series *Big Town*. "That's the press, baby! . . . And there's nothing you can do about it!" says the editor to the mobster who controls the city in *Deadline, U.S.A.* "Nothing's riding on this except the First Amendment to the Constitution, freedom of the press, and maybe the future of the country," editor Ben Bradlee tells Woodward and Bernstein in *All the President's Men*. "We are not descended from fearful men, not from men who feared to write, to associate, to speak, and to defend the causes that were for the moment unpopular," says Edward R. Murrow in taking on McCarthy in *Good Night, and Good Luck*.[42] "The survival of the government isn't my concern," reporter Mikael Blomkvist tells the Swedish prime minister in the novel *The Girl Who Kicked the Hornet's Nest*. "My role is to expose shit."[43] Journalists stand up to the powers that be no matter the cost to themselves—for example, reporter Cal McAffrey in the British *State of Play* reveals that a member of Parliament is responsible for the death of a young woman, no matter that the man is his best friend and that the exposé will forever alienate the woman McAffrey loves.

Works such as these indicate that "doing journalism is honorable and that honorable journalism can do good," as the introduction to a historical anthology of muckraking journalism asserts.[44] From a more critical perspective, they reproduce what has been called the "free press/free people myth."[45] According to Robert McChesney and Ben Scott, that myth is the idea that the existing commercial press system has been "ordained by the Founding Fathers as the engine of participatory self-government. . . . It is an article of faith if one believes in America, in freedom, in democracy."[46] Journalism's "most hallowed" task—to serve as democracy's watchdog—is exalted.[47]

The Press and Economic Power

According to critics, the problem with the myth of a free watchdog press is not only that the press "sometimes sleeps when it should bark, and too often barks at nothing."[48] It also is that "the near total elision of public service priorities by commercial imperatives" goes unaddressed, resulting in a whole host of ills: "a decline in hard news, a lack of investigative and process stories, staff cuts, concentrating ownership structures, closure of independent papers, more advertising, more tabloid fare, trends toward infotainment, and bias in the name of balance." From that perspective the only solution for promoting public service and deemphasizing commercialism is structural overhaul of the media, including increased government regulation and state subsidies to encourage not-for-profit journalism.[49]

However, in some nations with commercial media and especially in America, a "free press" typically has been taken to mean one that is privately owned and free of direct government subsidy. A state-subsidized media system is viewed as a potential means of oppression and even totalitarianism.[50] For example, the 1980s comics series and 2006 movie *V for Vendetta* depict a dystopian Great Britain that has fallen under a fascist dictatorship. In the comics series control is imposed by a state-run radio service known as the "Voice of Fate." In the movie the xenophobic Lewis Prothero (Roger Allam) performs the same function through the state TV network. "Immigrants, Muslims, homosexuals, terrorists—disease-ridden degenerates—they had to go," he tells his viewers. "Strength through unity! Unity through faith! I'm a God-fearing Englishman and I'm goddamn proud of it!" It is only when the mysterious mask-wearing "V" (Hugo Weaving) seizes control of the network that the people can hear a liberating message: "Where once you had the freedom to object, to think and speak as you saw fit, you now have censors and systems of surveillance coercing your conformity and soliciting your submission. . . . Fear got the best of you." In the end the people rise up against the fascist regime, as is symbolized by the fiery demolition of the Houses of Parliament.[51]

According to its director, James McTeigue, *V for Vendetta* "showed what could happen when society is ruled by government, rather than the government being run as a voice of the people." Yet he also said that the state TV network in the film was partially inspired by organizations such as America's Fox News and Britain's Sky News, both owned by Rupert Murdoch's News Corporation.[52] That example points to the potential of open collusion between the state and big business in controlling the news media and freedom of expression. It also highlights a regular popular culture theme: many times, private ownership can have a pernicious effect on journalism.

In an overview of how popular culture has depicted media ownership, Loren Ghiglione notes a dichotomy: the owner's "independence brings applause, his villainy jeers." There is a "soft spot for the editor-owner of the small-town paper, the one-man band who sells the ads, writes the stories, prints the paper, and then distributes it too," much as *Mr. Smith Goes to Washington* lionizes Senator Smith's late editor father and the children's handmade newspaper. On the other hand, when the owner represents "rapacious capitalism" or a vast conglomerate, he or she is typically portrayed negatively.[53]

That dichotomy is demonstrated by arguably the most famous media owner in pop culture history, the Hearst-like publisher Charles Foster Kane in Orson Welles's *Citizen Kane*. Film scholar Robert Ray has said that the movie encapsulates "the irresolvable conflict between American myths of success (celebrating energy and ambition) and of the simple life (warning that power and wealth corrupt)."[54] The young Kane shows the energetic and ambitious side as he vows to use his paper to "see to it that the decent, hardworking people in this community aren't robbed blind by a pack of money-mad pirates." The aging Kane shows the corrupt side as his media empire abandons muckraking in favor of promoting Kane's political ambitions and as his high-minded "Declaration of Principles" descends into megalomania (he proclaims that people will think "what I tell them to think!"). It is with good reason that *Citizen Kane* has been praised for

Orson Welles as Charles Foster Kane in *Citizen Kane*. (Courtesy of the Academy of Motion Picture Arts and Sciences)

highlighting "fundamental contradictions within monopolistic journalism . . . founded on distortion and hypocrisy."[55] At the same time, a critic has remarked upon the film's "vast, melancholy nostalgia for self-destructive talent."[56] Kane himself observes during his declining years that "if I hadn't been very rich, I might have been a really great man"—and perhaps a really great journalist.

Such complex portrayals of media owners are comparatively rare. More common are money- and power-obsessed publishers and moguls who always have been favorite popular culture villains. The negative depictions date back to nineteenth-century novels such as William Dean Howells's *Their Silver Wedding Journey,* whose uncouth newspaper owner, Jacob Stoller, is described as "a robber baron by nature."[57] Such portrayals carried over in the next century to the stage, silent films, and early Hollywood talkies. The venal publisher Bernard Hinchecliffe in the play and movie *Five Star Final* bears the wrath of the guilt-stricken editor for the tragedies the tabloid has wrought. "I'm through with your dirty rag, and I'm through with you," the editor tells Hinchecliffe in the film. "Oh, I'm not ducking any of the blame for this thing. You thought up the murder, and I committed it. But I did it for smaller profit, for wages. You did it for circulation. . . . I want you to wake up in the night and see your own squashy, putrid little soul!"[58]

If possible, the media mogul in Frank Capra's *Meet John Doe* is even more venal. D. B. Norton (Edward Arnold) acquires the *Bulletin* newspaper. A pneumatic chisel blasts the newspaper building's plaque ("The BULLETIN/'A free press means a free people'") into dust, and a new plaque takes its place: "THE NEW BULLETIN/A STREAMLINED PRESS FOR A STREAMLINED ERA." The "streamlining" results in mass layoffs, including columnist Ann Mitchell (Barbara Stanwyck). She fabricates aggrieved everyman "John Doe" for her column as a ploy to save her job, and she convinces the paper to hire an ex-baseball player (Gary Cooper) to play the part and boost circulation. The John Doe movement sweeps the nation, promoting neighborliness and self-sufficiency. However, Norton—who is first seen watching the drills of his own SS-like paramilitary corps—seeks to exploit the movement to create a fascist America under his rule: "What the American people need is an iron hand. Discipline!" When "Doe" tries to reveal the truth about Norton to a John Doe convention, Norton uses his newspapers to brand Doe a fake, and the crowd turns viciously upon the hapless man.[59]

Even Superman demonstrated the potential evils of private power over freedom of expression. In a 1943 comic book that seemed to prophesy "rapacious capitalism" being taken to its logical conclusion, the arch-villainous "Prankster" managed to copyright the alphabet. A Superman historian describes the consequences: "Immediately the nation is thrown into a panic as everyone has to pay the Prankster exorbitant royalties whenever they wish to write something. The *Daily Planet* is faced with the prospect of going broke; skywriters are suddenly out of work, not to mention typists, librarians, novelists. . . . Civilization teeters on the verge of total collapse because—as even Superman is forced to admit—the Prankster's racket seems totally legit. Not until the Prankster breaks the law by trying to kill Clark [Kent] and Lois [Lane] can Superman intervene."[60]

In the 1970s and subsequent decades, conspiracy-themed works cast suspicions on corporate control of the media, just as they questioned political control. Indeed, they implied that political and corporate control could not be separated.[61] As examples, Loren Ghiglione points to novels such as Jeff Millar's *Private Sector* (1979), Jack Anderson's *Control* (1988), Michael M. Thomas's *Hard Money* (1985), and David Aaron's *Agent of Influence* (1989). A common thread in those novels is corporations working in league with antidemocratic governments, if not obliterating the notion of "governments" altogether. According to an evil mogul in *Agent of Influence,* individual nations "are dangerously overarmed anachronisms. The earth will be ruled by global corporate organizations. And the key to global economic and political power is the media."[62]

Network may be the best-known expression of such fears. In the film, written by Paddy Chayefsky, TV programming head Diana Christensen (Faye Dunaway) takes over her network's news division and raises its ratings through the angry declamations of "The Mad Prophet of the Airwaves," anchor Howard Beale (Peter Finch). When Beale uses his on-air pulpit to rally national support against a lucrative corporate deal with the Arabs, the boss of the network's parent corporation, Arthur Jensen (Ned Beatty), demands that he atone for having "meddled with the primal forces of nature." Says Jensen to Beale: "There is no America. There is no democracy. . . . We no longer live in a world of nations and ideologies, Mr. Beale. The world is a college of corporations, inexorably determined by the immutable bylaws of business." Jensen commands Beale to use his news program to preach the gospel of "one vast and ecumenical holding company" that will render "all anxieties tranquilized, all boredom amused." Beale obliges, but when his ratings plummet (viewers find him too depressing), his bosses have him gunned down on live television.

Arthur Jensen's counterpart in the 1997 James Bond film *Tomorrow Never Dies* is multibillionaire mogul Elliot Carver (Jonathan Pryce). Carver adores calamity, much of which he and his media empire create themselves. "Good morning, my golden retrievers! What kind of havoc shall the Carver Media Group create in the world today?" he asks his news division. "Floods in Pakistan, riots in Paris, and a plane crash in California," comes the answer. "Excellent!" exults Carver. The mogul launches an elaborately nefarious scheme to control the planet through an exclusive worldwide flow of information. He finally is stopped by Agent 007 (Pierce Brosnan) with the aid of a giant drill. "You forgot the first rule of mass media, Elliot," Bond tells Carver just before the mogul is ground to death: "Give the people what they want!"[63]

Tomorrow Never Dies, Network, and *Agent of Influence* are all works of fantasy (even though it has been frequently remarked that *Network* was eerily prophetic regarding what would become of television in the years following the film's release).[64] In contrast, the film *The Insider* (1999) relates a true-life story. In 1995 the CBS news program *60 Minutes* broadcast an explosive interview with whistleblower Jeffrey Wigand. The former tobacco company executive revealed that the tobacco industry had increased nicotine levels in cigarettes even as industry representatives testified to Congress that nicotine was not addictive. The uncensored interview aired only after CBS had first prevented it from being broadcast, sparking a controversy that nearly tore *60 Minutes* apart. That is the focus of *The Insider,* as CBS producer Lowell Bergman (Al Pacino) clashes with journalist Mike Wallace (Christopher Plummer) and *60 Minutes* head Don Hewitt (Philip Baker Hall). Bergman has managed after long effort to persuade Wigand (Russell Crowe) to appear on the program, but CBS executives fear the broadcast will invite a massive tobacco lawsuit that could derail a planned merger between CBS and Westinghouse. To Bergman's shock and dismay, Hewitt and Wallace agree to postpone the broadcast.

Bergman is the film's journalistic conscience. "I'm just a commodity to you, aren't I?" Wigand asks him while hesitating to agree to the interview. "To a network, probably we're all commodities," Bergman replies. "To me, you're not a commodity. What you are is important." When Wigand retorts that Bergman is only putting up words, the journalist angrily says he has spent his career "giving my word, and backing it up with action!" And Bergman does act after the network kills the interview: he leaks the Wigand story and CBS's suppression of it to rival news organizations, embarrassing *60 Minutes* into finally airing it in its entirety. Don Hewitt calls him an "anarchist," whereas Wallace tries to justify not supporting him: "History only remembers most what you did last. And should that be fronting a segment that allowed a tobacco giant to crash this network—does it give someone at my time of life pause? Yeah."[65]

Owner interference with the news has continued as a theme in the popular culture works of the twenty-first century. The CEO of Sweden's largest paper orders editor Erika Berger to quash a story that reveals the CEO's connection to child labor abuses in *The Girl Who Kicked the Hornet's Nest.* A newspaper publisher orders the paper's editor to stop editorializing against top advertisers in the TV series *Boss* (2012): "This is about the bottom line—ours. . . . You might consider apologizing for your misguided opinion. Ask them to reconsider pulling their ads from our publication." Media conglomerate chief Leona Lansing (Jane Fonda) orders the head of her TV news division to squelch an outspoken anchor in the first season of the HBO series *The Newsroom.* "I told you to get him to lighten up on [conservative members of Congress], or a context would be created whereby his firing would look reasonable," she says, adding that the government is already threatening to eliminate tax loopholes and other policies that are favorable to her company.[66]

Again, more often than not, the endings to such stories are nominally happy (for example, the exposé is published and the corrupt CEO is forced out in *The Girl Who Kicked the Hornet's Nest*, and Lansing's attempt to silence her anchor fails in *The Newsroom*—indeed, eventually she heroically stands by the news team in connection with a threatened lawsuit). Nonetheless, there often is a bittersweet tinge to the endings, even in tales about press triumphs: a sense that perhaps the forces of greed will have the last laugh. In *Deadline, U.S.A.* the crusading paper is sold to a tabloid and put out of business, with the last image being the light atop the newspaper building being extinguished. In *Good Night, and Good Luck* Edward R. Murrow's beloved news program, *See It Now,* loses its prime-time slot ("I don't want to get a constant stomachache every time you take on a controversial subject," CBS head William Paley tells him), and the film concludes with Murrow warning a group of TV professionals about the medium's misuse for commercial ends: "If this instrument is good for nothing but to entertain, amuse, and insulate, then the tube is flickering now, and we will soon see that the whole struggle is lost." At the end of *The Insider,* after the Wigand interview finally has aired, Mike Wallace tries to persuade Lowell Bergman to stay at CBS. Bergman is unmoved: "What do I tell a source on the next tough story? 'Hang in with us. You'll be fine—maybe.' What got broken here doesn't go back together again." Then he turns away from the speechless Wallace and strides out of the CBS building into the sunlight.

*　*　*

A central dilemma of journalism has been "reconciling private ownership with public responsibility."[67] The social responsibility model of the press assumes that journalists will remain autonomous from their owners and advertisers and that they will act conscientiously and ethically—in brief, that they will responsibly exercise their socially sanctioned power on behalf of the public. According to Theodore Peterson, that model was intended to address a rising tide of fears about journalism in the first half of the twentieth century: that the press "wielded its enormous power for its own ends," that it was "subservient to big business" and "let advertisers control editorial policies and editorial content," that it "paid more attention to the superficial and sensational than to the significant," that it "invaded the privacy of individuals without just cause," and that it was "controlled by one socioeconomic class, loosely the 'business class.'"[68] Social responsibility was supposed to check the abuses of media barons like Hearst, raise journalism above the excesses of the tabloid press, and tackle the complex problems and issues of the post–World War II era.

To critical observers the social responsibility model never operated consistently well, in part due to increasingly concentrated ownership of the news media, and it certainly does not operate well in an age when anyone can create and distribute news. "The gates that the gatekeepers kept are coming down, and the authority of the gatekeepers is coming down with them," John Nerone writes, adding that because "hegemonic [mainstream] journalism has rarely worked for the powerless . . . it is hard to be especially saddened by its weakening."[69] As for the "free press/free people myth" that celebrates a privately owned news media, critics say that it too has served the powerful at the expense of the powerless. For politicians and owners it has been "useful because it is easier to deregulate the owners of media empires (who also sponsor politicians) behind a convincing show of support for truth and popular sovereignty." For the press it has granted journalists "a ready-made role in the ideal picture of . . . democracy," even if that idealized role "is tarnished in the eyes of the public."[70]

According to the free press myth, problems with the press largely stem from bad journalists as opposed to fundamental flaws in the media structure: "While individual editors or publishers along the way may be castigated for failing to do their jobs well, the system itself is beyond reproach."[71] Popular culture's stories about press misdeeds have followed a similar course in focusing on "evil individuals, easily identifiable."[72] A key role of myth in any culture is to address contradictory values or principles and try to reconcile them. Casting out "evil individuals" aligns the ideal of a privately controlled press with that of a publicly spirited one, as does honoring conscientious journalists who stand up to mendacious politicians and heartless corporations. An independent press devoted to competition and profit (but not to greed or exploitation) is celebrated, providing symbolic reassurance that the media system works.[73]

In the process the press is shown to have extraordinary power. Movies and television repeatedly show images of newspaper presses in full roar and newscasters broadcasting into millions of homes. (Such images appear in Frank Capra's silent film *The Power of the Press*; *Mr. Smith Goes to Washington*; *Deadline, U.S.A.*; *Absence of Malice*; *Network*; and both the British and American versions of *State of Play*, to list only a few examples.) The consequences are direct and immediate—theories of limited media effects hold little sway in popular culture.[74] Nixon's men fall one by one at the end of *All the President's Men*. Innocent men are saved from death row in *Call Northside 777*, *True Crime*, and the TV series *Deadline*. The government takes prompt action after a baby-selling racket, a dog-fighting ring, and a toxic waste dump are exposed in TV's *Lou Grant*. Evil is regularly uncovered and corrected.[75]

Significantly, though, there are also limits to journalism's power. The editor in *Deadline, U.S.A.* and Murrow in *Good Night, and Good Luck* can do nothing to save their newspaper and news program, just as (in one episode) Lou Grant and his staff have no power to stop the potential sale and loss of independence of their paper.[76] Charles Foster Kane fails to get himself elected to public office or turn his wife into an opera star in *Citizen Kane*. Megan Carter cannot keep herself or her newspaper from being disgraced in *Absence of Malice*. Mattie Storin and Zoe Barnes are unable to report unspeakable crimes or even save their own lives in the British and American versions of *House of Cards*. Howard Beale tells his audience to turn off their TV sets in *Network*, and instead his ratings soar; when he later urges them to acquiesce to a dehumanized world, they tune him out and his poor ratings lead to his assassination. The news media's exposés fix things only momentarily. After the reporters go on to other stories, the homeless are still there, the environment is still polluted, and the politicians are still corrupt.

Ironically, such tales of impotence often reproduce the same myths. Journalists who abuse their power see it vanish, whereas others who are more virtuous suffer the sorry consequences of "cutthroat capitalists" failing to "keep out of the pros' way."[77] Frequently there is a strong undercurrent of longing for a vanished era. The closing credits of the 2009 American version of *State of Play* show a newspaper being printed and shipped as the wistful song "Long As I Can See the Light" plays on the soundtrack. "It turns out to be a fond homage to old-school journalism, and it plays like a eulogy for a sadly dying industry," one critic wrote of the film, adding that it evoked "nostalgia for a more optimistic, prosperous time—especially for those of us who work in this business."[78] That is consistent with the belief of media scholars that journalists frequently "respond nostalgically and defensively to disruptive change,"[79] and that they seek relief from "the contradictions of journalistic life" through "a return to an idealized past."[80]

Not all journalists see things that way, of course. "My [first] instinct was to be defensive—to protect the world I knew and treasured," writes veteran magazine editor and journalism educator Stephen Shepard about the dramatic changes in the news industry. "I have come to believe that digital technology will enrich journalism, creating an interactive, multimedia form of storytelling that can invite community participation."[81] In a similar vein, longtime *Washington Post* editor Leonard Downie Jr. and journalism scholar Michael Schudson see "abundant opportunity" for a "genuine reconstruction of what journalism can and should be," with multiple sources of financing (including from the state and philanthropic foundations) to support "accountability journalism" that "targets those who have power and influence in our lives—not only governmental bodies, but businesses and educational and cultural institutions."[82]

In sustaining such optimistic views of the future, in which journalism serves as a genuinely responsible watchdog of power in partnership with the public, the "free press myth" as promoted by popular culture has its benefits. Such myths again can be understood not simply as falsehoods but as "inspirational, hopeful, ennobling" sentiments that provide "substance to a national history that would otherwise become vague in the minds of new generations."[83] They keep alive the idea that the press is the "essential nurturer of an informed citizenry."[84] By venerating journalism for using its power well and vilifying it for using that power badly, popular culture offers visions in which a free press and a free people cannot be separated.

5

Image

Journalism's relationship to the visual image has been a source of both fascination and apprehension. "For well over a century," says Kiku Adatto, people "have vacillated between celebrating pictures and worrying about their contrived nature, their association with commercialism, and their tendency to crowd out words."[1] The worries have grown more acute in an era of digital media, televised politics, and globalization, as the ease with which images can be digitally altered has raised questions about photojournalism's authenticity and whether "in the long run the new technologies might diminish the public's trust in journalism."[2] Television has been said to have had an especially pernicious impact in promoting worldwide "corporate colonization of the public sphere, undermining public journalism" through a "powerful, seductive discourse of diversion" that promotes infotainment over serious reporting provided by the quality print media.[3]

Others, though, warn against an "elite bias on behalf of the medium of print and against visual media."[4] Barbie Zelizer argues that news images "allow journalists, news executives, officials, politicians, and viewers to engage with public events as much with their hearts and guts as with their brains."[5] According to journalists themselves, that emotional power can be harnessed to serve the press's noblest ends. One writes that the best photojournalists "adopt a humanist point of view as they strive to make the world better with their pictures," upholding the "tradition of crusading journalism to expose problems and create understanding."[6] Another declares that television news can employ "the power of storytelling [to] connect with the viewer's heart" and at the same time tell "the truth as fully and courageously as possible."[7]

In this chapter we look more closely at the drama and conflicts that have surrounded photojournalists and television journalists in popular culture. They sometimes are portrayed as doing exactly what journalists say they should do: they promote accuracy and fairness, document wrongdoing and evil, and push citizens toward empathy and justice. Other times they represent the worst fears about visual media: an oppressive force that lends itself to fabrication, trivialization, and dehumanization.

Early Photojournalists

Photography became widely used in journalism in the early twentieth century through technological improvements in cameras and printing.[8] By the 1920s journalists embraced photography as a way of documenting reality, but there were already fears about its ability to deceive. As early as the Civil War, photographers had staged pictures for the camera, and then the yellow press at the turn of the twentieth century and the tabloid press of the post–World War I years shamelessly manipulated images.[9] Newsreel films were also well established by the 1920s and brought dramatic depictions of the news to cinemagoers. From their origins the newsreels had combined actual footage of events filmed under sometimes dangerous circumstances with reenactments of events and occasional outright fakery.[10]

Popular culture depictions of journalism followed suit. Bonnie Brennen notes that newsreel shooters are portrayed in the movies of the 1920s and 1930s "as heroes who risk their lives to bring images of news and information to the public," while also managing to "capture kidnappers, confront gangsters, solve mysteries, prevent crimes, and discover murderers." Simultaneously, the shooters are shown to be "ruthless, unethical, and corrupt, willing to do anything including faking news coverage to get a scoop."[11] *Too Hot to Handle* (1938) stars Clark Gable at the height of his career. He plays newsreel photographer Chris Hunter, who uses firecrackers and toy airplanes to fake footage of the bombing of Shanghai. ("I didn't distort the truth," he avows. "I merely heightened the composition.") He also unhesitatingly climbs onto the wing of a flying airplane to shoot film of a burning ship just before it explodes, and he manages to save his girlfriend's brother from a horrible death in a South American jungle. Hunter's ethical shortcuts notwithstanding, a reviewer described *Too Hot to Handle* at the time of its release as a "feature-length glorification of the newsreel cameraman."[12]

In contrast, according to Brennen, movies portrayed those who shot still photos instead of moving pictures as "second-class workers" who were "rou-

James Stewart plays the voyeuristic photojournalist loved by Grace Kelly in *Rear Window*.

tinely included as comic relief, falling out of cabs, knocking over their cam-eras, making a mess, and generally failing to get the picture."[13] Such portrayals indicated the low status and terrible working conditions of photojournal-ists in early twentieth-century journalism. Earle Bridger argues that movies showing photographers as "clumsy, trouble-making oafs" reflected the lot of real-world photojournalists, who "were poorly paid and had little job security."[14] Even when films showed them displaying skill and nerve, they still were portrayed as sensationalistic: James Cagney in *Picture Snatcher* sneaks a camera under his pants leg to photograph an execution, mimick-ing the true-life feat of a New York tabloid photographer who had captured a woman's death in the electric chair.[15]

In 1945 the National Press Photographers Association (NPPA) was formed partly to counter the "stereotype of a sharp-elbowed lout with a cigarette dangling from his lower lip, a press card jammed in the brim of his upturned hat, and a perpetually popping flash." It also was intended to confront the "common prejudice against photographs" in newsrooms—"that as a simplistic form of communication that appealed to the uneducated, they were inferior to the written word."[16] Such efforts did not significantly improve the negative image of photojournalists in popular culture. If anything, by the 1950s a new negative image had emerged of "egocentric, narrow-focused loners" with "an exaggerated sense of importance about their profession."[17] In Alfred Hitchcock's *Rear Window* (1954) the injured and wheelchair-bound Jeff Jefferies insists that few people could cope with the hardships that he faces in his assignments around the world: "In this job you carry one suitcase, your home is the available transportation, you don't sleep very much, you bathe less, and sometimes the food that you eat is made from things that you couldn't even look at when they're alive!" He passes the time by peeking at his neighbors with his telephoto lens, consistent not only with the idea of photojournalists as being unethical, but also with broader fears about cameras being used to spy on others. "The pleasure he derives from watching his neighbors without their knowledge or permission is essentially sadistic," one critic has written,[18] whereas another has called *Rear Window* an "ode to voyeurism."[19]

Robert Capa–Inspired Photojournalists

Whatever the faults of Jeff Jefferies, he is markedly more couth than his grubby pop culture predecessors, particularly as played by James Stewart and as ardently wooed in the film by Grace Kelly. One magazine historian has identified the character as a variation on another, more attractive photojournalist stereotype: the suave man with a camera who was "presentable—even desirable—in any situation," given that he was "a wry, funny, sexy sort (brave, too, terribly brave, of course) who had been *everywhere* where he had done *everything*." The most prominent model for such characters was the "cocky, debonair, woman-conquering" Robert Capa, who would be killed while covering the early stages of the Vietnam War.[20] The famous photojournalist had been the romantic obsession of film star Ingrid Bergman, and the Capa-Bergman romance was said to have inspired the relationship between the Stewart and Kelly characters in *Rear Window*.[21]

Capa-type photojournalists—daring and dashing, but also often damaged or doomed—have persisted as popular culture staples to this day. They have appeared in the comics,[22] on television,[23] and in scores of novels, including mysteries and romances.[24] In Barbara Taylor Bradford's *Remember,* Cleeland "Clee" Donovan sees Capa as "the single most important influence in his life." Donovan lives up to that legacy not only through "the powerful images on film for which he was famous," but also through his being devastatingly attractive to women, especially the novel's protagonist, television reporter Nicky Wells.[25] Things end happily for Wells and Donovan, but frequently the photojournalists in these works have witnessed too much trauma in their travels to be able to mend their lives easily (although the women who love them do their best to help). They return home with "battered body and mind," in "a state of depression and despair," and "yearning to shut out the world."[26] Tom Davis's novel *Scared* (2009) tells of the "celebrated and award-winning" Stuart Daniels, who is crippled by guilt over his best-known photograph showing brutality in Africa: a "haunting image that indicts him as a passive witness to gross injustice."[27]

In Ward Just's book *Exiles in the Garden* (2009) it is the photojournalist's decision *not* to witness overseas horrors that haunts him. Alec Malone turns down the opportunity to cover the Vietnam War, having no desire to be like Robert Capa and declaring, "I was damned if I was going to the war as a good career move." His decision ends up casting a long shadow over his life and career, and his wife leaves him. Years later, while looking at some of the favorite photos he has taken, Malone realizes "finally with the most open dismay that the common theme was the absence of conflict." He dies alone on a boat at sea—whether by accident or suicide is unclear.[28]

Hollywood has typically shunned ennui as a dramatic subject. Instead, it focuses on the turmoil of photojournalists who do embrace conflict. Themes similar to those of novels emerge: the unanticipated impact of photos, the obsession with getting a career-defining shot, and the emotional toll of seeing awful things through the viewfinder.

For example, in *Under Fire* (1983) rugged Russell Price (Nick Nolte) lands in Nicaragua during the 1979 revolution. He and his fellow reporter and sometime lover, Claire Stryder (Joanna Cassidy), are taken by Sandinista rebels to their leader, "Rafael," who turns out to have been killed. The rebels want Price to stage a photo making it seem as though Rafael is still alive in order to inspire their followers. Price initially refuses ("I'm a journalist!" he indignantly exclaims), but Stryder helps persuade him to shoot the picture by telling him that although he has won plenty of prizes, "you haven't won a war." The faked photo turns the tide in favor of the Sandinistas, even as Price is shocked to learn that other pictures he has taken are being used by the Somoza government to target rebels for elimination.

In Oliver Stone's *Salvador* (1986) Richard Boyle (James Woods) takes the old image of the unkempt photojournalist to an entirely new level. ("Nothing is legal about your car," a police officer who has stopped him for speeding tells him. "Even your press card is out of date.") Abandoned by his wife and child, Boyle heads to El Salvador in search of good times, only to be plunged into a brutal civil war and radicalized by American complicity with the bloodshed.

Along the way he meets fellow photojournalist John Cassady (John Savage), who represents another instance of Capa worship: "You know what made photographers like Robert Capa great, Rich? They weren't after the money. They captured the nobility of human suffering. . . . You gotta get close, Rich, to get the truth. You get too close, you die. Someday I want a shot like Capa. Someday." That day comes: Cassady snaps a sensational photo of a strafing airplane, but at the cost of his own life.[29]

Photojournalists also pay the ultimate price in *The Bang Bang Club* (2010). The film relates the true story of four photographers who covered the final violent years of apartheid in South Africa. Greg Marinovich (Ryan Phillippe) wins a Pulitzer Prize for a photo of a man being hacked and burned alive; Kevin Carter (Taylor Kitsch) wins a Pulitzer for a picture of a starving child apparently being stalked by a vulture. The men alternate between celebrating their professional exploits with booze, drugs, and sex, and brooding over their complicity with the horrors they record. Carter is particularly troubled by pointed questions over why he had not done more to help the starving child he photographed. He tells an interviewer that a great photo is "not just a spectacle; it's more than that. . . . You go out and you see bad things, evil things. And you want to do something about it. So what you do is you take

The photojournalists who make up *The Bang Bang Club* (from left to right): Ken Oosterbroek (Frank Rautenbach), João Silva (Neels Van Jaarsveld), Kevin Carter (Taylor Kitsch), and Greg Marinovich (Ryan Phillippe).

the picture that shows it. But not everybody is going to like what they see. You have to understand that they might want to shoot the messenger." To Marinovich, though, Carter says that those who disapprove are right, "all of the people that say that it's our job to sit there and watch people die." After fellow photographer Ken Oosterbroek is killed on the job, Carter leaves a suicide note saying he is "haunted by the vivid memories of killings and corpses and anger and pain," and he asphyxiates himself.[30]

Under Fire, Salvador, and *The Bang Bang Club* disturbed some journalists with their depictions of news photographers. The ready willingness to stage a photo for the sake of a cause was said to promote "a more hospitable public climate for claims that real journalists have all along been feeding us misinformation and disinformation."[31] The utter obliviousness to personal safety amounted to a romanticized "glorification of the iconic hero willing to die for his profession."[32] The self-flagellation over not directly intervening in events "belittle[d] the idea that documenting history is not necessarily inferior to actively participating in it."[33] However, critic Pauline Kael praised *Under Fire* for highlighting the existential struggles of the "automaton" photojournalist who finally becomes humanized by allowing himself to "be governed by his own core of generosity."[34]

Female Photojournalists and Male Paparazzi

Works like *The Bang Bang Club* depict an all-boys club (even with the presence in that film of a female photo editor, who exists primarily as a love interest). In fact, photojournalism historically has been male-dominated, according to Claude Cookman: "Patriarchal attitudes, good-old-boy networks, and men's desire to protect their dominance combined to keep the numbers of women in photojournalism small and to consign them to covering women's news and soft features, typically at lower salaries."[35] Women news photographers do appear frequently in popular culture, though, and they often experience the same kinds of conflicts that their male counterparts do.[36]

As is usual in portrayals of female journalists, home versus work is a constant concern. In the TV movie *Margaret Bourke-White* (1989) Farrah Fawcett plays the celebrated photojournalist. She has achieved distinction for her work that includes photos of Nazi death camps, but her marriage to novelist Erskine Caldwell is less successful, with his frequent protests about how she continually puts her work ahead of all else. Another globetrotting photojournalist (Sissy Spacek) returns to her hometown for the first time in years in the film *Violets Are Blue* (1986). She begins an affair with her old

boyfriend, who is now married. The romance ends, and the photojournalist leaves town once more after trying to explain herself to her father: "I've
missed every Christmas except one for the past thirteen years. And you know
why? . . . Because I want to be the best. To be the best, you've got to be there
[where news happens]. So *I'm* there."

Once in a great while a female photojournalist achieves a share of both
personal and professional happiness, as with the protagonist of Danielle Steel's
novel *Bittersweet* (1999). At the start India Taylor has willingly forsaken her
prizewinning photography career to devote herself to her husband and four
children. Inevitably she is drawn back to her work, including documenting
a graphic case of child sexual exploitation. Her enraged husband brands the
photos as "total smut," "sheer pornography," and "absolute filth," and he leaves
her. Fortunately for Taylor, she has met a Wall Street tycoon (albeit a married
one) who loves her for herself and her work, and after the requisite complications, it all appears to end happily.[37] In other instances the excitement of the
job seems more than enough for the photojournalist. The young eponymous
star of the "Jade del Cameron" historical mysteries, by Suzanne Arruda, has
a "lithe, well-muscled figure" and "eyes the color of brilliant moss," but her
"real beauty [lies] in her strength of character" and her "easy grace and confidence."[38] In 1919 del Cameron travels to Africa, where she not only takes
pictures but also "mingles with the colonial elite, kills a hyena, learns Swahili,
fingers a drug smuggler, romances a man twice her age, uncovers a murder
and attracts the attention of a local witch"—all in one book.[39]

Still, stereotypes of the female photojournalist as demonstrating a "lack
of personal and professional ethics" and as being in "need of male companionship" have persisted for years.[40] Also persistent have been stereotypes of
slovenly male photojournalists. The hairy, hippie-like character "Animal"
on the *Lou Grant* TV series raised the ire of real news photographers, never
mind that he was a competent professional. "Long after Lou Grant leaves the
network," protested one photographer, "will we carry the stigma his show
has given us in the public eye?"[41]

Whatever stigma accrued from that show could not match that from other
depictions of news photographers as scummy lowlifes. The Federico Fellini
film *La Dolce Vita* (1960) christened the term "paparazzo" through the name
of a tabloid photographer character, and scores of novels, movies, and television episodes since then have graphically portrayed the excesses of such
types. In the film *The Public Eye* (1992) they are labeled "shutterbugs" because
"they're insects. They're vermin, scavengers. They've got no morality."[42] In
Christopher J. Heassler's aptly named novel *The Antagonist's Handbook,* they

form a powerful union and prey on celebrities. The TV series *The Naked Truth* (1995–98) focuses on a onetime Pulitzer Prize nominee (Téa Leoni) who suffers a reversal of fortune and ends up taking pictures for a sleazy tabloid, whereas *Dirt* (2007–08) features a schizophrenic paparazzo who is lost in delusions about a dead actress and a cat. The movie *Paparazzi* (2004) is particularly scathing, as photographers set out to ruin a movie star and his family. ("I'm going to destroy your life and eat your soul," one hisses. "And I can't wait to do it!") After the film star's wife and child are critically injured in a paparazzi-triggered auto accident, the star takes his revenge by allowing one photographer to fall to his death and gorily dispatching another with a baseball bat.[43]

Television Journalists:
Development of a Stereotype

Badgering, paparazzi-ish photographers packed alongside hectoring, tabloid-esque TV reporters constitute a typical negative image of the press in popular culture.[44] However, whereas the negative portrayals of photojournalists are tempered with positive representations of them as courageously noble professionals, TV journalists are a regular source of ridicule. Television itself is depicted as a dangerous, mind-deadening medium that values trivia over significance and profit-taking over humanity. That is not to say that conscientious TV journalists do not exist—rather, they face formidable challenges that make for ideal pop culture fodder.

Before TV journalists there were radio journalists, and they too were a source of skepticism if not derision. In *Behind the Headlines* (1937) newspaper reporters try to steal the microphone of the radio news protagonist, and the papers threaten to drop ads for radio programs unless the radio reporter is fired. ("You're an utter cockroach," a print reporter tells the radio reporter. "And we did the world a good turn today by stepping on you.") Other movies, like *Two Against the World* (1936), depicted villainous radio station owners, precursors to tales of venal TV barons in the years to come.[45]

By the late 1950s films about radio would be largely supplanted by those about television. That was signified by *A Face in the Crowd* (1957), in which a charismatic folksinging radio personality (Andy Griffith) becomes a megalomaniacal TV star and a despotic political kingmaker while the radio reporter (Patricia Neal) who discovered him falls under his spell and is powerless (until the end) to stop him.[46] Novels followed suit. One study notes that "the first generation of fiction about television journalism—from the 1950s and 1960s—focused on the medium itself, not the people who report television news," with subjects such as television's perversion of politics or its susceptibility to political coercion.[47] In 1969, at the end of a decade of televised protests, assassinations, and warfare, the movie *Medium Cool* used the character of a TV news videographer to examine television's desensitizing role in American life. The videographer (Robert Forster) is obsessed with his work to the point of callousness. "Jesus, I love to shoot film," he murmurs while watching footage related to Martin Luther King Jr.'s assassination, and when he comes across a woman who has been seriously injured in a car accident, he films her before thinking about calling for help. The videographer's TV station fires him after he discovers that the station is sharing his film of draft resisters with the FBI, and at the end he suffers a terrible car wreck of his own. A passing car slows just long enough to allow a passenger to snap a photo of the wreck before it drives away.[48]

The most common images of the television journalist would take shape in the 1970s. They borrowed elements from depictions of the newsreel photographer (the excitement of capturing the story as well as the temptation toward fakery), the photojournalist (the Capa-type allure as well as the arrogance and often battered psyche), and the radio journalist (the lack of respect from the print media). Those all were projected onto the ongoing fears about TV's toxic impact on society. Familiar character types emerged: the male anchor who is lost without his teleprompter; the female reporter who is prized more for her looks than for her brains; the veteran journalist (most often male) who bemoans how the legacy of Edward R. Murrow is dying; and the unscrupulous producers, news directors, and managers who will do anything—including destroying people—for ratings.

Fluff, Lust, and Angst

Television news often is the stuff of parody, with TV itself establishing the model for the dimwitted anchor with Ted Baxter in *The Mary Tyler Moore Show*. As played by Ted Knight, Baxter is lovable but hopelessly incompetent on camera. ("In order for the bill to pass, it must be ratified by two-thirds of the forty-eight states. Oh—two more? Correction: Make that four-thirds!")[49] Will Ferrell pays homage to Baxter-like buffoons as the spectacularly coiffed Ron Burgundy in *Anchorman* (2004) and *Anchorman 2* (2013), a man who reads anything the teleprompter says, regardless of mistakes in punctuation: "I'm Ron Burgundy?" Other examples include the bloviating anchors Kent Brockman on *The Simpsons* (1989–) and Tom Tucker on *Family Guy* (1998–),

Television reporter Kermit the Frog interviews Elmo on *Sesame Street.*

not to mention the ruthless mockery of TV news content and conventions on *The Daily Show* (1996–), *The Colbert Report* (2005–14), and *Saturday Night Live's* "Weekend Update" (1975–). Even the venerable children's series *Sesame Street* (1969–) has poked gentle fun through its "News Flash" segments that featured a harried Kermit the Frog reporting live from the scenes of nursery rhymes. With "Hickory Dickory Dock," Kermit is chagrined when the mouse does not show up as expected and a horse attempts to run up the clock instead, thereby destroying it. "How come I always get [assigned] these nursery rhyme things?" the frog fumes before storming away.[50]

In other instances the glitz and glamour of TV news have offered a convenient backdrop for unbridled lust. Bonnie Tucker's novel *Stay Tuned: Wedding at 11:00* (1998) features Margaret St. James, who "can't stand gorgeous John Hennessey, her co-anchor on the news. After all, he'd loved her and left her in the past—and now he wants her job! She can't help it if the chemistry between them crackles over the airwaves."[51] In Montana Mills's *Need* (2011) reporter Mona Andrews "discovers that her handsome cameraman Roger has a little side project going on that involves filming other news anchors at a replica of the Channel 5 Action News room. What the anchors do there not only shocks Mona, but also turns her on. And now she wants in."[52]

Some novels look past the apparent sexual insatiability of TV journalists in suggesting that glitz and glamour can come at a price, with women chagrined to learn that being a good journalist is not enough. In Venise Berry's *All of Me* (2000) reporter Serpentine Williamson is humiliated by being forced to watch video of a focus group criticizing her appearance. Her news director informs her that, like it or not, her weight matters. "Television is not only about reporting skills, it's about the total package: skills, looks, voice tone, even personality," he says. "Viewers have to want to invite you into their living room on a daily basis." When Williamson learns that she likely will be passed over for an anchor spot, she explodes in anger ("No matter how you dress it up, shit stinks!"), but afterward she is "glad that she didn't accept [the] business-as-usual garbage."[53]

Reporter Riley Spartz likewise confronts the "garbage" as the star of a series of mystery novels. Author Julie Kramer, who herself once worked in broadcast journalism, says the books are "set in the desperate world of television news," in which "news and gossip have more in common" than ever before.[54] Spartz constantly deals with ratings pressures, including the need to come up with "sweeps" pieces that will attract viewers and generate revenue for her station. Fortunately or not, she keeps coming across murders that she not only helps solve but also turns into compelling news stories.

Network condemns television through the relationship between veteran news executive Max Schumacher (William Holden) and programming chief Diana Christensen (Faye Dunaway). It is Christensen who puts Howard Beale (Peter Finch) in prime time and exults in his success, no matter that in fits of revelation Beale berates his viewers for being television's slave: "You even think like the tube! This is mass madness, you maniacs! In God's name, you people are the real thing—we are the illusion!" For his part, Max Schumacher is besotted by the beautiful Christensen and briefly leaves his wife to be with her, even though Christensen admits to being a "lousy lay" and is able to climax during sex only by talking incessantly about TV. Finally, Schumacher sees the light and leaves her: "You're television incarnate, Diana. . . . War, murder, death—all the same to you as bottles of beer. And the daily business of life is a corrupt comedy. . . . You're madness, Diana . . . and everything you touch dies with you. But not me. Not as long as I can feel pleasure, and pain, and love."[55]

Both Max Schumacher and Howard Beale are of the Edward R. Murrow generation, and just as Murrow decried how TV's capacity to "illuminate" and "inspire" was being frittered away (as dramatized by 1986's *Murrow* and 2005's *Good Night, and Good Luck*), so too do other veteran male journalists lament what television news has become. Beale brands it as "a goddamn amusement park." In *The Insider* a despairing Lowell Bergman (Al Pacino) dismisses it as "infotainment [that] is so fucking useless—all of it."[56] In *Wrong Is Right* (1982) star reporter Patrick Hale (Sean Connery) sardonically observes that TV news is "show business, baby. Make 'em laugh; make 'em cry. Make 'em buy, buy, and buy!" In Aaron Sorkin's HBO series *The Newsroom*, anchor Will McAvoy (Jeff Daniels) tells his viewers that even though "some of history's greatest American journalists are working right now," they are "a small minority" who "don't stand a chance against the circus when the circus comes to town"—that circus, of course, being what the brunt of TV has to offer.[57]

If older men deliver jeremiads about TV, younger women like Diana Christensen are regularly made to represent "television incarnate"—the main attraction of the circus. Her epitome is Suzanne Stone (Nicole Kidman) in *To Die For* (1995). The film was based on Joyce Maynard's novel of the same name and was inspired by the true-life case of Pamela Smart, a twenty-two-year-old television wannabe who used sex to lure a teenage boy into murdering her husband.[58] In the movie Stone is just as desperate to be on the air: "On TV is where we learn about who we really are. Because what's the point of doing anything worthwhile if nobody's watching? And if people are watching, it makes you a better person." Trying to advance her career beyond her lowly job as a weatherperson on a local cable outlet, she starts a documentary about a sad-sack group of local teens, seduces one of them, and then manipulates him into killing her husband. When it appears as though Suzanne will get away with her evil deed, her late husband's parents call on the Mafia to eliminate her. In *To Die For* there is no Max Schumacher type on hand—only a sleazy TV executive (George Segal) who intones platitudes about the television journalist "bringing the world into our homes and our homes into the world" while leering at Suzanne and feeling her up under the table.[59]

In contrast with *To Die For, Broadcast News* (1987) features two conscientious news professionals, one male and one female. Both, though, are forced to adjust to the changing demands of TV journalism. Jane Craig (Holly Hunter) is a ferociously hardworking producer in a network Washington news bureau. Although her career is going well, her personal life (true to form) is a disaster; she schedules regular breaks during her day to cry. Her best friend is Aaron Altman (Albert Brooks), a talented reporter in the bureau who is secretly in love with her. They both are disconcerted by the arrival of Tom Grunick (William Hurt), who comes to the bureau from local TV sports and who freely admits that he knows nothing about news. Jane is appalled by his ignorance and the apparent decline in network news standards that he represents, but at the same time, she is powerfully attracted to his charm and good looks. Aaron is also appalled by Tom while envying his grace on camera and his hold on Jane. Complicating matters is a network cutback that terminates several employees but results in promotions for Jane and Tom. Aaron quits the network in disgust and then effectively sabotages Jane and Tom's romantic relationship by revealing to her that Tom faked part of a story. For his part, Tom is unrepentant; when Jane tells him that he crossed the line, he retorts, "They keep moving the little sucker, don't they?"

The romantic triangle in *Broadcast News* points to a clash in values. Aaron appeals to Jane's professional sensibilities by comparing Tom to the devil and telling her that Satan will look very much like a news anchor or presenter: "He will be attractive. He'll be nice and helpful. He'll get a job where he influences a great, God-fearing nation. He'll never do an evil thing. . . . He'll just bit by little bit lower our standards where they're important—just a tiny little bit, just coast along—flash over substance!" Yet Jane has a unique professional rapport with Tom, as is shown when he anchors live news coverage of a Libyan attack on an American military base. Jane tells him exactly what to do and say through a microphone connected to his earpiece. "There was like a rhythm we got into," he exultantly tells her afterward. "It was like—great sex!" For the film's writer-director, James L. Brooks, the point was that the only real connection the two characters could make was "far apart and electronically," suggestive again of television's dehumanizing powers.[60] At the end of *Broadcast News* (which flashes ahead seven years from the main events of the film), Tom is named nightly news anchor and Jane agrees to become his managing editor, ethical concerns apparently forgotten. Although it represents another promotion for Jane, it appears that Aaron's fears have come true: she has made her pact with the devil.

Principled Television Journalists

Some works eschew such barbed critiques of TV news, suggesting that good journalism can be done by both women and men in spite of everything. Again, television itself helped originate such positive portrayals. Both *The Mary Tyler Moore Show* and *Murphy Brown* starred female characters who were very good at their jobs, with *The Mary Tyler Moore Show* also featuring the upstanding news director Lou Grant (Edward Asner) and news writer Murray Slaughter (Gavin MacLeod). *Murphy Brown* featured a positive portrayal of an investigative reporter in Frank Fontana (Joe Regalbuto). That series also took characters that could have represented stock caricatures—the pompous older male anchor, the silly young female cub—and made them richer and more multidimensional. Reporter Corky Sherwood (Faith Ford) became a capable journalist, and anchor Jim Dial (Charles Kimbrough) turned out to be the antithesis of Ted Baxter. Well-known TV journalists such as Walter Cronkite and Mike Wallace greeted Dial and Murphy Brown

Mackenzie McHale (Emily Mortimer, standing far left), Will McAvoy (Jeff Daniels, second from left), and the rest of the news team trying to reclaim television journalism as an honorable profession in *The Newsroom*.

as friends and colleagues, and that gave the fictional journalists credibility and legitimacy.[61]

Similarly principled male anchors appeared in the TV movies *News at Eleven* (1986) and *The Image* (1990). In the first film Frank Kenley (Martin Sheen) publicly excoriates his station's role in exploiting the story of a high school student who has accused her teacher of rape; in the second, anchor Jason Cromwell (Albert Finney) uncovers a savings and loan scandal that his station originally misreported. Cromwell tells his viewers that "commitment to truth can be compromised in the race for the ratings. We have to ensure that the truth—the whole truth—will always be part of our process."

More recently the BBC's *The Hour* has featured a romantic triangle similar to that of *Broadcast News,* with a female TV producer (Romola Garai) torn between a handsome but seemingly shallow anchor and a brilliant but insecure reporter. Still, the team's news program (with help from another strong woman, who runs the foreign desk) exposes high-level state corruption. In *The Newsroom* it is producer Mackenzie McHale (Emily Mortimer) who helps persuade Will McAvoy (with whom she previously has had a romantic relationship) to leave the "circus" and do a news program with the loftiest of goals: "Reclaiming the Fourth Estate. Reclaiming journalism as an honorable profession. A nightly newscast that informs a debate worthy of a great nation. Civility, respect, and a return to what's important. The death of bitchiness, the death of gossip and voyeurism. Speaking truth to stupid. No demographic sweet spot—a place where we all come together."[62]

In at least one instance, popular culture has taken an example of television tragedy and excess and transformed it into glossy romance. It was inspired by the story of Jessica Savitch, who rose from local TV news in the 1970s to become a network anchor at NBC. Although Savitch was popular with viewers, many at the network scorned her, and she suffered drug addiction and an abusive relationship with TV journalist Ron Kershaw before dying young in an auto accident. Savitch's story was first told by the TV movie *Almost Golden* (1995), in which Sela Ward played the journalist. That film depicts a memorable blot on Savitch's career: she threw a tantrum during a commercial break in the middle of a newscast, and crew members who detested her surreptitiously taped the incident and circulated the tape around the country.

In *Up Close & Personal* (1996) screenwriters John Gregory Dunne and Joan Didion—neither of whom was known for sentimentality—transformed the Savitch story into a more uplifting tale. It became that of TV journalists Warren Justice (Robert Redford) and Tally Atwater (Michelle Pfeiffer). Warren mentors Tally while overlooking that she has fabricated her audition tape: "I figure if you're hungry enough to fake it, you might be hungry enough to do it." Her career skyrockets, and they fall in love and marry. After Warren dies tragically while pursuing a story in Panama, his wife pays him tribute at a TV industry event: "I thought if I ever stood up at something like this, it would be about glory or showing people. It's different; I know that now. I'm only here for one reason, to tell the story. My husband told me that not so long ago."[63]

Despite such portrayals of TV news as a (mostly) respectable profession, the old stereotypes persist. For example, a 2013 episode of the TV series *NCIS* features a reporter who becomes a copycat serial killer to generate sensational news coverage and resurrect his career—another incarnation of the utterly amoral, ratings-obsessed television journalist.[64] And even when the characters have been far more benign, the commercial imperatives and peculiar priorities of television news still rear their heads: in the final episode of *The Mary Tyler Moore Show,* the news team is fired for poor ratings, with only Ted Baxter somehow keeping his job.

*   *   *

The enduring stereotypes of photojournalists and television journalists highlight the uneasy place of the visual image in our culture. According to

Kiku Adatto, as far back as the nineteenth century critics were arguing that "pictures threatened to overwhelm words, to crowd out serious reflection with titillation, sensation, and distraction." Now, in the twenty-first century, "the line between news and entertainment, serious news and tabloid news has eroded," and "the producers of the news are embracing theater rather than apologizing for it" by putting "pretty faces, and, in the case of women, pretty bodies on display."[65] From such a perspective it is small wonder that popular culture presents grimy male news photographers and shallow female broadcasters, not to mention packs of nameless journalists who shove cameras and microphones into the face of anyone who seems to present a potential story. Small wonder, too, that quality journalism has appeared more likely to be the province of the print media—after all, Lou Grant had to escape Ted Baxter and join a newspaper (and an hour-long drama series as opposed to a half-hour comedy) in order to produce serious news coverage on a consistent basis.[66]

Adatto also notes that we are surrounded today by images that have been "Photoshopped" or otherwise digitally altered. "We know the images are fake," she argues, "but, on another level, we are seduced by what we see, and we measure ourselves by the images around us."[67] Although Photoshop is a comparatively new technology, photos and moving pictures always have been altered or staged by those who have not held weighty concerns about journalism ethics. The sometimes tenuous relationship between image and reality has been another long-standing pop culture subject, as has the seductiveness of the image. Stories showing the ease with which images can be manipulated suggest that photos do not always mirror reality or live up to "the professional ideology of objectivity."[68] Yet even though working with images and projecting one's image to others may not always seem as reputable as working with words, it still can be sexy and exciting. Thus the popularity of photojournalists and television journalists as the protagonists of adventures, romances, mysteries, and other popular genres should come as no surprise, particularly given the dramatic possibilities that are inherent in coping with the pressures of a job in which the quest for the best image—no matter how shallow, gruesome, or even phony it might be—can be all-encompassing.

Dramatic, too, are the fears about visual media being used for suppression and pacification. In her influential 1977 book, *On Photography,* Susan Sontag asserted that cameras "define reality in the two ways essential to the workings of an advanced industrial society: as a spectacle (for masses) and as an object of surveillance (for rulers)." The surveillance function gathers "unlimited amounts of information" in order to maintain order and control, whereas the spectacle provides "vast amounts of entertainment in order to stimulate buying and anesthetize the injuries of class, race, and sex."[69] Today, when smartphone cameras are everywhere, spectacle and surveillance have folded into one and spread to the masses; as one scholar observes, "now we're all paparazzi."[70] Concerns over the use and abuse of visual media have been acknowledged by popular culture for years, whether it be Jeff Jefferies in *Rear Window* wondering aloud "if it's ethical to watch a man with binoculars and a long-focus lens" (after which he goes right on watching), or Howard Beale in *Network* telling his viewers that they are "beginning to believe the illusions we're spinning here" and urging them to turn off their TV sets (whereupon his studio audience erupts in cheers and his ratings go through the roof).

Recent scholarship has pointed toward a more constructive role for news photos and those who take them. "Journalism and its visuals have existed for too long in an uneven relationship that has kept images fastened as second-class citizens," Barbie Zelizer writes, arguing that images engage the public precisely because they appeal to "emotions [and] the imagination" as opposed to providing just dry, factual information.[71] For her part, Susan Sontag would come to reassess her assertion in *On Photography* that the spectacle of graphic news photos hardened people to human suffering. Although the photos by themselves could not change things, at least they could offer "an invitation to pay attention, to reflect, to learn, to examine the rationalizations for mass suffering offered by established powers."[72] In short, they could foster the "humanist point of view" that the best photojournalists are said to possess and promote through their work.[73] That humanist viewpoint has been represented again in popular culture through the depictions of heroic, Capa-like news photographers, who often pay a steep price through their repeated exposure to other people's pain.

Television has not achieved the same degree of respectability. The regular appearance of characters such as Suzanne Stone in *To Die For* reflects that television "has been historically and pejoratively constructed as a feminine medium" that is not so serious or sober as the print medium.[74] If popular culture is prone to characterize print news in terms of "rumpled masculinity,"[75] as, for example, with portrayals of macho male photojournalists, television news is depicted as an occupation in which "beauty presides over brains" and "the *image* of authority/trust/sincerity/knowledge/credibility [is] superior to the actual thing."[76] Even when a brainy and principled female television journalist excels at her work as in *Broadcast News,* it is implied that "choosing a career constitutes a denial of essential womanhood that will make one's life miserable,"[77] which, to be sure, is also true of depictions of female print journalists.

Beyond concerns that by consuming television we are "amusing ourselves to death," as Neil Postman famously put it,[78] there are also fears about the global spread of infotainment, much as had been foretold by *Network*. The French social theorist Pierre Bourdieu warned of "the extraordinary extension of the power of television over the whole of cultural production, including scientific and artistic production," and suggested that those TV professionals "who would like to defend the values of independence, freedom from market demands, freedom from made-to-order programs, and from managers" were becoming increasingly powerless.[79]

Popular culture has addressed the struggles of conscientious professionals through the complaints (again typically coming from older males) about TV news having degenerated into an "amusement park" or "circus." In media scholar Todd Gitlin's words, "the old, good, smart, honest television" is contrasted with "the new, bad, dumb, deceptive one," the implication being that we could return to the good and the smart and the honest if the bad and dumb would just step aside and allow the old virtues to reassert themselves.[80] Frequently such thinking is extended beyond the television world to the broader culture. Howard Beale in *Network* lambastes his viewers—"an entire generation that never knew anything that didn't come out of this tube!"—for no longer reading books or newspapers. Will McAvoy in *The Newsroom* tells an unfortunate college student that she is "without a doubt a member of the worst-period-generation-period-ever-period," and then waxes eloquent about when America was great: "We sacrificed, we cared about our neighbors, we put our money where our mouths were, and we never beat our chest. . . . We were able to be all these things and do all these things because we were informed. By great men, men who were revered."[81]

Such speechifying can be easy to mock, and in fact one reviewer of *The Newsroom* branded it as "bona-fide baloney—false nostalgia for an America that never existed."[82] In a like vein, *Good Night, and Good Luck*'s veneration of Edward R. Murrow and his perorations about the frittering away of television's potential were criticized as having drawn upon "the usual nostalgia for newsrooms choking on their own cigarette smoke" in such a way as to inflate "the considerable accomplishments of a mortal and flawed newsman into modern miracles."[83] As for *Broadcast News*, Todd Gitlin suggested that the professional acumen of Jane Craig and Aaron Altman was employed in the service of superficial news coverage even before Tom Grunick appeared on the scene. Gitlin added that the movie's appeal to actual TV news professionals reflected their fervently held belief that that they were "custodians of serious information, guardians of the public weal, tribunes of democracy," even though the strictures of the television industry were such that they had never really been those things and never could be.[84]

Of course, popular culture and Hollywood in particular do not make a habit of delivering downbeat stories to a paying public. In his memoir about the making of *Up Close & Personal,* John Gregory Dunne recalled the difficulties of fitting the depressing details of Jessica Savitch's life into the screenplay. The story did not jell until producer Scott Rudin said that at heart it should be "about two movie stars": Robert Redford and Michelle Pfeiffer. Both negative and positive reviews characterized the film as "schmaltzy, shallow, and predictable," but the positive reviews went on to praise it as a throwback to the star-driven romances of Hollywood's golden age, and the movie was a box office hit.[85] Although *Up Close & Personal* aimed a few barbs at the TV news business, ultimately the film made it seem romantic and even heroic by peddling myths that proved as lucrative as ever: if you work hard enough, you can make it to the top and also find your true love.[86]

Treasured myths are also at the heart of works such as *The Newsroom.* The idea that America was once informed by great and revered men implicitly pays homage to the likes of Murrow, and although the legends that have been built up around Murrow have been rightfully criticized,[87] his example is still used to stir television news professionals. Journalist Al Tompkins consciously echoes Murrow in saying the best TV news stories "don't just inform; they teach, illuminate and inspire viewers." Decades after the legend's passing, and with fears about television as acute as ever, the notion that the medium can be much more than "merely wires and lights in a box" is sustained in journalism and in popular culture.[88]

So, too, are the notions put forth by producer Mackenzie McHale in *The Newsroom:* that there can be informed debate characterized by civility and respect, that truth can triumph over stupidity, that we can rise above bitchiness and gossip and voyeurism, and that we all can finally come together. Those are central not just to the ideal of a free and vigorous press but also to that of a free and vigorous democracy. According to popular culture, the visual media, with their appeal to the emotions, can rouse the rabble to catastrophic ends, but in the right hands they can move us as a people toward greatness.

6

War

Real-world war photographers witness unimaginable horrors and suffer for it just as their popular culture counterparts do. For many, the price they might pay on the job is a necessary risk. João Silva was part of the South African "Bang Bang Club" immortalized in the film of the same name, and in 2010 he lost both legs to a land mine while covering the war in Afghanistan. Silva summarized the rationale for recording humanity at its worst: "We do it because it's there, we do it because we can, and because there is a need for the world to know."[1]

It is not only photojournalists who seek out the rigors—and the thrills—of covering warfare. War reporting commands unique prestige, having been viewed as "the ultimate journalistic challenge" and "a glamorous specialism of journalism" that is practiced by "an elite, specialized class apart and above regular reporters."[2] Simultaneously, according to Stuart Allan and Barbie Zelizer, "it is beset by an array of problems associated with allegiance, responsibility, truth, and balance."[3] Those on the political left have criticized war reporting for amounting to nothing but propaganda. In the words of one scholar, it demonstrates "the incredible consistency of journalists, editors, and news outlets in internalizing and disseminating official views, and at the expense of dissenting public views."[4] Those on the political right have questioned the news media's patriotism during wartime, in effect demanding to know of journalists, "are you with us, or are you against us?"[5] At worst, journalists have been accused of actively undermining the war effort, or (as was the case with the American military and the Vietnam War) even contributing to outright defeat.[6]

In this chapter we examine how popular culture reflects the conflicted image of war reporting. Although there have been notable exceptions, the war correspondent has been regularly portrayed as a hero whose job requires day-to-day courage and toughness. At the same time, those correspondents have confronted both pointed questions about their loyalties and blatant attempts to manipulate or intimidate them. Their efforts to remain as neutral observers fail again and again, and the terrible things they witness threaten to do them irrevocable harm.

Pre–World War II Correspondents

Popular culture depictions of war correspondents date back to the fiction of the late nineteenth century.[7] Novels of that period portrayed correspondents as what have been described as "knights-errant" at the center of "boy-gallops-horse, boy-fights-baddies, boy-gets-glory romance[s]."[8] Rudyard Kipling's *The Light That Failed* (1890) was a prime example. The book's hero, Dick Heldar, accompanies British troops who are attempting to suppress a revolt in Sudan. Although Heldar is supposedly there only to record the action, he takes up arms against the rebels, suffers a wound that costs him his eyesight, and finally gets his wish to die "in the forefront of the battle" thanks to "the crowning mercy of a kindly bullet through his head."[9]

Other early war correspondent fiction was produced by the likes of Stephen Crane and Richard Harding Davis, both of whom (like Kipling) had worked as journalists themselves.[10] In fact, Davis was the most celebrated foreign correspondent of his era, embodying "America's idea of the journalist as hero and model." He died in 1916, though, and did not shape the popular image of the war journalist to the extent that his successor Floyd Gibbons did.[11] A star correspondent for the *Chicago Tribune*, Gibbons survived the sinking of the British liner *Laconia* after it was torpedoed by the Germans in February 1917; his dramatic account of the incident was read aloud in Congress and helped make the case for America's entry into the war. Later Gibbons lost an eye on the battlefield in France and won the Croix de Guerre before returning to America to become a radio commentator and newsreel narrator.[12] He wrote *The Red Napoleon* (1929) about a fictional dictator with himself as first-person journalistic narrator. In the 1930s Gibbons played the "Headline Hunter" in a series of *Your True Adventures* movie shorts, and after his death in 1939 his legacy continued to be celebrated in films, comic books, and television shows. For example, the movie *The Angel Wore Red* (1960) features foreign correspondent "Hawthorne" (Joseph Cotten) reporting on the Spanish Civil War. He carries four glass eyes that he rotates to suit any occasion.[13]

The image of the pre–World War II correspondent was not always glamorous. In his survey of war correspondent fiction, Howard Good observes that irony always has been a key component of such depictions, with the journalists frequently portrayed as "fools and liars." Indeed, even as authors such as Kipling, Crane, and Davis venerated war correspondents, they also parodied them.[14] That satire carried over to the stage and cinema. The Broadway play *Clear All Wires* (1932) was written by Samuel and Bella Spewack, both of whom had previously worked as Moscow correspondents. The play was then turned into a 1933 movie starring Lee Tracy as reporter Buckley Joyce Thomas of the *Chicago Globe*. Posted to Moscow, Thomas stops at nothing to produce sensational stories, even staging the fake assassination of the Russian leader. His actions prompt a reporter colleague to brand him "a public enemy," but Thomas is unbowed: "I'm news. I disappear for a week and all America boils. Millions of people out there waiting for me, praying for me. . . . I'm the only color in the lives of the masses!"[15]

Tongue-in-cheek portrayals like *Clear All Wires* paled next to Evelyn Waugh's *Scoop* (1938). The book has become a favorite of actual foreign correspondents, having been called "a novel nearly every one of them reads, rereads, and recommends to newcomers."[16] That is ironic in that it presents "a vision of correspondents as blindly competitive, morally obtuse and criminally negligent."[17] Just before writing it, Waugh had worked as a journalist covering the Italo-Ethiopian War. His novel depicts war reporters as willingly allowing themselves to be manipulated by government and military officials in return for information—a depiction that anticipated similar charges of collusion to be leveled against journalists in the decades to come.[18] Protagonist William Boot gets the "scoop" of the title only after his newspaper, the *Daily Beast,* sends him to an African war zone by mistake (he is a nature writer by trade and author of such indelible prose as, "*Feather-footed through the plashy fen passes the questing vole*"). As for Boot's colleagues, they do not hesitate to manufacture stories outright when necessary. A famous war correspondent who oversleeps on a European train and accidentally arrives at a nation at peace nonetheless produces a "thousand-word story about barricades in the streets, flaming churches, machine guns answering the rattle of his typewriter as he wrote, a dead child, like a broken doll, spreadeagled in the deserted roadway below his window." The false story creates such a commotion that it triggers an actual revolution in the country, and the reporter wins the Nobel Peace Prize "for his harrowing descriptions of the carnage."[19]

Still, *Scoop*'s damning depiction of war correspondents represented more the exception than the rule in popular culture's portrayals before World War II. John Maxwell Hamilton's history of overseas reporting asserts that the "golden age of foreign correspondence" was "in the period between the two world wars, when outlets for foreign news swelled and a large number of experienced, independent journalists circled the globe."[20] Pop culture's portrayals followed suit, particularly in Hollywood films with such titles as *Viva Villa!* (1934), *Paris Interlude* (1934), *I Cover the War* (1937), *The Last Train from Madrid* (1937), *Barricade* (1939), *Espionage Agent* (1939), and *Comrade X* (1940). In those movies, even when foreign correspondents are "deceitful, bent on success, and hedonistic," they still are "basically good people who want to get the story but have a broader commitment to fellow human beings" and who manage in the end to "save the day."[21] That image reached its apotheosis during the world war itself.

Correspondents in World War II

War correspondents became folk heroes during the war years, being perfect movie protagonists whose daily work involved patriotism and danger. Such movies appeared even before America's entry into the war. *Arise, My Love* (1940) featured a heroic woman war correspondent (Claudette Colbert) reporting on the end of the Spanish Civil War and the start of the world war while being romanced by a pilot (Ray Milland). Alfred Hitchcock's *Foreign Correspondent* (1940) was inspired by Vincent Sheean's 1935 memoir, *Personal History*, which told of the famed journalist's overseas adventures. A group of writers including Ben Hecht adapted the memoir into a story about an American crime reporter, Johnny Jones (Joel McCrea), who is sent to Europe because his editor wants a "fresh, unused mind" there. The reporter is rechristened with an appropriately distinguished-sounding new name: "Huntley Haverstock." Following a series of adventures involving Nazi spies, kidnapped diplomats, and shot-down airplanes, Haverstock is transformed into an Edward R. Murrow–like correspondent broadcasting from a blacked-out London during an air raid: "Hello, America! Hang onto your lights! They're the only lights left in the world!" The finished movie (which debuted just before the London Blitz began in earnest) bore little relation to *Personal History*, but as John Maxwell Hamilton observes, "the broader theme—the independent journalist willing to take sides in a conflict between good and evil—was pure Sheean."[22]

Journalists wholly on the side of good (i.e., the Allies) and wholly against the side of evil (i.e., fascism) predominated on screen. *Keeper of the Flame* (1942) starred Spencer Tracy as a reporter who uncovers the story of an American fascist plotting a national coup. Other pictures put reporters di-

Actor Burgess Meredith (left) meets journalist Ernie Pyle during the making of *The Story of G.I. Joe,* based on Pyle's World War II reporting. Pyle would be killed in the war before the film was released.

rectly on the front lines. They fit well into the formula of the World War II combat film, which typically focused on a diverse group of soldiers following a heroic leader on an important mission while being accompanied by a sympathetic observer, such as a journalist.[23] If that journalist was blatantly jingoistic or even racist, it was a price that everyone seemed willing to pay. In *Objective, Burma!* (1945), a reporter who has been a thoughtful chronicler of men in battle becomes hysterical after witnessing enemy atrocities. He calls the Japanese "stinking little savages" and screams, "Wipe 'em out! Wipe 'em off the face of the earth!"

The Story of G.I. Joe (1945) offered a more sober perspective by focusing on the most beloved war journalist of his day, Ernie Pyle. The movie, which appeared in cinemas just six months after Pyle was killed at the front, relates his experiences in reporting on the war in Tunisia and Italy for a syndicated newspaper column. There is no John Wayne–like character singlehandedly whipping the enemy. Instead there is rain and muck and getting miserably bogged down under fire, which was true to the actual details of the Italian campaign and Pyle's accounts of it. The movie even highlights one of the most notorious blunders of that campaign: the Allied bombing of the Abbey of

Monte Cassino, which was mistakenly thought to be an enemy observation post. In what Pyle (played by Burgess Meredith) describes in a voice-over as "one of the grim ironies of war," the "rubble of the monastery became a fortress for the Nazis," leaving the Americans "right back where we started from." In such ways the journalist conveys much of the war's tragedy and gloom, with personal glory—such as his winning a Pulitzer Prize—mattering little. To be certain, he does not report all that he sees, including the combat fatigue that befalls one of the soldiers. A Pyle biographer suggests that *The Story of G.I. Joe* "blended myth and reality in about the same proportions as the column that inspired it."[24] Even as the movie and Pyle himself both showed the "grim ironies" of war, they also indicated that the men fighting it on the ground were noble and that the press's proper place was on the men's side.

So it was in a host of other Hollywood movies that were produced during the war. *Berlin Correspondent* (1942), *Cairo* (1942), *The Lady Has Plans* (1942), *Once Upon a Honeymoon* (1942), *Somewhere I'll Find You* (1942), *Passage to Marseille* (1944), and *Blood on the Sun* (1945) featured such stars as Dana Andrews, Robert Montgomery, Robert Young, Cary Grant, Clark Gable, Lana Turner, Paulette Goddard, Humphrey Bogart, and James Cagney playing the journalists. The film *Guadalcanal Diary* (1943), based on the book of the same name by war correspondent Richard Tregaskis, provided an Ernie Pyle–like perspective on the war in the Pacific. War correspondents also appeared in comic books of the day via characters such as "Chase Yale: Commando Yank" and "Liberty Belle" (aka "Libby Lawrence"), both of whom fought the enemy by doubling as reporters and action heroes.

Portrayals of World War II as a just and necessary conflict that was covered by brave and conscientious journalists have endured to this day. The HBO TV movie *Hemingway & Gellhorn* (2012) tells of the tempestuous relationship

Martha Gellhorn (Nicole Kidman) and Ernest Hemingway (Clive Owen) cover the Spanish Civil War and later World War II in *Hemingway & Gellhorn*.

between journalist Martha Gellhorn (Nicole Kidman) and novelist Ernest Hemingway (Clive Owen). Gellhorn's distinguished career as a correspondent spanned from the Spanish Civil War of the 1930s to the Central American wars of the 1980s. Much of the film is set in Spain, and although the politics and agonies of the conflict there are addressed, it serves more as a backdrop for passion between the two protagonists, who hungrily consummate their romance as bombs and plaster fall all about them. The world war, though, is portrayed with more gravity. It is not only that the romance and subsequent marriage have collapsed (amid Hemingway's complaints that there is "no home and hearth for my wife—she'd rather be married to war"). It is also that Gellhorn comes face-to-face with Dachau and Auschwitz, with images of Kidman in character as the journalist superimposed over documentary footage of the death camps.[25] "It was an unbelievable horror, I think so horrendous that you could not take it all in without becoming frenzied and hysterical and mad," Gellhorn says in the film. Still she perseveres in her work, with renewed conviction that neutrality in the face of evil is impossible and that objectivity in war reporting is "shit."[26]

Vietnam-Era Correspondents

The image of the war correspondent in the post–World War II era grew more complex and conflicted, just as wars themselves no longer commanded the same degree of public support or commitment. The 1950–53 stalemate in Korea inspired nothing that remotely approached the number of depictions of the World War II correspondent.[27] Decades after the armistice, the TV series *M*A*S*H* (based on the 1970 Robert Altman film of the same name) did feature a handful of episodes with reporters. In "The Interview" (1976) and "Our Finest Hour" (1978), war correspondent Clete Roberts played himself and interviewed the staff of the army field hospital in Korea that was the focus of the series. Roberts asks commanding officer Sherman Potter (Harry Morgan) in "The Interview" if anything good will come out of the conflict, and the colonel bluntly replies, "Not a damn thing."[28] *M*A*S*H*'s strongly antiwar tone reflected the skepticism toward involvement in overseas conflicts that had developed during the next major American war after Korea—the quagmire of Vietnam.[29]

Graham Greene's 1955 novel, *The Quiet American,* anticipated the grief that Vietnam would bring and the moral conundrums of the journalists who covered that war. Like many others before and since, Greene had worked as a journalist himself before drawing upon his experiences in his fiction;

he reported on the First Indochina War, which resulted in the French relinquishing colonial control over the region. Greene's novel would be similar to *Scoop* in that it became a favorite among actual war correspondents (*New York Times* Vietnam correspondent David Halberstam called the book "our bible").[30] Its protagonist Thomas Fowler is a middle-aged British reporter in Vietnam in the early 1950s. He harbors no illusions, and his observations are consistent with what Halberstam and other journalists would discover in the following decade after the American military had replaced the French in the country. In response to a suggestion that the Vietnamese do not want communism, Fowler retorts, "They don't want to be shot at. They want one day to be much the same as another. They don't want our white skins telling them what they want." He also sees through the lies that French war command tells during its news conferences. A French officer tells him privately that the war never can be won even though they "have to go on fighting till the politicians tell us to stop. Probably they will get together and agree to the same peace that we could have had at the beginning, making nonsense of all these years."[31]

Still, Fowler steadfastly refuses to take sides of any kind. He is no longer interested in the war's progress, saying that "grenades had staled on me." Most of all, he declares himself to be "not *engagé*" or involved: "It had been an article of my creed. The human condition being what it was, let them fight, let them love, let them murder, I would not be involved. My fellow journalists called themselves correspondents; I preferred the title of reporter. I wrote what I saw. I took no action—even an opinion is a kind of action."[32] That stance finally crumbles through Fowler's relationship with Alden Pyle, the young and idealistic "quiet American" of the title and the one who suggests to Fowler that Vietnam does not (or at least should not) want communism. An undercover CIA agent, Pyle has been profoundly influenced by the writings of one York Harding, whom Fowler contemptuously describes as "a superior sort of journalist—they call them diplomatic correspondents. He gets hold of an idea and then alters every situation to fit the idea." That "idea" is that nations like Vietnam must find a middle path between colonialism and communism. After Pyle's anticommunist efforts lead to a car bombing that kills dozens of innocent Vietnamese (and after Pyle also steals Fowler's young Vietnamese lover), Fowler sets up Pyle to be assassinated. "I had betrayed my principles," the journalist says at the end. "I had become as *engagé* as Pyle, and it seemed to me that no decision would ever be simple again."[33]

The Quiet American has been viewed as another rejection of the pretense of journalistic objectivity, particularly during wartime.[34] Yet the stand that

Fowler finally takes is ambivalent at best; it does not seem to be rooted in any particular idealism. ("God save us always from the innocent and the good," the journalist drily observes after Pyle's death.[35]) As Howard Good notes, the novel presents "a world without obvious heroes, where good motives share qualities with their opposites, and where every action, however seemingly right or noble, casts a shadow of guilt."[36] Such ambiguous depictions of war correspondents would not become the norm for many years. The first movie version of *The Quiet American* appeared in 1958 and starred Michael Redgrave as Fowler and Audie Murphy as Pyle. Produced by Hollywood during the cold war and before America became fully involved in Vietnam, the film completely altered the novel's ending to make Pyle a heroic martyr to the communists and Fowler an unwitting communist patsy. Graham Greene complained that "one could almost believe that the film was made deliberately to attack the book and the author."[37]

During the height of the Vietnam War, popular culture for the most part continued to eschew explicit antiwar sentiments so far as the press was concerned. *The Bedford Incident* costarred Sidney Poitier as a journalist on board a destroyer whose captain (Richard Widmark) is obsessively stalking a Soviet submarine. Although the film contains a critique of cold war tensions (it ends with nuclear torpedoes vaporizing the ship after the submarine is accidentally destroyed), it does not address Vietnam in detail. In contrast, *The Green Berets* (1968) represented John Wayne's fervent desire to direct and star in a movie that promoted America's involvement in the war. The result was a critically reviled but commercially popular World War II combat picture that just happened to be set in 1968, with the North Vietnamese substituting for the Japanese and David Janssen's reporter substituting for the similar character in *Objective, Burma!*[38] At first the newsman is skeptical about the U.S. military intervention, but soon he is helping load mortars and even toting a gun. That proved to be too much even for the Pentagon, which told the filmmakers that the reporter's gun wielding "violate[d] the rules under which he operates as a news correspondent," although the scene remained in the film.[39]

After the American withdrawal and the takeover by the north, some popular culture stories alluded to the perception that a critical, unsupportive press had contributed to the U.S. defeat. (In reality, according to Daniel Hallin, "in the early years the media strongly supported American involvement in Vietnam, which they interpreted in a Cold War framework similar to the geopolitical framework of the Second World War." Coverage did become more critical later, but only after "changes in elite and mass opinion" against the war already had occurred.[40]) In the film *Full Metal Jacket* (1987)—which features a young marine who doubles as a reporter and as a combatant—a marine officer says of the 1968 Tet Offensive that "the civilian press are about to wet their pants, and we've heard even [CBS News anchor Walter] Cronkite's going to say the war is now unwinnable." In the movie *Angkor: Cambodia Express* (1982), a general brands reporters as "pencil-pushing assholes" and adds, "You guys cost us the war. . . . We could have won. But every time we shot one of those motherfuckers, there was a national protest back home. Do you know why? Because of the goddamn press! You didn't care about our guys as long as you could sell newspapers!"[41]

However, a majority of pop culture tales from the 1970s onward have reflected a more critical perspective on the war while vividly portraying the "pain, doubt and disillusionment of correspondents in the Vietnam War era."[42] That appeared on television in the series *China Beach* with a 1989 two-part episode featuring a photojournalist who arrives at the front and announces that she is there "to let the folks back home know how you boys are really doing." She experiences the terrors of jungle combat while inadvertently attracting enemy fire with her camera and then sees a young combatant whom she has befriended get mortally wounded.[43] The stage play *The Columnist* portrays syndicated columnist Joseph Alsop as a York Harding type, a journalist who is utterly convinced of the rightness of the American course of action despite mounting evidence to the contrary. "I saw the endlessly resourceful military of a great and benevolent power in a twilight struggle for freedom against an inhuman enemy," Alsop proclaims after a visit to Vietnam, where he has spoken only to the officials in charge of the war effort. In due course he sees his professional credibility irrevocably diminished and his beloved stepdaughter join the antiwar movement.[44]

Marti Leimbach's novel *The Man from Saigon* (2009) tells of a "women's interest" magazine that sends reporter Susan Gifford to Vietnam in 1967 to do soft feature stories. She soon ends up on the front lines and is captured by the North Vietnamese. Before Gifford is freed, she develops a close friendship with a Vietnamese photojournalist who has been captured with her, even after she learns that he has been working with the Vietcong. Meanwhile, Gifford's lover (a married television reporter) grows ever more disillusioned with the American military command: "*They stand there at the briefing and lie. About everything. About the outcome of every firefight or set piece or bombing or engagement. Nobody is winning. We* certainly *are not winning.*"[45]

Finally, in the movies, *The Quiet American* was remade with Michael Caine as Fowler and Brendan Fraser as Pyle. The film—which premiered in 2002 just before the American invasion of Iraq after first being delayed by the 9/11 terrorist attacks—restored Graham Greene's original ending. It included a closing montage of newspaper headlines and pictures detailing how the Americans repeated the mistakes of the French in Vietnam and ultimately met the same sorry fate. That same year, *We Were Soldiers* (2002) depicted a war reporter (based on the actual Vietnam correspondent Joe Galloway) who takes up arms in the heat of battle. That echoed *The Green Berets,* and in fact one observer has characterized the depiction of the war correspondent in *We Were Soldiers* "as a return to the certainties of a bygone age."[46] Regardless, the film was markedly less jingoistic and simpleminded than the John Wayne movie had been, and the Galloway character underscored the damage that combat can inflict upon both its participants and its witnesses: "We who have seen war will never stop seeing it. In the silence of the night, we will always hear the screams."[47]

War Correspondents in the Post-Vietnam Age

Popular culture's portrayals of journalists ensnared in post-Vietnam conflicts have maintained the themes of courage mixed with angst. Occasionally there are arrogant or inept correspondents who are more concerned with themselves than with the people they cover or who get in the way of those who are doing the fighting. More often "the narrative focus is on the heroism of the reporter, and the risks he or she takes in acting as witness."[48] The reporter "starts detached or indifferent to circumstances," but grows increasingly involved, and finally "becomes a human being exactly at the moment that he [or she] stops being a journalist," or at least a detached or indifferent one.[49] Many times the role of Western powers—especially the United States—is explicitly questioned, reflecting perceptions among many in the world that America acts "as an imperial nation and often as an aggressor."[50]

Several stories center on the anguish suffered by smaller nations that have been engulfed by civil war, with Western indifference or interference often a culprit. The journalist, who frequently has become emotionally involved with one or more natives of the country, is caught in the middle. Such is the case with the photojournalists in the movies *Salvador* and *Under Fire.* In *Salvador* the cavalier attitude of Richard Boyle (James Woods) toward his life and work is forever altered by his romantic relationship with a Salvadoran woman and his shock at the horrors perpetrated by the U.S.-backed Salvadoran military. "I don't want to see another Vietnam. I don't want to see America get another bad rap," he tells U.S. military advisers. "I believe that we stand for something. For

Dith Pran (Haing S. Ngor, left) and Sydney Schanberg (Sam Waterston) witness the Khmer Rouge takeover of Cambodia in *The Killing Fields*.

a constitution. For human rights—not just for a few people, but for everyone on this planet!" It does no good; Boyle has to flee the country for his life, only to see immigration officials haul his lover and her child away and presumably return them to the hell that they have desperately tried to escape.[51] In *Under Fire* Russell Price (Nick Nolte) similarly sees his detachment challenged. When Price angrily asks an American mercenary whether he gets "paid by the hour or by the body," the mercenary retorts, "I get paid the same way you do"; in effect, both are hired guns roaming from war to war. When Price sees a journalist friend murdered by Nicaraguan soldiers, his photos of the murder help swing U.S. public opinion against the Somoza government. ("Maybe we should have killed an American journalist fifty years ago," a Nicaraguan woman says.) When finally the Sandinista rebels win with the help of another Price photo—this one faked to help the rebel cause—Price's fellow journalist and lover asks him if "we fell in love with too much." His response is emphatic: "I'd do it again!"[52]

Often a native of the country at war is made to be a paragon of virtue or even a martyr, in contrast to the morally compromised foreign correspondent. The film *The Killing Fields* (1984) relates the true story of *New York Times* reporter Sydney Schanberg (Sam Waterston) and his assistant, Dith Pran (Haing S. Ngor), during the Khmer Rouge takeover of Cambodia. Schanberg is often brusque toward Pran and does not actively intervene to get him out of the country until it is too late. To the reporter's grief and guilt, Pran disappears amid the killing fields even as Schanberg wins professional accolades for his Cambodian reporting. After four years Pran manages to escape, and he and Schanberg are tearfully reunited, with the reporter asking for forgiveness.[53] In *The Year of Living Dangerously* (1982) journalist Guy Hamilton (Mel Gibson) attempts to report an impending communist incursion in Indonesia and thereby endangers his girlfriend, who has tipped him off to the story. The reporter's Indonesian photographer, Billy Kwan (Linda Hunt), scolds him for "making a fetish of your career and making all relationships temporary lest they disturb that career. Why can't you give yourself?" After Kwan is killed while protesting social conditions, Hamilton abandons the story and leaves the country with the woman he loves.[54] In Lara Santoro's novel *Mercy* (2007), a dissolute and alcoholic correspondent is shamed into living a more selfless life through the example of her African housekeeper (the "Mercy" of the title). The housekeeper develops AIDS and allows herself to die to protest the high cost of HIV medicines.

At times the war correspondent tries to alleviate the misery that she or he witnesses, whether it be through honest, hard-hitting reporting or through revenge. The film *Blood Diamond* (2006) costars Jennifer Connelly as reporter Maddy Bowen, who is trying to expose the deadly illegal diamond trade in Sierra Leone. She tells a gunrunner (Leonardo DiCaprio) with whom she has an ongoing flirtation that she is tired of writing stories that accomplish nothing: "I need names, I need dates, I need pictures, I need bank accounts. . . . I can't write that story until I get facts that can be verified, which is to say until I find someone who will go on record. So if that is not you, and you're not really going to help me, and we're not really going to screw, then why don't you get the fuck out of my face, and let me do my work?" (Eventually he gives her the information she needs.) In 1997's *Welcome to Sarajevo*—again based on a true story—journalist Michael Nicholson (Stephen Dillane) strives at first to be objective: "We're not here to help; we're here to report!" Soon he decides that he no longer can stand idly by and watch children suffer. He smuggles a girl out of Sarajevo and takes her home to England, where his family adopts her.[55]

The Bosnian war is also the backdrop for two tales in which journalists try to get even with murderous brutes. The film *The Hunting Party* (2007) shows a small group led by reporter Simon Hunt (Richard Gere) managing to capture the man who had killed Hunt's Bosnian lover and their unborn child. No such luck visits the title character in Michael Ignatieff's novel *Charlie Johnson in the Flames* (2003). Johnson has vowed to find and kill the man who burned alive a woman who had tried to help Johnson while he was reporting on the war. For the journalist, all that he has seen in war zones— "those chopped and desecrated bodies, those eyes of weeping women, those forlorn barefoot orphans"—obsesses him beyond redemption. He dies at the hands of the man he has come to kill. A journalist colleague observes that Johnson had "owed the woman [who was murdered] something better than vengeance"—namely, a promise not to forget her and to seek justice for her.[56]

Justice and fairness from the news media can seem remote to the people enmeshed in war, especially to those doing the fighting. The TV movie *War Stories* (2003) portrays a fictional conflict between a U.S.-backed government in Uzbekistan and Al Qaeda–backed rebels. The rebels detain a male and female journalist and demand to know why the press does not report government atrocities. Shouting about their family members who have been raped, they go so far as to yank down the pants and underwear of the woman journalist before relenting: "Maybe you [will] write with more feeling now."[57] When the press in the Bosnian film *No Man's Land* (2001) tries to report on a bizarre standoff between two opposing soldiers in the Bosnian war, it ends in disaster. One of the soldiers calls the journalists "vultures" and yells, "Does our misery pay well?" The soldiers then shoot each other dead before the news cameras.[58]

The theme of war's miseries being packaged and sold as a media show is especially prominent in stories about Iraq. The Gulf War of 1991 has been pointed to as an example of warfare turned into entertainment for mass consumption, especially through television—"valuable not only for high ratings but for high excitement in the community and the newsroom alike."[59] *Live from Baghdad* (2002) shows that excitement through the inside story of CNN's live coverage of the bombing of Baghdad at the war's start, an event that cemented CNN's reputation as a journalistic force.[60] The crew, led by CNN producer Robert Wiener (Michael Keaton), pauses to gaze somberly at the destruction the bombing has wrought, but on the whole the movie celebrates the TV network's triumph. Still, concerns about television's "extremely seductive" portrayal of war were reflected in such works as *Three Kings* (1999), a film set in the Persian Gulf in 1991.[61] It features yet another example of a female journalist trading sex in return for stories, this time from an army major (George Clooney). The journalist's actions raise the ire of her colleague, a Christiane Amanpour–like correspondent (Nora Dunn). As the two reporters bicker, a colonel scolds the major: "This is a media war—a *media* war—and you better get on board!" In *Wag the Dog*, of course, the notion of "media war" is taken to its logical conclusion, with the media manufacturing an entire televised conflict by themselves without any actual combat taking place.[62]

Controversies concerning media complicity with waging war came to a head after the 9/11 terror attacks and the subsequent new military campaigns in Iraq and Afghanistan. Critics viewed the press as helping facilitate the 2003 Iraq War through uncritical reporting of U.S. government claims about weapons of mass destruction.[63] The film *Lions for Lambs* (2007) addressed those debates through a story about a U.S. senator (Tom Cruise) who tries to "spin" a journalist (Meryl Streep) into providing favorable coverage of a new military plan in Afghanistan. The journalist urges her boss to reveal the senator's ploy for what it is, but he overrules her, and the story airs just as the senator intended it, even as the new military strategy is shown to have disastrous consequences.

Similar controversies arose around the U.S. policy of "embedding" journalists with military units, a policy that was developed for the Iraq War after concerns arose about unescorted journalists trying to cover the war in Afghanistan.[64] Embedment granted the journalists access to the front lines while providing a measure of physical protection for them, but the policy also drew heated criticism. It was cited as another sophisticated case of news management by "creating a sense of breathless identification with the soldiers in combat, and leaving the high-level impressions of how the war was going almost entirely [up] to the Defense Department and the White House."[65]

Actor Tim Robbins's play *Embedded* (2004) presents a scathing critique of embedment. Journalists are put through basic training by a drill sergeant who forces them to shout in unison, "Sir! I am a maggot journalist, sir!" The embedded reporters then eagerly recite the propaganda fed to them by the U.S. military, including manufactured details about the rescue of Private Jessica Lynch from the Iraqis. When one reporter challenges allegations of Iraqi brutality concerning Lynch and cites a non-embedded British journalist as his source, the military informs him that "there is not one sentence of that that is suitable" to be reported to the public.[66] In other popular culture works, journalists (principled or not) who try to evade embedment restrictions land in serious trouble. In the *Law and Order* TV episode "Embedded,"[67] an arrogant reporter accused of criminally reckless and even fabricated reporting about Iraq rationalizes his actions: "What's really despicable is the Pentagon using some fake patriotism to eviscerate the First Amendment and then using the media to spread that fake patriotism like manure in a garden!" The TV series *Over There* (2005) features an embedded reporter who enrages the soldiers he is accompanying through no fault of his own; his wire service

Evan Wright (Lee Tergesen, far left) is embedded with American marines in Iraq in *Generation Kill*.

wants a juicy, salable story, and it edits his video without his permission to create the false impression that a soldier has committed war atrocities.[68]

The graphic novel *Shooting War* (2007) suggests that only a truly independent reporter can produce truthful reporting about the Iraq War. Set slightly ahead in a dystopian future, the novel portrays blogger Jimmy Burns being hired by Global News Network to report from the Persian Gulf. He comes to see himself as "a liar, a fake, and a fraud" who has "covered up the truth to protect my access, my ass, and my job." An Iraqi colleague scolds him—"This is bigger than me or you!"—and urges him to "tell the world what is happening. That is our job." He agrees and surreptitiously manages to upload video that shows Iraqi civilians who have been killed by the U.S. military, whether it represents an actual war crime or "just more unfortunate collateral damage." Burns's reporting prompts the U.S. president not to run for reelection and to blast the George W. Bush administration for starting the war. In turn, the media credit Burns for "literally changing the course of American history."[69]

At least one popular culture tale has presented a more positive take on embedded reporting in Iraq, suggesting it could produce a true, if necessarily only partial, picture of the war. The HBO miniseries *Generation Kill* (2008) tells of the experiences of *Rolling Stone* reporter Evan Wright (played by Lee Tergesen) in accompanying a U.S. Marine battalion across Iraq in 2003. In some ways the series seems to justify criticisms of embedded reporters growing too close to those they cover; the marines give Wright the nickname "Scribe" and consider him to be their good luck charm. On the other hand, the vulgarity of the marines is never whitewashed—they pass around a photo of Wright's girlfriend and gleefully call her a "whore" who has been "doing all of H&S Company." Nor is their antipathy toward certain officers or their pleasure in waging war (to the point of bloodthirstiness) downplayed. "I didn't want to write about these guys as heroes or as villains," Wright said in an interview. "My intent in [*Generation Kill*] is to try to connect people in an honest way to the troops that are fighting: not to glorify them and not to demean them, [but instead] just show them as they are."[70]

In the same interview, Wright said that witnessing combat in Iraq had not really changed him, for covering war overseas was no worse or more traumatizing than covering violence at home.[71] His may be a minority viewpoint, though. Both in real life and in popular culture, war correspondence exerts a heavy personal toll. "Those who were in the war cannot forget," former *New York Times* war correspondent Chris Hedges writes. "They become frozen in time, walking around newsrooms years later with eyes that see things others do not see, haunted by graphic memories of human cruelty and depravity, no longer sure what life is about or what it means, wondering if they can ever connect with those around them."[72] So it is in the multitude of pop culture works that show emotionally scarred war photojournalists trying to rebuild their lives, or—as was the case with Kevin Carter as depicted in *The Bang Bang Club*—eventually destroying themselves.[73]

At least on the surface the British protagonist of Anna Blundy's "Faith Zanetti" novels escapes such turmoil. Zanetti is described as "a war correspondent with plenty of libido, good looks, a great sense of humor, and a zest for life that never quits," and she lives by the motto "courage without equal, truth without bullshit, [and] vodka without tonic." Yet her first-person narration in *Vodka Neat* reveals a more damaged side. Thinking she can simply write and forget about war's tragedy, she finds that "it doesn't work. It stays in there festering and finds some other way out." Her vodka habit gets out of hand (at the end of the novel she ends up in Alcoholics Anonymous), and while reporting in Moscow she lies awake at night and ponders her life:

> What am I doing here? War after war and country after country. Am I out to pasture in Moscow? Would nobody else do the job? I won stuff. I won a big silver plate after I got shot in El Salvador. . . . Will I carry on? Will there be some flare-up in Abkhazia that I'll go to? I'll dodge some bullets, hide in a cave, sleep with an Atman, eat a goat, win some more hardware. And then what?
> I touched my face and found it wet with tears.[74]

In Kira Salak's novel *The White Mary* (2008), protagonist Marika Vecera is likewise coming to terms with her career choice. She is a war correspondent who has recently returned from the Congo, where she had witnessed "an endless stream of the worst, most inconceivable acts of inhumanity paraded in front of her. . . . Was it possible to see such things and be the same afterward? To live that 'normal life'? She didn't know."[75] When Vecera hears that her role model (renowned war correspondent Robert Lewis) may not have committed suicide as had been reported but instead may still be alive, she heads to New Guinea to search for him. It develops that Lewis faked his own death after being tortured in a war zone and then retreated from the world to live alone with his anguish.[76] "You know what my worst fear was, during all that pain?" Lewis says to her. "That I would lose my compassion. . . . And you know what? I did."

Vecera begs him to leave with her and return to the land of the living, but he insists that it is too late for him. As the book's ending reveals, Vecera will not succumb to the same fate: "Real courage isn't about visiting the world's hells and returning alive to tell about it—it's easy to risk her life, and even easier to get herself killed. What takes real courage is choosing to *live,* choosing to save herself at all costs. . . . And she won't do it just for herself, but for the world. For all the ugliness in it. And for all the grace."[77]

*   *   *

For all the ugliness in war, its pull remains undeniable. To media scholars the "reporting of war and peace has been of unique importance and fascination."[78] Journalists still aspire to cover war, and once the conflict of the moment ends, "cultural producers—film-makers, artists, writers, curators— shape the raw material of war into a source of inspiration or warning."[79]

Popular culture has told scores of inspiring stories about the war correspondent, whether they have focused on the noble people whom the reporter meets (the Dith Prans, Billy Kwans, and Mercys of the world) or on the reporter's own heroism. It is true that the stories of the post-Vietnam era can seem not so heroic as those of the first half of the twentieth century; as one study observes, whereas in the "golden age" correspondents were "portrayed as celebrities," in more recent times "they are less glamorous, even seedy."[80] Nevertheless, they still risk their lives and still bear witness, and their occasional seediness only underlines the danger and toil of their jobs.

Alongside the inspirational tales have been cautionary ones. Their messages align with that of Phillip Knightley's highly critical history of war correspondence, *The First Casualty.* Knightley took his title from Hiram Johnson's 1917 declaration that "the first casualty when war comes is truth."[81] Popular culture shows the press spreading misinformation during wartime due to state or military coercion, misplaced ambition, sheer laziness, or even—as in *Under Fire*—genuine conviction that deception is the one just course of action. The media's "supine and credulous" role in acting as "war's cheerleaders" is also portrayed,[82] as is their part in depicting war "as a cinematic spectacle to be appreciated rather than a humanitarian catastrophe to be denounced."[83] Pop culture even alludes to a hard truth about contemporary journalism: that "foreign news is one of the *most* expensive journalistic undertakings and one of the *least* rewarding in terms of audience interest," particularly when wars drag on or are not being fought at all.[84] "The American media have tried to do away with it altogether, despite the fact that they spend most of the time killing people abroad," Faith Zanetti tartly observes in the novel *The Bad News Bible* (2004). "We [in the British media] just try to grab people's attention with orangutans. That or a diagram of a tank or something. You know, big pieces written by the diplomatic editor and featuring weaponry for boys."[85]

When war correspondents persevere in the face of such apathy and strive to produce conscientious reportage, they still often find themselves in a damned-if-they-do and damned-if-they-don't predicament. If they choose detachment they can be "censured or condemned for their dispassionate stance often in the form of accusations of a lack of patriotism." If they choose involvement they can be "criticized for opening the door to mistaken accounts of the conflicts, and for being 'self-righteous' and 'moralizing.'"[86] More often than not in popular culture, the journalist chooses involvement, which after all is the more dramatically compelling course of action and the one that is more apt to seem heroic.

Some critics suggest that what the journalist really should choose is peace. "War correspondence would benefit not only from reporters who seek to place combat stories into a broader context of politics, economics, religion, and culture, but also from those whose work promotes peace and stability after the shooting stops," writes one observer, while also acknowledging that that is "a difficult task that runs counter to the long-term trends."[87] In fact, "peace journalism" advocates suggest that it requires a full-scale challenge to "relations of dominance in the world economic, political and social order."[88] War correspondents find that task daunting if not impossible. "We begin our careers as young crusaders, convinced our pens and cameras can persuade the world to live another way," says Michael Nicholson, who inspired *Welcome to Sarajevo*. "But in our middle age, as we hang up our boots, we leave it as we found it. All we have done is to advertise the world's many ills and offer nothing to cure them."[89] Small wonder that such reporters in reality and in fiction are so prone to anguish and despair.

Perhaps the most that war correspondents can realistically be expected to do is to contribute to our collective memory. Their best work reminds us that, as Susan Sontag writes, "This is what human beings are capable of doing—may volunteer to do, enthusiastically, self-righteously. Don't forget."[90] Popular culture's stories about war and journalism do their own part in that same task. They also offer the hope that amid all the world's evils, war correspondents and the rest of us can finally find a measure of grace.

CONCLUSION

Imagining the Future

It is taken for granted that journalism in the twenty-first century is confronting epochal change. What is less certain, according to journalists and journalism scholars, is whether that change will be for good or for ill. Paolo Mancini notes that the idea that "journalism is in crisis . . . has become the dominant image" of the Western news media. He adds that as a result of increased commercialization and technological change, media are becoming ever more fragmented and segmented. Journalism is more "'blurred,' more confused, and less stable in terms of both structure and professional identity," with unpredictable consequences for the press and participatory democracy.[1] For Bregtje van der Haak, Michael Parks, and Manuel Castells, such changes represent not "a crisis of journalism, but rather, an explosion of it. In fact, the profession seems to be more alive than ever and going through a multiplication of both forms and content at amazing speed." With the help of social networks and new ways of presenting and analyzing data, journalists can contribute to "the expanding body of reliable information" and offer "meaningful interpretation of this information in a world characterized by informed bewilderment."[2]

In considering the role and character of journalism in the years to come, we turn once more to popular culture. We will examine some of the ways pop culture has imagined the press of the future and has anticipated or addressed the transformations that journalism is grappling with now. We then will summarize what we know and do not know about the image of the journalist in popular culture, and we will suggest some paths that researchers of the future might take.

Speculative Fiction and Journalism

Press scholar Loren Ghiglione observes that speculative fiction (incorporating science fiction and other fantasy-based stories) is a fruitful way of thinking about journalism and the future, for it always has been "committed to the notion of extraordinary change in the world." It presents competing perspectives on media and news: "One voice embraces future communications technology and a utopian tomorrow, the other voice worries about the dangers of that technology to human privacy and envisions an apocalyptic future."[3] Much as popular culture's stories about the past inescapably speak to present-day concerns,[4] so do its stories about the future. Journalist and novelist Cory Doctorow speaks of science fiction's "radical presentism," which he describes as "literature that uses the device of futurism to show up the present"—that is, to expose and question how technology is disrupting our lives for better or worse.[5] In addition, as another student of the genre has noted, it never is just "producing arbitrary fantasy but rather reworking key metaphors and narratives already circulating in the culture."[6] Speculative fiction's tales about the press draw upon the same myths and conflicts that underlie other stories about journalism, and they present similar depictions of heroes and villains using and abusing the power of the press.

To be sure, the protagonists of those stories do not always resemble old-fashioned reporters and editors. Three character types that Ghiglione identified in 1990 remain relevant today: (1) the "human journalist" who "makes his living from investigating and reporting the news"; (2) the "nonhuman journalist—a robot, computer, or other device—that supplements, even replaces, the human journalist"; and (3) "the consumer of news" who employs technology to become his or her "own journalist."[7] Even with the nonhuman journalist and consumer of news, though, traditional notions of what a journalist ought to be and do are still present, just as real-world journalists of today are increasingly incorporating automation and citizen participation into their work.

The category of "human journalist" naturally has conformed most closely to the depictions of journalists in other pop culture genres. In Isaac Asimov's classic story "Nightfall" (1941), "Theremon 762" is a cynical columnist on the planet Lagash who strikingly resembles the cynical columnists on the planet Earth. He refuses to believe the assertions of scientists that an eclipse is about to plunge Lagash into darkness (the planet has experienced perpetual daylight from multiple suns and never has seen the coming of night). "You have led a vast newspaper campaign against the efforts of myself and my colleagues to organize the world against the menace which it is now too late to avert," an astronomer angrily tells Theremon. "You have done your best with your highly personal attacks to make the staff of this Observatory objects of ridicule." Inevitably the darkness comes, and the journalist goes mad.[8]

The movie *The Thing from Another World* (1951) presents another recognizable type: the reporter on the trail of a big story. In this instance, though, the journalist is far from a skeptic and is more than willing to side with authority figures. The climax shows Ned "Scotty" Scott (Douglas Spencer) breathlessly sharing his scoop about a terrifying and murderous alien that has been vanquished against all odds: "One of the world's greatest battles was fought and won today by the human race. Here at the top of the world, a handful of American soldiers and civilians met the first invasion from another planet. . . . Every one of you listening to my voice, tell the world! Tell this to everybody, wherever they are! Watch the skies, everywhere! Keep looking! Keep watching the skies!" According to one critic, Scotty represents cold war tensions in that he presents "pro-American propaganda" and "clearly exerts pride and approves the impulse of retaliating if the 'other' eventually attacks," while he also urges eternal vigilance against that same "other."[9]

The pop culture stories of subsequent decades have not always been so propagandistic, but they have continued to present familiar journalistic types who confront otherworldly phenomena or display special abilities of their own. Investigative reporters have used psychic powers to study the paranormal,[10] voyaged far into the cosmos to be stranded on a rapidly disintegrating planet,[11] and battled the Antichrist in a post-Rapture world.[12] There have been skeptical editors—sometimes too skeptical for their own good—in works such as the "Kolchak" TV series, TV movies, comic books, and novels, with a constant being that editor Tony Vincenzo cannot believe reporter Carl Kolchak's incredible-but-true stories of the supernatural. There have been cub reporters such as Sabrina Spellman (Melissa Joan Hart), who uses her powers as a half witch to get stories for her high school paper in TV's *Sabrina, the Teenage Witch* (1996–2003). The teen protagonist of the novel *Cindy Jones and the Secret of Craycroft* (2013) works as a television reporter and is "selected by an ancient and righteous force of aliens from the Planet Eton" to help break the story of a smuggling ring.[13]

Strong female journalists have regularly appeared, such as Sarah Jane Smith in the long-running British *Doctor Who* TV series and one of its TV spinoffs, *The Sarah Jane Adventures*. One of the many characters who have accompanied Doctor Who in his travels through time and space, Smith (played by Elisabeth Sladen) has been described as "an ardent feminist" and "a feisty, opinionated, strong equal to the Doctor."[14] Other women journalists confront the typical dilemma of balancing personal and professional demands. In James Dobson and Kurt Bruner's "Julia Davidson" novels, reporter Davidson tries to cover the strife-filled world of the year 2042 while finding herself "torn between the influence she craves and the husband she loves."[15] Predictably, some works also recycle and satirize the worst clichés regarding female journalists. The title character of Laura Knots's novel *Brandi Bloom Galactic Reporter Enslaved* (2013) hosts a scandalous tabloid TV news show that airs throughout the galaxy. Things go very wrong after "she insults the wrong alien," who "vows to make the young beauty pay."[16]

On the whole—as with the unfortunate Brandi—TV journalists are portrayed no better than they are in other genres and are constantly placed in opposition to "human privacy and dignity."[17] Television either has been depicted as an instrument of terror and subjugation, as in works by the likes of Ray Bradbury and Philip K. Dick,[18] or else it has been made the object of mockery, as in the *RoboCop* franchise of movies, TV series, video games, and comic books. "On the international scene, the Amazon nuclear power facility has blown its stack, irradiating the world's largest rain forest. Environmentalists call it a disaster," a male news anchor intones in the film *RoboCop 2* (1990). "But don't they always?" his female coanchor brightly responds.[19]

Likewise, media moguls are depicted negatively, with William Randolph Hearst himself featured in Kage Baker's "Company" stories. In "Welcome to Olympus, Mr. Hearst," the publisher receives a mysterious man named Denham at Sam Simeon in 1926. Denham turns out to be a cyborg representative of The Company, a twenty-fourth-century entity that employs time travel to exploit the past for profit. Hearst is promised immortality if he allows The Company to store historical artifacts in Hearst Castle and uses his media holdings to promote The Company's agenda. To help persuade him, Denham shows Hearst a snippet of journalism from the year 2106: "No newspapers anymore, you see; it'll all be online by then. Sort of a print-and-movie broadcast." Hearst is delighted by what he sees: "Even an illiterate stevedore could get this stuff. It's like a kindergarten primer. . . . And it occurs to me, Mr. Denham, that it must be fairly easy to sway public opinion with this kind of pap." The story concludes in the year 2333, with a forever-young Hearst reveling in his eternal sway over humanity and "smiling his terrible smile at the world he [is] making."[20]

If Kage Baker employs futurism to comment on long-standing concerns over media concentration and trivialization, Dan Abnett employs it to comment on fears about military manipulation of the press during wartime. In the novel *Embedded* (2011) war correspondent Lex Falk grows tired of being told by the armed forces that he "will, of course, report only what we permit you to report." He gets himself chipped into the head of a combat soldier on the colony planet Eighty-Six. Complications ensue when it appears that the soldier is killed in action, whereupon Falk somehow must make his way back to safety. In the end it all proves worthwhile; the journalist is able to uncover a military cover-up despite fervent efforts to stop him.[21]

Speculative fiction often portrays the press searching for better ways to see or witness the world,[22] just as the press does in actuality. For example, a 2013 episode of the TV series *Bones* shows a documentarian strapping a video camera around his head to record everything he experiences.[23] In real life a documentarian has had a miniature video camera inserted in place of his missing right eye, coupled the camera to the movement of his left eye, and sent the resulting pictures to a monitor.[24] Journalists also are experimenting with drones to gather material where they themselves cannot easily go,[25] and they are making extensive use of other technological tools. Computer programs help in gathering and studying government records and other data, including semantic analysis of Twitter feeds.[26] In addition, companies are using algorithms to produce simple news stories automatically, in theory freeing journalists to concentrate on more sophisticated forms of news.[27]

All of this is to suggest that the second category of speculative fiction Ghiglione identified in 1990—that focusing on the nonhuman journalist— is actually coming to fruition. However, whereas some observers view that as a hopeful trend that signifies a "dynamic landscape of continuous and diversified witnessing and reporting,"[28] popular culture has often cast it in a darker light, with the nonhumans threatening or competing with humans or replacing them outright. One of Superman's old nemeses is Metallo, an evil journalist-turned-cyborg.[29] At times robots assume the bodies and identities of journalists for nefarious ends,[30] or else reporters create automatons to help them in their work, only to see it go dreadfully awry.[31] Other examples—some gloomier than others—include the television series *Max Headroom* (1987–88), which depicts a computer-generated TV news anchor taking the place of the real thing, and novels that feature humans plugging themselves directly into global information networks unmediated by journalists.[32]

Ghiglione's third 1990 category, news consumers who help make their own journalism, clearly has been realized in the twenty-first century. Some specialize in data analysis and assist professional reporters and editors. As one study observes, "Journalists can better navigate in the ocean of information with the help of programmers, designers, and hackers who are more skilled at uncovering and penetrating digital information."[33] Furthermore, although some traditionalists have resisted seeing bloggers as "true" journalists, the distinction separating the two has become blurred if not moot.³⁴ Professional journalists have increasingly been expected to use blogs and other social media as resources in their work while also contributing to such media themselves.

Before the rise of the Internet, speculative fiction proved prescient in anticipating a culture in which anyone could engage in "creating, stealing, synthesizing the information he [or she] wants." Again, some portrayals were dystopian in suggesting that individuals would anesthetize themselves by manufacturing their own illusory worlds.³⁵ Once hackers and bloggers became accepted facts of life, popular culture often portrayed them more benignly or even heroically. Such is the case with Lisbeth Salander, the master hacker who helps investigative journalist Mikael Blomkvist in Stieg Larsson's *Millennium* novels and the movies based on the books. As far back as the 1980s, hacker Theora Jones (Amanda Pays) helped investigative reporter Edison Carter (Matt Frewer) uncover corruption and consumer exploitation in the *Max Headroom* TV series.³⁶

Bloggers and citizen watchdogs also have been portrayed as assisting traditional journalists in their work, suggesting that the two sides complement rather than compete with each other. In the movie *State of Play,* Della Frye (Rachel McAdams) blogs for her newspaper's online division and works with investigative reporter Cal McAffrey (Russell Crowe) in exposing a member of Congress who has been an accessory to murder.³⁷ In the last season of TV's *Enlightened* that aired in 2013, Amy Jellicoe (Laura Dern) works for the criminally corrupt Abaddonn Industries and blows the whistle on her employer with help from a coworker who hacks into the company's computer system. She gives the information to *Los Angeles Times* reporter Jeff Flender (Dermot Mulroney), who eagerly accepts the exclusive story while violating professional ethics (he indulges in a brief fling with Jellicoe and does not make it clear that the story will get her fired and sued). Notwithstanding, when she is confronted by her bosses, Jellicoe remains resolute: "I tried to make change from within. And you guys wouldn't listen. . . . I'm tired of watching the world fall apart because of guys like you. I tried to take a little power back." She is rewarded by seeing the publication of Flender's front-page story—headlined "Portrait of a Corporate Whistle Blower: How One Woman Took on a Giant"—and decides that anyone can be "an agent of change."³⁸

Would-be change agents have popped up in a host of other popular stories. The final season of the TV series *Damages* (2012) featured blogger Channing McClaren (Ryan Phillippe) as the founder of a controversial whistleblower website, with the character and website having been inspired by Julian Assange and WikiLeaks. ("Why do people hate you so much when you tell the truth?" McClaren asks.)³⁹ In TV's *Terriers* (2010) a blogger works with two private investigators in uncovering wrongdoing in a California town; in *The Cape* (2011) a blogger helps a superhero fight crime and corruption; and in *Dark Angel* (2000–02) a journalist uses his blog to alert the citizenry in a way that no other medium can or will in a postapocalyptic America.⁴⁰

Such depictions imply a largely positive role for new media, consistent with an upbeat perspective on the future of journalism. Other stories are more cautionary. In the American TV version of *House of Cards,* Zoe Barnes blogs for the *Washington Herald* newspaper, where she is openly disdainful of journalism ethics. Her editor wants to fire her. "Zoe Barnes, Twitter, blogs, enriched media—they're all surface," he tells the paper's publisher. "They're fads. They aren't the foundation this paper was built on, and they aren't what will keep it alive. We have a core readership that thirsts for hard news. Those are the people I work eighty hours a week for. And I won't be distracted by what's fashionable." The publisher, who sees Barnes as a cutting-edge means toward generating buzz for the paper, is unmoved. "That's your resignation letter," she tells the editor.⁴¹

Even when principled journalists work for new media, they face pressure to go down the wrong path. In Gwendolyn Zepeda's novel *Lone Star Legend* (2010), a journalist is hired by the website *¡LatinoNow!,* where "she can't wait to write hard-hitting pieces to combat all those stupid Latino stereotypes." Unfortunately, the website is soon taken over by a new editor—"the infamous Dolores Villanueva O'Sullivan"—who turns *¡LatinoNow!* into a gossip-and-fluff-laced site aimed only at generating as many online visits as possible.⁴² Likewise, Jessica Grose's debut book, *Sad Desk Salad* (2012), tells of a writer for the website *Chick Habit,* for which "she is required to churn out 10 posts daily on everything from meth head former beauty queens to women giving birth in bathtubs." She then must decide whether to publish compromising information about the teenage daughter of a self-proclaimed parenting expert. Grose had worked for the online sites *Slate* and *Jezebel* and said she wanted to explore "how difficult and somewhat oppressive" toiling for a news website could be.⁴³

Some popular culture stories appear to confirm the nastiest preconceptions about bloggers and so-called citizen journalists: that they spread "unconfirmed, incomplete rumors" along with "celebrity gossip" and "news reports [poached] from other publications"; that they "carp and whine" in "satisfying their juvenile egos"; or that they are "socially inadequate, pimpled, single, slightly seedy, bald, cauliflower-nosed young men sitting in their mother's basements and ranting."⁴⁴ In a 2009 episode of television's *NCIS,* a muckraking blogger is murdered after he makes up stories.⁴⁵ In Nick Laird's novel

Glover's Mistake (2009), David Pinner is a lonely college teacher who creates a blog (*The Damp Review*) through which he can post sardonic commentary on London culture. Pinner feels that "*they* might have the television, the newspapers, the books, but the internet was his. Democratic, public, anonymous—it was his country and he felt grateful to be born in the generation that inherited it." Yet he also dimly recognizes that he is "searching not for things to love but a place to put his rage." Pinner posts a scathing critique of an art show featuring the work of one of his former teachers, with whom his roommate is now having an affair. "How foolish they were to think they could become purposeful and whole through another human being," he thinks to himself regarding his two ostensible friends.[46]

So it is with other bloggers who represent the latest incarnations of the gossip mongers who always have been popular culture targets. They drive a successful chef mad with a humiliating online review,[47] brag about their sexual liaisons (including those in exchange for money) with powerful men in government,[48] and make themselves pests—or worse—at school. Jacob Ben Israel (Josh Sussman) is the ubergeek video blogger in the TV series *Glee* (2009–), dishing out news and dirt about his high school classmates and sometimes stalking the female ones. The title character of Cecily von Ziegesar's *Gossip Girl* novels (2002–11) and the associated TV series (2007–12) anonymously posts news about a group of rich teens on Manhattan's Upper East Side.[49] In a 2011 episode of the series *Harry's Law*, a teen who runs a blog aptly called *The Snark Queen* drives a lesbian classmate to kill herself. The young blogger is found not guilty of negligent homicide after her attorney, Harriet "Harry" Korn (Kathy Bates), tells the jury that the teen is the product of a society in which "cable news shows trade on [being] mean."[50]

Social media being used as instruments for cruelty and cyberbullying represent a serious concern.[51] The same is true of the social impact of video games, which even their enthusiasts acknowledge can at times be "vulgar, crude, disgusting and thoroughly unredeeming," not to mention gory.[52] Journalist characters appear in video games that present speculative realities that are rife with violence. News photographer Scarlet Lake in *Alpha Protocol* (2010) has won multiple awards for her images taken in hotspots worldwide—and has time left over to work as a hired assassin.[53] In *Mass Effect* (2007) and *Mass Effect 2* (2010) TV journalist Emily Wong investigates corruption and organized crime in the twenty-second century. (Eventually *Mass Effect*'s makers killed off the character.)

The *Dead Rising* games feature journalists confronting zombies. *Dead Rising* (2006) and *Dead Rising: Chop Till You Drop* (2009) portray freelance photojournalist Frank West heroically risking his life while covering the rav-

Rebecca Chang takes time out from her reporting duties to wield a gun in the *Dead Rising* video games.

enous flesh-eaters. Similarly, in three installments of *Dead Rising 2* (2010–11), reporter Rebecca Chang investigates a zombie outbreak in Fortune City. (The zombies have been featured on the *Terror Is Reality* TV show, which pits them against contestants who either can win "enormous cash prizes and short-lived fame" or else "get devoured alive by the undead on live pay-per-view.") Just as Chang is about to expose the man who deliberately has triggered the outbreak, he fatally shoots her in the face.[54]

Of course, not all video games center on death and destruction.[55] Some journalists see them as useful devices for promoting citizen involvement with the news. "Our job as journalists is to inform the public," one writes. "By using emotion and empathy, games allow us to inform readers in a new way—and one in which they both remember and understand." Journalist-created examples have invited players to try to balance the federal budget, experience the dangers of texting while driving, and decide how to transport cardiac patients safely and efficiently to New York City hospitals.[56]

Both real-world news organizations and virtual news organizations have participated in the MMORPG (massively multiplayer online role-playing game) *Second Life,* which was founded in 2003. The game offers an online virtual reality in which players create avatars and interact in a wide range of activities and milieus. CNN and Reuters were among the actual press outlets that created Second Life bureaus to report on the alternative world, although some of those bureaus were short-lived.[57] Simultaneously, virtual newspapers like the *Alphaville Herald* (with the slogan "Always Fairly Unbalanced") were established. The paper's website acknowledges that it "is often called a muck-raking tabloid or worse, but its loyal readers (numbering several thousand per day) love—and often love to hate—the unique service it provides: to take a good, close, often snarky look at the online worlds that are becoming a more and more important part of everyone's offline lives."[58] In a 2010 study Bonnie Brennen and Erika dela Cerna argued that the *Herald* and other *Second Life* newspapers raised "important questions about freedom of expression in virtual worlds" (particularly considering censorship), and that the papers also played a notable role in "community building and education." They thus set a potentially useful example for traditional journalists to follow.[59]

In such ways new media again are invoked as methods of reinventing and reinvigorating journalism. For the most part, though—and just as is true of other media—video and online games have tended to reproduce traditional images of the journalist, even when the journalist is doing extraordinary things or following a vocational path that real journalists rarely get to take. Nintendo's *Imagine: Reporter* (2010) invites children to experience life in the news business: "Build your career from a local newspaper reporter all the way to hosting your very own national TV show! Develop exciting news stories, track information in the field, and take photos. Interview movie stars, athletes and more, then report breaking news stories to your audience!"[60]

Just as a child's video game reproduces the characters of the reporter, photojournalist, and TV journalist on the trail of big stories, so do the more violent, adult-oriented games. *Dead Rising 2*'s Rebecca Chang is described as "an ambitious, beautiful news reporter" who works to "get the scoop in any way." She "always wears the same shirt with 3 buttons undone, showing cleavage"—recycling the usual stereotypes of the female journalist as being talented and aggressive, but hardly averse to using her looks and sexuality to her professional advantage.[61] Male journalists similarly conform to traditional type. As one study notes, video games propel "the fictional hero journalist into the next generation while at the same time holding on to the conventions and images of the past."[62] Speculative fiction's journalism of tomorrow is not so different from popular culture's journalism of today or yesterday.

Future Research on Journalism's Popular Image

Having considered journalism's future, we turn now to potential future directions for scholarship as to the image of the journalist in popular culture. In particular, we point toward research areas of which more should be known.

First, additional scholarship is needed on pop culture stories in media other than films. We have attempted to redress that paucity of research with this book, but we still need more detailed analyses of radio and television programs, novels, plays, cartoons, comics, commercials, and online and interactive stories and games. Again, those analyses ideally should pay heed to the social, cultural, and historical contexts in which the stories were produced and link the findings to other research areas regarding the news media.

Second, more work should be done on the depiction of the journalist in countries other than the United States. We have included a few examples here from Britain and elsewhere, but many other countries have produced stories about journalists and press systems outside the Anglo-American realm.[63] Studies of those stories along with cross-cultural analyses of the journalist's image across nations not only will broaden our understanding of journalism's place in popular culture but also will meet the calls for more comparative and non-Westernized scholarship in journalism studies.[64]

Third, we need to learn more about the effects that popular culture may or may not have on public perceptions of journalism and how people interpret such portrayals of the news media. Do they affect attitudes or beliefs regarding press credibility? Is there a "Mean Journalist" syndrome whereby popular culture cultivates the impression that journalists are sleazier than they are in real life?[65] Are people able to "see through" such depictions? Do those depictions actually make journalism seem more intriguing, much as *The Front Page* captivated many prospective young reporters?[66] We do not really know. It will take well-designed surveys, experiments, and audience ethnography studies to start providing some answers.[67]

On the other hand, there is plenty that we do know about journalism's image, and what we know should be kept in mind by future researchers. Media scholar James Carey asserted that an essential way of "comprehending the popular arts is against the cultural tradition in which they are embedded," a tradition "that insists on reasserting itself" no matter how much else might change.[68] In popular culture stories about journalism, as we have demonstrated here, certain characters and themes repeatedly appear. There are heroes and scoundrels who embody specific journalistic roles, whether it is that of the reporter, editor, photojournalist, or other recurring types. The portrayal of those types varies according to time and place, but still they persist. The conflicts between them speak to broader hopes and fears regarding the news media.

Heroes and scoundrels express dueling myths: "official" characters who can be upstanding and respectable or else unctuous and venal, and "outlaw" characters who can be independent and incorruptible or else slimy and creepy. They illustrate both "Progressive" perspectives on media history, with brave journalists furthering press freedom, and critical perspectives, with hapless journalists buffeted by strife and uncertainty. They demonstrate professionalism's virtues of ethical, independent journalism and its vices of bland and neutered reporting. They celebrate difference while pointing to intractable rifts rooted in race and gender and sexuality. They show the power of the press as an instrument of justice and as a tool of oppression. They highlight the potency of images in moving citizens toward enlightenment or imbecility, and the horrors of war in moving journalists and others toward righteousness or madness. Finally, they suggest that those sorts of tensions will continue long into the future and will continue to be portrayed by popular culture in familiar ways.

The persistence of such characters and themes is especially striking given the flux affecting not only journalism but also other professions. For example, law is similarly confronting technological upheaval, with the Internet increasing the availability of lower-cost legal services and in some cases lessening the need for lawyers.[69] Medicine is witnessing heated discussions over the level of training needed to provide certain kinds of care.[70] Both medicine and law are debating what to include in a professional education and whether to reduce the number of years of schooling required to earn a degree. A decline in law school applications has prompted one professor to observe that they "are going through a revolution in law with a time bomb on our admissions books."[71] In all the professions the ideals of meritocracy and public service seem to be increasingly under siege.

Then again, public ambivalence toward the professions is nothing new. For decades people have looked up to professionals but also distrusted their authority and their entanglements with dominant interests, casting an ever wary eye toward what has been called "the inevitable complicity of knowledge and power."[72] If the recurrence of heroic doctor and lawyer characters in popular culture is not surprising, neither is the recurrence of professional villains who make a mockery out of medicine and law.[73] As for journalists—despite their hazy professional status in comparison with doctors and lawyers—they too have enjoyed a privileged place and consequently have drawn similar skepticism. As John J. Pauly has observed, "Professional journalists attract attention and criticism because they claim the right to sort out competing definitions of the world for the rest of society, and thus they bear the brunt of our anger when they do it in a fashion we dislike."[74] That is, they help define what is supposedly true and what is not true, and when they commit blatant falsehoods in doing so or violate the public interest, popular culture makes them pay the price. Moreover, the journalist is a handy "symbolic prop" for addressing a host of other social concerns,[75] including the impact of new technologies, the changing roles of women and of ethnic and sexual minorities, and the uses and abuses of institutional power.

When journalists in popular culture do exactly what they are supposed to do—uncover the truth and serve the public interest—they help reinforce a host of treasured myths and beliefs: that we can govern ourselves, that citizens can influence events and policymaking, that technology and the professions can better our lives, that freedom of speech and the press can flourish, that the system can work, and that the truth can emerge triumphant.[76] That is why the image of the heroic journalist on the trail of the big scoop will never go out of style, regardless of what sorts of journalistic practices, organizations, and technologies might predominate at any given moment. In reviewing the film *State of Play,* critic Roger Ebert observed that "no matter what happens to newspapers, the newspaper movie is a durable genre. Shouting 'stop the presses!' is ever so much more exciting than shouting 'stop the upload!'"[77]

*   *   *

We began this book by rhetorically asking why scholars should study the image of the journalist in popular culture. We neglected to provide one important answer: it's fun. What could be more enjoyable than immersing oneself in movies, TV shows, novels, comics, or video games, and seeing journalists doing thrilling, appalling, extraordinary things? Still, it never is all fun. One cannot simply pick and choose what one would normally like, as is ordinarily the case with popular culture. One must accept occasional exposure to material that may come across as silly or offensive or just plain dull; popular culture has produced no small share of junk. Nevertheless, the casual spectator's junk can be the serious scholar's artifact, worthy of careful analysis with an eye toward developing a fuller and more nuanced grasp of the field. And careful, critical analysis as opposed to casual spectatorship is always the scholar's main responsibility, requiring the investment of time and hard work.

That investment pays off in providing unique insight into journalism. In the original version of *The Front Page*—which solidified pop culture's running themes about the news media and shaped countless works that followed—the incorrigible editor Walter Burns expounds upon the "unseen power" of the press. "Bigger men than you have found out what it is!" he tells the mayor and sheriff. "Presidents! Yes—and Kings!"[78] On the face of it, Walter's boast is preposterous; he and reporter Hildy Johnson are in police custody for harboring an escaped fugitive whom they have hidden not out of any sense of justice but because he represents a fabulous exclusive. That exclusive has

Walter Burns (Adolphe Menjou, far right) and Hildy Johnson (Pat O'Brien) invoke the
"unseen power" watching over the press in the 1931 film version of *The Front Page*.
(Courtesy of the Academy of Motion Picture Arts and Sciences)

been the product of dumb luck (it literally climbed in through the window)
rather than hard work. The press seems as much a public menace as a public servant. And yet the journalists still print their scoop, oust the corrupt
officials, and free the condemned man. As for Walter Burns, he would be
embodied by no less a star than Cary Grant in the 1940 film version of the
play, *His Girl Friday*. "Walter, you're wonderful, in a loathsome sort of way,"
Hildy (Rosalind Russell) tells him in the movie. Walter truly is loathsome,
but he is just as wonderful: he is played by Cary Grant, after all.

Hero and scoundrel, delightful and despicable, public servant and public
menace—that is the image of the journalist that popular culture gives us.
Pop culture routinely makes the press matter by showing good journalism
saving the day and bad journalism wreaking pain and havoc. It suggests that
in spite of formidable obstacles and occasional wrenching change, the press
and its noblest ideals will somehow endure. Therein lies the "unseen power"
of journalism's popular image, and that is why it is necessary that we continue
to study and care about it.

Appendix

List of Works

Following is a complete list of the works that are referred to in this book, including the endnotes. The list is by category, with the works listed chronologically and alphabetized by title within each year. When a work has run multiple years, it is listed according to the year that it first appeared. For more details regarding each work, consult the book's index and the Image of the Journalist in Popular Culture (IJPC) Database (www.ijpc.org).

Animated Cartoon Series

1941–42:	*Superman*
1966–70:	*The New Adventures of Superman*
1967–70:	*Spider-Man*
1981–82:	*Spider-Man*
1981–83:	*Spider-Man and His Amazing Friends*
1988:	*RoboCop; Superman*
1989– :	*The Simpsons*
1994–98:	*Spider-Man: The Animated Series*
1996–2000:	*Superman: The Animated Series*
1999–2003, 2005– :	*Family Guy*
2002–10, 2013– :	*Cyberchase*
2003:	*Spider-Man: The New Animated Series*
2007– :	*Hoofy & Boo's News & Views*
2008–09:	*The Spectacular Spider-Man*
2012– :	*Ultimate Spider-Man*

Comic Strips, Comic Books, and Graphic Novels

1927–68: *Jane Arden*

1938– : *Superman* (comic books)

1939–66,
   1978–85: *Superman* (comic strips)

1940–2004: *Steve Roper*

1940–2011: *Brenda Starr*

1942: *Liberty Belle*

1942–48: *Chase Yale: Commando Yank Comics*

1949: *King of Reporters: Floyd Gibbons (True Comics)*

1962– : *Spider-Man* (comic books)

1967–2007: *The Question*

1968–2007: *Jack Ryder—The Creeper*

1970– : *Doonesbury*

1977– : *Spider-Man* (comic strip)

1982–89: *V for Vendetta*

1984–1991: *Transformers Comic Books*

1987–91: Don Lomax, *Vietnam Journal*

2001–02: Tim LaHaye and Jerry B. Jenkins, *Left Behind: A Graphic Novel of the Earth's Last Days*

2003: *Kolchak: The Night Stalker* (comic book)

2003–12: *Kolchak: The Night Stalker* (graphic novel series)

2007: Anthony Lappé and Dan Goldman, *Shooting War*

2008: Mat Johnson and Warren Pleece, *Incognegro*

2009– : *Wolverine* (Melita Garner episodes)

Drama

430 BC: Sophocles, *Women of Trachis*

1625: Ben Jonson, *The Staple of News*

1926: Maurine Watkins, *Chicago*

1928: Ben Hecht and Charles MacArthur, *The Front Page*

1930: Louis Weitzenkorn, *Five Star Final*

1932: Manuel Seff and Forrest Wilson, *Blessed Event*; Bella Spewack and Samuel Spewack, *Clear All Wires*

1938: Cole Porter, Samuel Spewack, and Bella Spewack, *Leave It to Me!* (musical)

1940: Ernest Hemingway and Benjamin Glazer, *The Fifth Column*

1945: Howard Lindsay and Russel Crouse, *State of the Union*

1946: Garson Kanin, *Born Yesterday*

1955: Jerome Lawrence and Robert E. Lee, *Inherit the Wind*

1958: Yigal Mossinson, *Throw Him to the Dogs (Zrok oto la-klavim)*

1966:	Charles Strouse, Lee Adams, David Newman, and Robert Benton, *It's a Bird . . . It's a Plane . . . It's Superman* (musical)
1975:	John Kander, Fred Ebb, and Bob Fosse, *Chicago* (musical)
1979:	Amlin Gray, *How I Got That Story*
2002:	Marvin Hamlisch, Craig Carnelia, and John Guare, *Sweet Smell of Success* (musical)
2003:	Tracey Scott Wilson, *The Story*
2004:	Tim Robbins, *Embedded*
2006:	Peter Morgan, *Frost/Nixon*
2010:	Douglas Carter Beane, *Mr. and Mrs. Fitch*
2011:	Bono and the Edge, Julie Taymor, Glen Berger, and Roberto Aguirre-Sacasa, *Spider-Man: Turn Off the Dark* (musical)
2012:	David Auburn, *The Columnist*; Gabe McKinley, *CQ/CX*; Alan Menken, Jack Feldman, and Harvey Fierstein, *Newsies* (musical)
2013:	Nora Ephron, *Lucky Guy*

Movies

1914:	*The Active Life of Dolly of the Dailies* (series)
1914:	*Making a Living*
1915:	*The Gentleman from Indiana*
1927:	*Chicago*
1928:	*The Cameraman; Hot News; Let 'Er Go, Gallegher; The Power of the Press*
1929:	*Big News*
1931:	*Five Star Final; The Front Page; Hot News Margie; Scandal Sheet*
1932:	*Blessed Event; The Final Edition; Is My Face Red?; Love Is a Racket; Okay, America; Scandal for Sale*
1933:	*Above the Clouds; Clear All Wires; Headline Shooter; King Kong; Picture Snatcher; Professional Sweetheart*
1934:	*Burn 'Em Up Barnes; The Friends of Mr. Sweeney; Hi, Nellie!; It Happened One Night; Paris Interlude; Viva Villa!*
1935:	*Broadway Melody of 1936; Ladies Crave Excitement; Page Miss Glory; Too Tough to Kill*
1936:	*A Face in the Fog; Here Comes Carter; Libeled Lady; Mr. Deeds Goes to Town; Murder with Pictures; Two Against the World; A Woman Rebels*
1937:	*Anything for a Thrill; Bank Alarm; Behind the Headlines; Hollywood Hotel; I Cover the War; The Last Train from Madrid; Love and Hisses; Love Is on the Air; Nothing Sacred; They Wanted to Marry; Wake Up and Live*
1937–39:	*Torchy Blane* (series); *Your True Adventures* (featuring Floyd Gibbons, "The Headline Hunter")
1938:	*Here's Flash Casey; Time Out for Murder; Too Hot to Handle*
1939:	*Adventures of Jane Arden; Barricade; Chasing Danger; Espionage Agent; The Light That Failed; Mr. Smith Goes to Washington; Nancy Drew,*

Reporter; Scandal Sheet; Sued for Libel; That's Right—You're Wrong; The Women

1940: *Arise, My Love; Behind the News; Comrade X; A Dispatch from Reuters; Foreign Correspondent; His Girl Friday; Mystery in Swing*

1941: *Citizen Kane; Meet John Doe; Murder with Music* (aka *Mistaken Identity*)

1942: *Berlin Correspondent; Cairo; Keeper of the Flame; The Lady Has Plans; Once Upon a Honeymoon; Roxie Hart; Somewhere I'll Find You; Woman of the Year*

1943: *Guadalcanal Diary*

1944: *Laura; Passage to Marseille*

1945: *Blood on the Sun; Objective, Burma!; The Story of G.I. Joe; Week-End at the Waldorf*

1946: *Without Reservations*

1947: *Gentleman's Agreement*

1948: *Call Northside 777; June Bride; State of the Union; Superman* (serial)

1950: *All About Eve; Atom Man vs. Superman* (serial); *Born Yesterday; The Lawless* (aka *The Dividing Line*); *Sunset Boulevard*

1951: *Ace in the Hole* (aka *The Big Carnival*); *Come Fill the Cup; The Day the Earth Stood Still; The Man from Planet X; Superman and the Mole Men; The Thing from Another World*

1952: *Assignment: Paris; The Captive City; Deadline, U.S.A.; Park Row; Red Planet Mars; Scandal Sheet; The Turning Point; Washington Story*

1953: *Francis Covers the Big Town; Sabre Jet*

1954: *Rear Window*

1955: *The Big Knife; Headline Hunters; Love Is a Many-Splendored Thing; Tarantula*

1956: *The Gamma People; Godzilla, King of the Monsters!; The Great Man; High Society*

1957: *The Deadly Mantis; A Face in the Crowd; Funny Face; The Land Unknown; Sweet Smell of Success*

1958: *The Quiet American; Teacher's Pet; War of the Colossal Beast*

1959: *Island of Lost Women; -30-*

1960: *The Angel Wore Red; Inherit the Wind; La Dolce Vita*

1962: *The Man Who Shot Liberty Valance*

1964: *Black Like Me*

1965: *The Bedford Incident*

1968: *Anzio; The Green Berets; The Legend of Lylah Clare*

1969: *Medium Cool*

1974: *The Front Page; The Odessa File; The Parallax View*

1975: *Friday Foster; The Lost Honour of Katharina Blum* (*Die verlorene Ehre der Katharina Blum*); *Three Days of the Condor*

1976: *All the President's Men; Futureworld; Network*

1977: *Capricorn One; A Special Day* (*Una giornata particolare*)

1978: *Eyes of Laura Mars; Superman*

1979: *Apocalypse Now; The China Syndrome*

1980: *Death Watch; Superman II; Where the Buffalo Roam; Without Love (Bez milosci)*

1981: *Absence of Malice; Marianne and Juliane*

1982: *Angkor: Cambodia Express; Another Way (Egymásra nézve); Tenebre; Wrong Is Right; The Year of Living Dangerously*

1983: *The Right Stuff; Superman III; Under Fire*

1984: *The Killing Fields*

1985: *Fletch; The Year of the Dragon*

1986: *Heartburn; Salvador; Violets Are Blue*

1987: *Broadcast News; Full Metal Jacket; RoboCop; Street Smart; Superman IV: The Quest for Peace*

1988: *À corps perdu; Evil Angels (aka A Cry in the Dark); Switching Channels; Virgin Machine (Die Jungfrauenmaschine)*

1989: *Fletch Lives; Wired*

1990: *RoboCop 2*

1991: *Livin' Large!*

1992: *Bob Roberts; Hero; The Living End; Newsies; The Public Eye*

1993: *Born Yesterday; Deadly Exposure; Kalifornia; The Pelican Brief*

1994: *Blankman; The Paper*

1995: *The Bridges of Madison County; Nixon; Thin Ice; To Die For*

1996: *The People vs. Larry Flynt; Pretty Village, Pretty Flame (Lepa sela lepo gore); Up Close & Personal*

1997: *Hong Kong Night Club (Hon Kon daiyasokai: Tatchi and Magi); In & Out; Mad City; Tomorrow Never Dies; Wag the Dog; Welcome to Sarajevo*

1998: *Fear and Loathing in Las Vegas; High Art; The Velvet Goldmine*

1999: *Aimée & Jaguar; Dick; The Insider; Three Kings; True Crime*

2000: *Harrison's Flowers; Left Behind; The Weight of Water*

2001: *The Cat's Meow; Kissing Jessica Stein; The Map of Sex and Love (Qingse ditu); No Man's Land*

2002: *Black and White; Chaos and Desire (La turbulence des fluides); Chicago; Left Behind II: Tribulation Force; Mr. Deeds; The Quiet American; Road to Perdition; Spider-Man; The Trip; We Were Soldiers*

2003: *The Far Side of the Moon (La face cachée de la lune); Shattered Glass; Veronica Guerin*

2004: *Anchorman: The Legend of Ron Burgundy; Closer; Kis Kis Ki Kismat; Lakshya; November; Paparazzi; Spider-Man 2*

2005: *Capote; Good Night, and Good Luck; Harry Potter and the Goblet of Fire; Left Behind: World at War; Page 3; Thank You for Smoking*

2006: *Blood Diamond; Boys Love; The Devil Wears Prada; Infamous; Superman Returns; V for Vendetta; Whispering Moon (Das Flüstern des Mondes); The Yacoubian Building (Omaret yakobean)*

2007:	*The Bourne Ultimatum; The Hunting Party; Lions for Lambs; A Mighty Heart; Spider-Man 3*
2008:	*The Baader Meinhof Complex (Der Baader Meinhof Komplex); Dostana; Frost/Nixon; Nothing but the Truth; The Reflecting Pool*
2009:	*Balibo; Brüno; The Girl Who Kicked the Hornet's Nest (Luftslottet som sprängdes); The Girl Who Played with Fire (Flickan som lekte med elden); The Girl with the Dragon Tattoo* (Swedish-language version, *Män som hatar kvinnor); He's Just Not That Into You; Julie & Julia; State of Play*
2010:	*The Bang Bang Club; Bitter Feast; Harry Potter and the Deathly Hallows, Part 1; Peepli (Live)*
2011:	*The Girl with the Dragon Tattoo* (English-language version); *Harry Potter and the Deathly Hallows, Part 2; No One Killed Jessica*
2012:	*Cloud Atlas; Rock of Ages*
2013:	*Anchorman 2: The Legend Continues; The Fifth Estate; Man of Steel; Philomena*

Novels and Short Stories

1832:	James Kirke Paulding, *Westward Ho*
1838:	James Fenimore Cooper, *Home as Found* and *Homeward Bound*
1843:	Honoré de Balzac, *Lost Illusions*
1843–44:	Charles Dickens, *The Life and Adventures of Martin Chuzzlewit*
1862:	William Makepeace Thackeray, *The Adventures of Philip*
1864:	Bayard Taylor, *John Godfrey's Fortunes*
1871:	Harriet Beecher Stowe, *My Wife and I*
1873:	Mark Twain and Charles Dudley Warner, *The Gilded Age*
1874:	Rebecca Harding Davis, *John Andross*
1875:	Harriet Beecher Stowe, *We and Our Neighbors*
1881/1908:	Henry James, *The Portrait of a Lady* (original and updated versions)
1890:	Richard Harding Davis, "Gallegher" (short story); Rudyard Kipling, *The Light That Failed*
1899:	Stephen Crane, *Active Service*; Booth Tarkington, *The Gentleman from Indiana*; William Dean Howells, *Their Silver Wedding Journey*
1900:	Irving Bacheller, *Eben Holden*
1902:	Richard Harding Davis, "A Derelict"
1907:	Richard Harding Davis, *Gallegher* (novel); Emily Lafayette McLaws, *The Welding*
1921:	Ben Hecht, *Erik Dorn*
1929:	Floyd Gibbons, *The Red Napoleon*
1931:	Emile Gauvreau, *Hot News*; Mildred Gilman, *Sob Sister*
1932:	Emile Gauvreau, *Scandal Monger*
1938:	Evelyn Waugh, *Scoop*

1940:	Frank Bell (aka Mildred A. Wirt), *Flash Evans and the Darkroom Mystery* and *Flash Evans: Camera News Hawk*
1941:	Isaac Asimov, "Nightfall"
1947:	R. F. Delderfield, *All Over the Town*; Laura Z. Hobson, *Gentleman's Agreement*
1950:	Ray Bradbury, "The Veldt"
1955:	Graham Greene, *The Quiet American*
1964:	Philip Dick, *The Penultimate Truth*
1970–91:	Joseph Hansen, the "David Brandstetter" novels
1974:	D. G. Compton, *The Continuous Katherine Mortenhoe*; Arthur Lyons, *The Dead Are Discreet*; Heinrich Böll, *The Lost Honour of Katharina Blum*
1974–94:	Gregory Mcdonald, the "Fletch" novels
1976:	Les Whitten, *Conflict of Interest*; Danielle Steel, *Passion's Promise*
1978:	Christopher Koch, *The Year of Living Dangerously*
1979:	Jeff Millar, *Private Sector*
1980– :	Loren D. Estleman, the "Amos Walker" novels
1982–88:	Vicki P. McConnell, the "Nyla Wade" novels (including *The Burnton Widows*, 1984)
1983:	Nora Ephron, *Heartburn*
1984:	Ward Just, *The American Blues*
1984–93:	Susan Moody, the "Penny Wannawake" novels
1985:	Michael M. Thomas, *Hard Money*
1986–2005:	C. C. Risenhoover, the "Matt McCall" novels
1987:	Robert Inman, *Home Fires Burning*
1987–2003:	Val McDermid, the "Lindsay Gordon" novels
1988:	Jack Anderson, *Control*; Isaac Asimov, *Prelude to Foundation*
1989:	David Aaron, *Agent of Influence*; Michael Dobbs, *House of Cards*
1989–97:	Mike Phillips, the "Sam Dean" novels
1990:	Danielle Steel, *Message from Nam*
1991:	Barbara Taylor Bradford, *Remember*; Barbara Paul, "Who What When Where Why" (in *Invitation to Murder*)
1991–2002:	Stephen F. Wilcox, the "Elias Hackshaw" novels
1992:	Robert James Waller, *The Bridges of Madison County*; John Grisham, *The Pelican Brief*; John Varley, *Steel Beach*
1993–2011:	Jan Burke, the "Irene Kelly" novels
1994:	Jackie Collins, *Hollywood Kids*
1994–95:	Lisa Haddock, the "Carmen Ramirez" novels (including *Edited Out*, 1994, and *Final Cut*, 1995)
1994–97:	Claudia McKay, the "Lynn Evans" novels
1994–2005:	Penny Mickelbury, the "Mimi Patterson" novels (including *Night Songs*, 1995)
1994–2011:	Maud Tabachnik, the "Sandra Khan" novels

1995:   Andrew Klavan, *True Crime*

1995–99:   R. D. Zimmerman, the "Todd Mills" novels

1995–2007: Tim LaHaye and Jerry B. Jenkins, the *Left Behind* series

1996:   Colin Harrison, *Manhattan Nocturne*; Christopher John Farley, *My Favorite War*

1996–2008: John Morgan Wilson, the "Benjamin Justice" novels

1997–99:   Jo Bannister, the "Rosie Holland" novels

1997–2004: Michael Craft, the "Mark Manning" novels

1997–2007: J. K. Rowling, the "Harry Potter" novels

1998:   Bonnie Tucker, *Stay Tuned: Wedding at 11:00*; Kim McLarin, *Taming It Down*

1998–2001: Carlene Miller, the "Lexy Hyatt" novels

1999:   Danielle Steel, *Bittersweet*; Michael D. O'Brien, *Plague Journal: Children of the Last Days*

2000:   Venise Berry, *All of Me: A Voluptuous Tale*; JoAnn Ross, *Fair Haven*

2000–04:   Isaac Adamson, the "Billy Chaka" novels

2000– :   James Butcher, *The Dresden Files* series; Larry Keys and Matt Wolf, the "Geronimo Stilton" novels

2001:   Jack McDevitt, *Deepsix*; Kim McLarin, *Meeting of the Waters*

2001–07:   Nancy Fairbanks, the "Carolyn Blue" novels

2002:   Christopher J. Heassler, *The Antagonist's Handbook*; Jeffrey Frank, *The Columnist*; Janet Boling, *Deadly Sources*

2002–04:   Jon P. Bloch, the "Rick Domino" novels

2002–05:   Yolanda Joe, the "Georgia Barnett" novels; Elizabeth Sims, the "Lillian Byrd" novels

2002–06:   Bill Kent, the "Andrea Cosicki" novels

2002–11:   Cecily von Ziegesar, the *Gossip Girl* series

2003:   Michael Ignatieff, *Charlie Johnson in the Flames*; Lauren Weisberger, *The Devil Wears Prada*; Kathleen Lamarche, *The Plot*; Chris Benson, *Special Interest*

2003–06:   Janet Evanovich and Charlotte Hughes, the "Jamie Swift" novels

2004:   John Robert Marlow, *Nano*; Ruth Langan, *Retribution*; Lindsey Davis, *Scandal Takes a Holiday*

2004–07:   Sheryl J. Anderson, the "Molly Forrester" novels

2004–09:   Anna Blundy, the "Faith Zanetti" novels (including *The Bad News Bible*, 2004, and *Vodka Neat* [aka *Neat Vodka*], 2008)

2005:   Dan Marsh, *Klandestined*; Jessica Cutler, *The Washingtonienne*; John Blanchard, *Without Fear or Favor*

2006:   James Siegel, *Deceit*; Deborah Schoeneman, *4% Famous*; Patricia Potter, *Tempting the Devil*

2006–10:   Suzanne Arruda, the "Jade del Cameron" novels

2006– :   Morgan St. James and Phyllice Bradner, the "Godiva Olivia DuBois" novels

2007: Janet Boling, *Breaking News*; Jamie Malanowski, *The Coup*; Kage Baker, *Gods and Pawns* (includes "Welcome to Olympus, Mr. Hearst"); Lara Santoro, *Mercy*; Kage Baker, *The Sons of Heaven*

2007–08: Roberta Isleib, the "Rebecca Butterman" novels

2007–11: Persia Walker, the "Lanie Price" novels

2008: Ally Blake, *Falling for the Rebel Heir*; Stieg Larsson, *The Girl with the Dragon Tattoo*; Allan McLeod, *The Money Washers*; Jill Monroe, *Primal Instincts*; Kira Salak, *The White Mary*; Roxanne Rustand, *Wildfire*

2008– : Julie Kramer, the "Riley Spartz" novels

2009: Ward Just, *Exiles in the Garden*; Helen Brenna, *First Come Twins*; Stieg Larsson, *The Girl Who Played with Fire*; Nick Laird, *Glover's Mistake*; Kathryn Lilley, *Makeovers Can Be Murder*; Marti Leimbach, *The Man from Saigon*; John Barth, *Northland: A City within a Nation*; Adriana Kraft, *Return to Purgatory Point*; Diana Kingham, *The Road to Imphal*; Tom Davis, *Scared: A Novel on the Edge of the World*

2009–12: Glen Albert Ebisch, the "Laura Magee" novels

2010: Gary B. Hudson, *Brief*; BethAnn Buehler, *Broken Together*; David Hagberg, *The Cabal*; Kimberly Kaye Terry, *Hot to Touch*; Mike Lawson, *House Justice*; Jan Neuharth, *The Kill*; Karen Hawkins, *Lois Lane Tells All*; Gwendolyn Zepeda, *Lone Star Legend*; Tatjana Soli, *The Lotus Eaters*; Kristin Hanna, *Winter Garden*; Louis Hillary Park, *Wolf's Run*

2011: Dawn Atkins, *The Baby Connection*; Patricia Spencer, *Day Three*; Dan Abnett, *Embedded*; Dawn Reno, *Foxglove*; Ray Flynt, *Kisses of an Enemy*; Montana Mills, *Need*; JoAnn Ross, *One Summer*

2012: Teri Wilson, *Alaskan Hearts*; Larry Matthews, *Brass Knuckles*; Douglas Fetterly, *Breach of Justice*; Leroy Smith, *Constant Jay: Embedded Reporter in Hell*; Joshua Graham, *Darkroom*; Donna Hill, *Everything Is You*; Stieg Larsson, *The Girl Who Kicked the Hornet's Nest*; Carol L. Johnston, *A Lifetime of Tomorrows*; Jessica Grose, *Sad Desk Salad*; Jim Hipps, *Tenacious Bulldogs*; Thomas Mallon, *Watergate*

2012– : Nancy G. West, the "Aggie Mundeen" novels

2013: Laura Knots, *Brandi Bloom Galactic Reporter Enslaved*; Don Chase, *Cindy Jones and the Secret of Craycroft*; Rachel Bailey, *No Stranger to Scandal*

2013– : James Dobson and Kurt Bruner, the "Julia Davidson" novels

Poetry and Music

81–103: Martial (author), "The Newsmonger" (*The Twelve Books of Epigrams*, Book 9, No. 35)

1930: Cole Porter (composer), "Let's Fly Away"

1933: Al Dubin and Harry Warren (composers), "Shuffle Off to Buffalo"

1937: Richard Rodgers and Lorenz Hart (composers), "The Lady Is a Tramp"

1982:	Don Henley (singer), "Dirty Laundry"
2007:	Britney Spears (singer), "Piece of Me" music video
2008:	Lady Gaga (singer), "Paparazzi"
2011:	Britney Spears (singer), "I Wanna Go" music video

Radio

1937–52:	*Big Town*
1940–51:	*Adventures of Superman*
1942–44:	*Hot Copy*
1943–50, 1954–55:	*Flashgun Casey* (aka *Casey Crime Photographer*)
1944:	*The George Burns and Gracie Allen Show* (September 12 episode with Louella Parsons)
1950–52:	*Night Beat*
2009:	*Scoop*

Television Movies and Plays

1965:	*Inherit the Wind*
1975:	*The Lives of Jenny Dolan*
1981:	*Word of Honor*
1983:	*V*
1985:	*The Hearst and Davies Affair*; *Malice in Wonderland*
1986:	*Annihilator*; *Murrow*; *News at Eleven*
1987:	*Scoop*
1988:	*Inherit the Wind*
1989:	*Margaret Bourke-White*
1990:	*The Image*; *Somebody Has to Shoot the Picture*
1993:	*Message from Nam*; *Remember*
1995:	*Almost Golden: The Jessica Savitch Story*
1996:	*Devil's Food*
1999:	*Inherit the Wind*; *RKO 281*
2000:	*Mary and Rhoda*
2002:	*Live from Baghdad*
2003:	*War Stories*
2005:	*Embedded Live!*; *ShakespeaRe-Told: Much Ado about Nothing*
2008:	*He Kills Coppers*
2012:	*Hemingway & Gellhorn*

Television Series and Episodes

| 1950–56: | *Big Town* |
| 1952–58: | *Adventures of Superman* |

1955:   *I Love Lucy,* "The Hedda Hopper Story" (March 14)

1958–60:   *Man with a Camera*

1962:   *The Untouchables,* "The Floyd Gibbons Show" (December 11)

1962–63:   *Man of the World*

1963–89,

  1996,

  2005– :   *Doctor Who*

1965–68:   *Walt Disney's Wonderful World of Color,* "Gallegher" series

1968–71:   *The Name of the Game*

1969– :   *Sesame Street,* "News Flash" segments (including "Hickory Dickory Dock," January 3, 1975)

1970–77:   *The Mary Tyler Moore Show* (including "Will Mary Richards Go to Jail?" September 14, 1974; "You Sometimes Hurt the One You Hate," September 28, 1974)

1972:   *Scoop*

1973:   *Cannon,* "Press Pass to the Slammer" (March 14)

1974:   *Owen Marshall: Counselor at Law,* "The Ghost of Buzz Stevens" (April 6)

1974–75:   *Kolchak: The Night Stalker*

1975– :   *Saturday Night Live,* "Weekend Update"

1976:   *City of Angels,* "The November Plan," parts 1–3 (February 3, February 10, February 17); *M*A*S*H,* "The Interview" (February 24)

1977–79:   *The Amazing Spider-Man*

1977–81:   *Eight Is Enough* (including "Much Ado about Garbage," January 18, 1978)

1977–82:   *The Incredible Hulk; Lou Grant*

1978:   *M*A*S*H,* "Our Finest Hour" (October 9)

1978–82:   *WKRP in Cincinnati* (including "Turkeys Away," October 30, 1978)

1979:   *Mrs. Columbo,* "Off the Record" (November 1); *The Omega Factor*

1982:   *M*A*S*H,* "Blood and Guts" (January 18); *Mork & Mindy,* "Cheerleader in Chains" (April 22)

1983:   *Goodnight, Beantown,* "Our Man in the Slammer" (November 6)

1984–85:   *V*

1987–88:   *Max Headroom*

1988–98:   *Murphy Brown* (including "Subpoena Envy," January 8, 1990)

1989:   *Anything but Love,* "Scared Straight," (October 18); *China Beach,* "How to Stay Alive in Vietnam," parts 1 and 2 (November 29 and December 6); *Major Dad,* "Major Mom" (November 13); *Night Court,* "Passion Plundered" (December 20); *Perfect Strangers,* "Prose and Cons" (March 10)

1990:   *House of Cards* (British version)

1993:   *Evening Shade,* "The Proof Is in the Pudding" (December 20)

1993–97:   *Lois & Clark: The New Adventures of Superman*

1993–2002: *X-Files*

1993–2004: *Frasier*

1994–95: *RoboCop*
1995–98: *The Naked Truth* (including "The Source," May 14, 1997)
1995–99: *NewsRadio*
1996–2003: *Sabrina, the Teenage Witch*
1996– : *The Daily Show*
1998–2004: *Sex and the City*
1998–2006: *Charmed*
1999–2001: *The Lot*
2000–01: *Deadline*
2000–02: *Dark Angel*
2001: *Law & Order*, "Deep Vote" (May 23); *The Lone Gunmen*
2001–07: *Crossing Jordan*
2001–11: *Smallville* (including "Gemini," December 13, 2007)
2002: *Queer as Folk*, "Hypocrisy: Don't Do It" (January 20)
2003: *Law & Order*, "Embedded" (November 19); *State of Play*
2003–04: *Da Ali G Show*
2004: *The West Wing*, "Gaza" (May 12)
2004–09: *The L Word*
2005: *Over There*
2005–14: *The Colbert Report*; *How I Met Your Mother*
2006: *Pepper Dennis* (including "Pepper Dennis behind Bars: Film at Eleven," June 20); *Veronica Mars*, "Versatile Toppings" (March 15)
2006–10: *Ugly Betty*
2007–08: *Dirt* (including "Ita Missa Est," March 27, 2007); *Women's Murder Club*
2007–11: *The Sarah Jane Adventures*
2007–12: *Gossip Girl*
2008: *The Andromeda Strain*; *Generation Kill*; *The Wire* (Season 5)
2009: *Dexter* (episodes featuring reporter "Christine Hill," September 29–December 6); *NCIS: Naval Criminal Investigative Service*, "The Inside Man" (October 6)
2009–11: *V*
2009– : *Glee*
2010: *Covert Affairs*, "Pilot" (July 13); *The Defenders*, "Whitten v. Fenlee" (November 17); *Terriers*
2011: *The Cape*; *Harry's Law*, "Queen of Snark" (October 12); *Hawaii Five-O*, "Ki'ilua" (November 21); *Rizzoli & Isles*, "Seventeen Ain't So Sweet" (December 12); *White Collar*, "Deadline" (June 21)
2011–12: *Boss*; *The Hour*
2012: *Bones*, "The Crack in the Code" (January 12); *Damages*, "But You Don't Do That Anymore" (September 12); *Downton Abbey* (Season 3); *NCIS: Naval Criminal Investigative Service*, "Secrets" (February 14); *Necessary*

Roughness, "A Load of Bull" (August 1); *Person of Interest*, "Bury the Lede" (November 1); *Political Animals*

2012– :	*Scandal*
2012–14:	*The Newsroom*
2013:	*Bones*, "The Blood from the Stones" (March 25); *Enlightened* (Season 2); *King & Maxwell*, "Stealing Secrets" (July 15); *NCIS: Naval Criminal Investigative Service*, "Prime Suspect" (March 5)
2013–14:	*House of Cards* (U.S. version, seasons 1–2)
2013– :	*The Bridge*

Video and Computer Games

1986– :	*Castlevania* series
1989:	*The Colonel's Bequest*
1992:	*The Dagger of Amon Ra*
1994:	*Who Killed Taylor French?*
1995:	*Full Throttle*
1996:	*Broken Sword*; *Ripper*
1997:	*Broken Sword II*
1998:	*Grim Fandango*
2000:	*Curious George Reads, Writes, and Spells*; *Donald Duck: Goin' Quackers*
2002:	*Eternal Darkness: Sanity's Requiem*
2003:	*Beyond Good & Evil*; *Resident Evil: Outbreak*
2003– :	*Second Life* (including the *Alphaville Herald*)
2004:	*Resident Evil: Outbreak—File #2*; *Spider-Man*
2006:	*Dead Rising*
2007:	*Global Conflicts: Palestine*; *Mass Effect*; *Uncharted: Drake's Fortune*
2008:	*Spider-Man*
2009:	*Dead Rising: Chop Till You Drop*; *Uncharted: Eye of Indra*; *Uncharted 2: Among Thieves*
2010:	*Alpha Protocol*; *Dead Rising 2*; *Dead Rising 2: Case Zero*; *Imagine: Reporter*; *Mass Effect 2*
2011:	*Dead Rising 2: Off the Record*; *Uncharted 3: Drake's Deception*
2012:	*The Amazing Spider-Man*

Notes

Introduction

1. Karin Wahl-Jorgensen and Thomas Hanitzsch, "Introduction: On Why and How We Should Do Journalism Studies," in *The Handbook of Journalism Studies,* edited by Karin Wahl-Jorgensen and Thomas Hanitzsch (New York: Routledge, 2009), 3.

2. Robert W. McChesney and John Nichols, *The Death and Life of American Journalism* (Philadelphia: Nation Books, 2010), x; Mark Deuze, "Liquid and Zombie Journalism Studies," *Journalism Studies Interest Group at the International Communication Association* (hereafter, *JSIG*), May 2006, http://www.icahdq.org/divisions/JournalismStudies/jsigweb4/newsletterS06/debatedeuzefull.html.

3. For a discussion of the decline in trust and the possible reasons behind it, see Jay Rosen, "Rosen's Trust Puzzler: What Explains Falling Confidence in the Press?" *PressThink,* April 17, 2012, http://pressthink.org/2012/04/rosens-trust-puzzler-what-explains-falling-confidence-in-the-press.

4. See "Press Widely Criticized, But Trusted More than Other Information Sources," *Pew Research Center for the People and the Press,* September 22, 2011, http://www.people-press.org/2011/09/22/press-widely-criticized-but-trusted-more-than-other-institutions.

5. Joseph Turow, *Playing Doctor: Television, Storytelling, and Medical Power* (New York: Oxford University Press, 1989), xv. See also Michael Pfau, Lawrence J. Mullen, Tracy Deidrich, and Kristen Garrow, "Television Viewing and Public Perceptions of Attorneys," *Human Communication Research* 21.3 (1995): 307–30; Barbara L. Ley, Natalie Jankowski, and Paul R. Brewer, "Investigating *CSI*: Portrayals of DNA Testing on a Forensic Crime Show and Their Potential Effects," *Public Understanding of Science* 21.1 (2012): 51–67; Brian L. Quick, "The Effects of Viewing *Grey's Anatomy* on Perceptions of Doctors and Patient Satisfaction," *Journal of Broadcasting and Electronic Media* 53.1 (2009): 38–55.

6. Michael Asimow, "Bad Lawyers in the Movies," *Nova Law Review* 24.2 (2000): 533; David Ray Papke, "Conventional Wisdom: The Courtroom Trial in American Popular Culture," *Marquette Law Review* 82.3 (1999): 488.

7. Glenn Flores, "Mad Scientists, Compassionate Healers, and Greedy Egotists: The Portrayal of Physicians in the Movies," *Journal of the National Medical Association* 94.7 (2002): 656.

8. Quick, "Effects of Viewing *Grey's Anatomy,*" 38. See also Turow, *Playing Doctor.*

9. Brian McNair, "Journalism in the Cinema," in *The Routledge Companion to News and Journalism,* edited by Stuart Allan (London: Routledge, 2010), 385.

10. See, for example, Dan Barry, "Real Reporters on the Screen? Get Me Rewrite!" *New York Times,* June 10, 2012, AR14.

11. See, for example, David Zurawik, "Aaron Sorkin's 'The Newsroom' and an American Press That Has Lost Its Sense of Purpose," *Baltimore Sun,* June 23, 2012, http://articles.baltimoresun.com/2012-06-23/entertainment/bal-aaron-sorkin-the -newsroom-hbo-failure-journalism-20120612_1.

12. For just one example, see Neda Semnani, "Hollywood's Utter Failure to Accurately Portray Female Journalists," *The Week,* April 30, 2013, http://theweek.com/article/ index/243421/hollywoods-utter-failure-to-accurately-portray-female-journalists.

13. See Stephen Vaughn and Bruce Evensen, "Democracy's Guardians: Hollywood's Portrait of Reporters, 1930–1945," *Journalism Quarterly* 68 (1991): 829–38.

14. Nora Sayre, "Falling Prey to Parodies of the Press," *New York Times,* January 1, 1975, 8.

15. Chip Rowe, "Hacks on Film," *Washington Journalism Review,* November 1992, http://www.ajr.org/article_printable.asp?id=2588.

16. James Fallows, *Breaking the News: How the Media Undermine American Democracy* (New York: Vintage, 1997), 44.

17. Barry, "Real Reporters on the Screen?" AR14. For other accounts of how popular culture has influenced journalists, see Don Hewitt, *Tell Me a Story: Fifty Years and 60 Minutes in Television* (New York: Public Affairs, 2001), 19–20, 46; Pete Hamill, *News Is a Verb: Journalism at the End of the Twentieth Century* (New York: Ballantine, 1998), 90–91; Loren Ghiglione, *The American Journalist: Paradox of the Press* (Washington, D.C.: Library of Congress, 1990), 8–9.

18. The following is based upon Matthew C. Ehrlich, "Studying the Journalist in Popular Culture," *The Image of the Journalist in Popular Culture Journal* (hereafter, *IJPC Journal*) 1 (2009): 5–8, http://ijpc.uscannenberg.org/journal/index.php/ijpcjournal/ article/view/7/9.

19. See Joe Saltzman, "Introduction to The Image of the Journalist in Popular Culture (IJPC) Online Database," http://ijpc.org/introdatabase.htm.

20. See, for example, Joe Saltzman, *Frank Capra and the Image of the Journalist in American Film* (Los Angeles: Image of the Journalist in Popular Culture, 2002); Matthew C. Ehrlich, *Journalism in the Movies* (Urbana: University of Illinois Press, 2004); Richard R. Ness, *From Headline Hunter to Superman: A Journalism Filmogra-*

phy (Lanham, Md.: Scarecrow, 1997); Brian McNair, *Journalists in Film: Heroes and Villains* (Edinburgh: Edinburgh University Press, 2010); Howard Good, *Outcasts: The Image of Journalists in Contemporary Film* (Metuchen, N.J.: Scarecrow, 1989); Howard Good, *Girl Reporter: Gender, Journalism, and the Movies* (Lanham, Md.: Scarecrow, 1998); Howard Good, *The Drunken Journalist: The Biography of a Film Stereotype* (Lanham, Md.: Scarecrow, 2000); Howard Good and Michael J. Dillon, ed., *Media Ethics Goes to the Movies* (Westport, Conn.: Praeger, 2002); Howard Good, ed., *Journalism Ethics Goes to the Movies* (Lanham, Md.: Rowman and Littlefield, 2008); Alex Barris, *Stop the Presses!: The Newspaperman in American Films* (South Brunswick, N.J.: A. S. Barnes, 1976); Larry Langman, *The Media in the Movies: A Catalog of American Journalism Films, 1900–1996* (Jefferson, N.C.: McFarland, 1998).

21. Qtd. in Donald G. Godfrey, "Researching Electronic Media History," in *Methods of Historical Analysis in Electronic Media,* edited by Donald G. Godfrey (Mahwah, N.J.: Lawrence Erlbaum Associates, 2006), 4. The quote is from University of Washington professor Milo Ryan, who created what would become known as the Milo Ryan Phonoarchive.

22. McNair, *Journalists in Film,* 13.

23. This book's appendix lists all the works to which we will refer. For one previous broad survey of the image of the journalist in popular culture, see Ghiglione, *American Journalist.*

24. Lawrence Lanahan, "Secrets of the City: What *The Wire* Reveals about Urban Journalism," *Columbia Journalism Review* (January-February 2008): 24, 31. See also David Simon, "Does the News Matter to Anyone Anymore?" *Washington Post,* January 20, 2008, B1; "The Wire Final Season," *Slate,* January 8, 2008, http://www.slate.com/articles/arts/tv_club/features/2008/the_wire_final_season/david_simon_responds.html.

25. Bob Franklin, Martin Hamer, Mark Hanna, Marie Kinsey, and John E. Richardson, *Key Concepts in Journalism Studies* (London: Sage, 2005), xv. For other overviews of journalism studies, see Wahl-Jorgensen and Hanitzsch, *Handbook of Journalism Studies*; and Allan, *Routledge Companion to News and Journalism.*

26. See Barbie Zelizer, *Taking Journalism Seriously: News and the Academy* (Thousand Oaks, Calif.: Sage, 2004).

27. James W. Carey, *Communication as Culture* (Boston: Unwin Hyman, 1989), 142, 204; John J. Pauly, "A Beginner's Guide to Doing Qualitative Research in Mass Communication," *Journalism Monographs,* no. 125 (February 1991): 5.

28. Chandra Mukerji and Michael Schudson, "Introduction: Rethinking Popular Culture," in *Rethinking Popular Culture,* edited by Chandra Mukerji and Michael Schudson (Berkeley: University of California Press, 1991), 23.

29. See, for example, Peter Dahlgren and Colin Sparks, eds., *Journalism and Popular Culture* (London: Sage, 1992); Martin Conboy, *The Press and Popular Culture* (London: Sage, 2002); John Hartley, "Journalism and Popular Culture," in Wahl-Jorgensen and Hanitzsch, *Handbook of Journalism Studies,* 310–24; John Hartley,

"Journalism, History, and the Politics of Popular Culture," in Allan, *Routledge Companion to News and Journalism*, 13–24; James W. Carey, "A Short History of Journalism for Journalists: A Proposal and Essay," *Harvard International Journal of Press/Politics* 12.1 (2007): 3–16.

30. Carey, "Short History of Journalism," 7.

31. Zelizer, *Taking Journalism Seriously*, 187. See also Thomas Hanitzsch, "What Is Journalism, and What Is Not . . ." *JSIG*, May 2006, http://www.icahdq.org/divisions/JournalismStudies/jsigweb4/newsletterS06/debatehanfull.html.

32. Zelizer, *Taking Journalism Seriously*, 190.

33. Peter Dahlgren, Introduction to *Journalism and Popular Culture*, edited by Peter Dahlgren and Colin Sparks (London: Sage, 1992), 1.

34. See Mitchell Stephens, *A History of News*, 3rd ed. (New York: Oxford University Press, 2007).

35. The following discussion of the journalist as depicted in fictional form from ancient times to the late nineteenth century is based upon Joe Saltzman, "Analyzing the Images of the Journalist in Popular Culture: A Unique Method of Studying the Public's Perception of Its Journalists and the News Media," *Image of the Journalist in Popular Culture*, 2005, http://ijpc.org/uploads/files/AEJMC%20Paper%20San%20Antonio%20Saltzman%202005.pdf.

36. See Sophocles, *Trachiniae*, 430 BC, translated by Richard C. Jebb, http://en.wikisource.org/wiki/Trachiniae.

37. Martial, *The Twelve Books of Epigrams*, translated by J. A. Pott and F. A. Wright (New York: E. P. Dutton, 1924), 273.

38. See Ben Jonson, *The Staple of News*, 1625, http://hollowaypages.com/jonson1692news.htm.

39. See Michael Schudson, *Discovering the News: A Social History of American Newspapers* (New York: Basic Books, 1978). See also Carey, "Short History of Journalism."

40. For a survey of American novels of the nineteenth century, see James G. Harrison, "Nineteenth-Century American Novels on American Journalism I," *Journalism Quarterly* 22.3 (1945): 215–24; James G. Harrison, "Nineteenth-Century American Novels on American Journalism II," *Journalism Quarterly* 22.4 (1945): 335–45.

41. Rebecca Harding Davis, *John Andross* (New York: Orange Judd, 1874), 12, 89.

42. James W. Carey, "The Mass Media and Democracy: Between the Modern and the Postmodern," *Journal of International Affairs* 47.1 (1993): 9–10.

43. For more on the newsroom fiction of this era, see Howard Good, *Acquainted with the Night: The Image of Journalists in American Fiction, 1890–1930* (Metuchen, N.J.: Scarecrow, 1986); Bonnie Brennen, "Cultural Discourse of Journalists: The Material Conditions of Newsroom Labor," in *Newsworkers: Toward a History of the Rank and File*, edited by Hanno Hardt and Bonnie Brennen (Minneapolis: University of Minnesota Press, 1995), 75–109; Thomas Elliott Berry, *The Newspaper in the American Novel, 1900–1969* (Metuchen, N.J.: Scarecrow, 1970); Donna Born, "The Image

of the Woman Journalist in American Popular Fiction: 1890 to the Present," paper presented to the Association for Education in Journalism, August 1981, http://www .ijpc.org/uploads/files/Donna%20Born%20—%20The%20Image%20of%20the %20Woman%20Journalist%20in%20American%20Popular%20Fiction.pdf.

44. See Maurine Watkins, *Chicago: With the* Chicago Tribune *Articles That Inspired It* (Carbondale: Southern Illinois University Press, 1997); Louis Weitzenkorn, *Five Star Final: A Melodrama in Three Acts* (New York: Samuel French, 1931); Ben Hecht and Charles MacArthur, *The Front Page* (New York: Covici-Friede, 1928).

45. See Ben Hecht, *Erik Dorn* (New York: G. P. Putnam's Sons, 1921).

46. Hecht and MacArthur, *Front Page*, 192.

47. One example of the ubiquity of the journalist in silent films was Charlie Chaplin's first movie, *Making a Living* (1914). It featured Chaplin as a ne'er-do-well who takes a reporting job, steals a rival journalist's camera, and gets a scoop.

48. For broad overviews of this era of journalism movies and the eras that followed, see Ehrlich, *Journalism in the Movies*; Ness, *From Headline Hunter to Superman*.

49. Capra addressed journalism in his films starting with the silent picture *The Power of the Press* (1928). For more on Capra's journalism movies, see Saltzman, *Frank Capra and the Image of the Journalist in American Film*.

50. See Larry Tye, *Superman: The High-Flying History of America's Most Enduring Hero* (New York: Random House, 2012).

51. See "Big Town," *Newspaper Heroes on the Air*, http://jheroes.com/detectives/ big-town. *Newspaper Heroes on the Air* (http://jheroes.com) is a superior resource regarding the golden age of radio's depictions of the journalist.

52. For an overview of Brenda Starr and its creator, Dale Messick, see Jackie Leger, "Dale Messick: A Comic Strip Life," *Animation World Magazine*, July 2000, http:// www.awn.com/mag/issue5.04/5.04pages/legermessick.php3.

53. See Tom DeFalco, *Spider-Man: The Ultimate Guide* (New York: Marvel/DK, 2001).

54. For a scholarly analysis of *The Mary Tyler Moore Show* and *Murphy Brown* from a feminist viewpoint, see Bonnie J. Dow, *Prime-Time Feminism: Television, Media Culture, and the Women's Movement since 1970* (Philadelphia: University of Pennsylvania Press, 1996), 24–58, 135–63.

55. See, for example, Howard Good, "The Image of Journalism in American Poetry," *American Journalism* 4.3 (1987): 132–32; Bill Knight, "MacLeish in McLuhan's World: Poetry and Journalism," *Image of the Journalist in Popular Culture*, n.d., http://ijpc.org/ uploads/files/Poetry%20and%20Journalism%20Bill%20Knight.pdf; Jake Gaskill, "Heroes at the Push of a Button: The Image of the Photojournalist in Videogames," *Image of the Journalist in Popular Culture*, n.d., http://ijpc.org/uploads/files/IJPC%20Student %20Journal%20-%20Jake%20Gaskill.pdf; Daxton R. Stewart, "Harry Potter and the Exploitative Jackals: Media Framing and Credibility Attitudes in Young Readers," *IJPC Journal* 2 (2010): 1–33, http://ijpc.uscannenberg.org/journal/index.php/ijpcjournal/ article/view/18/26; Ashley Ragovin, "N Is for News: The Image of the Journalist on

Sesame Street," *IJPC Journal* 2 (2010): 34–85, http://ijpc.uscannenberg.org/journal/
index.php/ijpcjournal/article/view/19/27; Judith A. Markowitz, *The Gay Detective
Novel: Lesbian and Gay Main Characters and Themes in Mystery Fiction* (Jefferson,
N.C.: McFarland, 2004), 112–21, 126–51.

56. "Alpha Protocol Wiki," Wikia.com, http://alphaprotocol.wikia.com/wiki/Alpha
Protocol%28video_game%29. See also "Scarlet Lake," Wikia.com, http://alpha
protocol.wikia.com/wiki/Scarlet_Lake. For samples of "Hoofy & Boo's News and
Views," see CoryBortnicker.com, http://corybortnicker.com/hoofy.html; for more
on Geronimo Stilton and the *Rodent's Gazette*, see The Stacks, Scholastic.com, http://
www.scholastic.com/titles/geronimostilton.

57. See, for example, Radhika Parameswaran, "Moral Dilemmas of an Immoral
Nation: Gender, Sexuality and Journalism in *Page 3*," *IJPC Journal* 1 (2009): 70–
104, http://ijpc.uscannenberg.org/journal/index.php/ijpcjournal/article/view/10/12;
Sukhmani Khorana, "The Female Journalist in Bollywood: Middle-Class Career
Woman or Problematic National Heroine?" *Metro Magazine* 171 (2012): 102–06.

58. See Carey, "Mass Media and Democracy"; Daniel C. Hallin, "The Passing of the
'High Modernism' of American Journalism," *Journal of Communication* 42.3 (1992):
14–25; Daniel C. Hallin, "The Passing of the 'High Modernism' of American Journalism Revisited," *Political Communication Report* 16.1 (2006), http://www.jour.unr
.edu/pcr/1601_2005_winter/commentary_hallin.htm.

59. For more on the BBC radio adaptation of *Scoop*, see "Scoop," *British Comedy
Guide*, http://www.comedy.co.uk/guide/radio/scoop_2009.

60. The following is based upon Saltzman, "Analyzing the Images of the Journalist
in Popular Culture."

61. Examples of those who have been depicted in multiple works include Woodward and Bernstein, Edward R. Murrow, Martha Gellhorn, Walter Winchell, and
many others.

62. See Dixon Wecter, *The Hero in America: A Chronicle of Hero-Worship* (New
York: C. Scribner's Sons, 1941); Orrin Edgar Klapp, *Heroes, Villains, and Fools: The
Changing American Character* (Englewood Cliffs, N.J.: Prentice-Hall, 1962). The basic dichotomy between hero and villain in the journalist's depiction has often been
noted. See, for example, Eric Newton, ed., *Crusaders, Scoundrels, Journalists: The
Newseum's Most Intriguing Newspeople* (New York: Times Books, 1999); Barris, *Stop
the Presses!*; Good, *Outcasts*; McNair, *Journalists in Film*.

63. Jack Lule, *Daily News, Eternal Stories: The Mythological Role of Journalism* (New
York: Guilford, 2001), 15.

64. See, for example, Rick Altman, *The American Film Musical* (Bloomington:
Indiana University Press, 1987); Thomas Schatz, *Hollywood Genres: Formulas, Filmmaking, and the Studio System* (New York: McGraw-Hill, 1981); Will Wright, *Sixguns
and Society: A Structural Study of the Western* (Berkeley: University of California
Press, 1975).

65. Robert B. Ray, *A Certain Tendency of the Hollywood Cinema: 1930–1980* (Princeton, N.J.: Princeton University Press, 1985), 58–62. See also Schatz, *Hollywood Genres,*

45–149; Richard Slotkin, *Gunfighter Nation: The Myth of the Frontier in Twentieth-Century America* (Norman: University of Oklahoma Press, 1998); Alan Kaufman, Neil Ortenberg, and Barney Rosset, eds., *The Outlaw Bible of American Literature* (New York: Thunder's Mouth, 2004).

66. Zelizer, *Taking Journalism Seriously*, 187; Ray, *Certain Tendency*, 60.

67. Vaughn and Evensen, "Democracy's Guardians," 829.

68. Zelizer, *Taking Journalism Seriously*, 176.

69. See Schatz, *Hollywood Genres*, 35; Lule, *Daily News, Eternal Stories*, 191–93.

70. Ness, *From Headline Hunter to Superman*, 5–6.

71. See, for example, James W. Carey, "The Problem of Journalism History," *Journalism History* 1.1 (1974): 3–5, 27; John Nerone, "Does Journalism History Matter?" *American Journalism* 28.3 (2011): 7–27; Bonnie S. Brennen, *Qualitative Research Methods for Media Studies* (New York: Routledge, 2013), 93–105.

72. See, for example, James W. Carey, "A Plea for the University Tradition," *Journalism Quarterly* 55 (1978): 846–55; Michael Schudson and Chris Anderson, "Objectivity, Professionalism, and Truth Seeking in Journalism," in Wahl-Jorgensen and Hanitzsch, *Handbook of Journalism Studies*, 88–101; Clifford G. Christians, John P. Ferré, and P. Mark Fackler, *Good News: Social Ethics and the Press* (New York: Oxford University Press, 1993).

73. See, for example, Jay Rosen, *What Are Journalists For?* (New Haven, Conn.: Yale University Press, 1999).

74. See, for example, Deborah Chambers, Linda Steiner, and Carole Fleming, *Women and Journalism* (London: Routledge, 2004); Juan González and Joseph Torres, *News for All the People: The Epic Story of Race and the American Media* (London: Verso, 2011); Marguerite Moritz, "Getting It Straight: Gay News Narratives and Changing Cultural Values," in Allan, *Routledge Companion to News and Journalism*, 320–30.

75. See, for example, Janet Malcolm, *The Journalist and the Murderer* (New York: Knopf, 1990); Robert W. McChesney, *The Political Economy of Media: Enduring Issues, Emerging Dilemmas* (New York: Monthly Review Press, 2008).

76. See, for example, Kiku Adatto, *Picture Perfect: Life in the Age of the Photo Op*, new ed. (Princeton, N.J.: Princeton University Press, 2008); Daya Kishan Thussu, "Television News in the Era of Global Infotainment," in Allan, *Routledge Companion to News and Journalism*, 362–73; Barbie Zelizer, *About to Die: How News Images Move the Public* (New York: Oxford University Press, 2010); Claude Cookman, *American Photojournalism: Motivations and Meanings* (Evanston, Ill.: Northwestern University Press, 2009); Al Tompkins, *Aim for the Heart: Write, Shoot, Report, and Produce for TV and Multimedia*, 2nd ed. (Washington, D.C.: CQ Press, 2012).

77. See, for example, Howard Tumber, "Covering War and Peace," in Wahl-Jorgensen and Hanitzsch, *Handbook of Journalism Studies*, 386–97; Stuart Allan and Barbie Zelizer, eds., *Reporting War: Journalism in Wartime* (London: Routledge, 2004).

78. See, for example, Paolo Mancini, "Media Fragmentation, Party System, and Democracy," *International Journal of Press/Politics* 18.1 (2013): 43–60; Bregtje van der

Haak, Michael Parks, and Manuel Castells, "The Future of Journalism: Networked Journalism," *International Journal of Communication* 6 (2012): 2923–38.

Chapter 1. History

1. Jerome de Groot, *Consuming History: Historians and Heritage in Contemporary Popular Culture* (New York: Routledge, 2009), 6–7.

2. Jerome de Groot, "All History Lies to Us, but at Least Historical Fiction Admits It," *History Extra*, October 4, 2011, http://www.historyextra.com/blog/all-history-lies-us -least-historical-fiction-admits-it.

3. Gary R. Edgerton, "Television as Historian: A Different Kind of History Alto- gether," in *Television Histories: Shaping Collective Memory in the Media Age,* edited by Gary R. Edgerton and Peter C. Rollins (Lexington: University Press of Kentucky, 2001), 8–9.

4. See Daniel C. Hallin, "The Passing of the 'High Modernism' of American Jour- nalism," *Journal of Communication* 42.3 (1992): 14–25.

5. Russel B. Nye, "History and Literature: Branches of the Same Tree," in *Essays on History and Literature,* edited by Robert H. Bremner (Columbus: Ohio State Univer- sity Press, 1966), 141, 159.

6. Hayden White, *Tropics of Discourse: Essays in Cultural Criticism* (1978; reprint, Baltimore: Johns Hopkins University Press, 1985), 121–22.

7. Warren I. Susman, *Culture as History: The Transformation of American Society in the Twentieth Century* (Washington, D.C.: Smithsonian Institution Press, 2003), 11. See also Richard Slotkin, *Gunfighter Nation: The Myth of the Frontier in Twentieth- Century America* (Norman: University of Oklahoma Press, 1998).

8. For radio, see, for example, Matthew C. Ehrlich, "'All Things Are as They Were Then': Radio's *You Are There,*" *American Journalism* 28.1 (2011): 9–33. For novels, see, for example, Jerome de Groot, *The Historical Novel* (London: Routledge, 2009). For television, see, for example, Edgerton and Rollins, *Television Histories*; and John E. O'Connor, ed., *American History/American Television: Interpreting the Video Past* (New York: Frederick Ungar, 1983).

9. See, for example, Leger Grindon, *Shadows on the Past: Studies in the Historical Fiction Film* (Philadelphia: Temple University Press, 1994); Robert A. Rosenstone, *Visions of the Past: The Challenge of Film to Our Idea of History* (Cambridge, Mass.: Harvard University Press, 1995); Mark C. Carnes, ed., *Past Imperfect: History Ac- cording to the Movies* (New York: Henry Holt, 1995); Robert Brent Toplin, *History by Hollywood,* 2nd ed. (Urbana: University of Illinois Press, 2009); Peter C. Rollins, ed., *Hollywood as Historian: American Film in a Cultural Context,* rev. ed. (Lexington: University Press of Kentucky, 1998); David Ellwood, ed., *The Movies as History: Vi- sions of the Twentieth Century* (Stroud, England: Sutton, 2000); Robert Brent Toplin, *Reel History: In Defense of Hollywood* (Lawrence: University Press of Kansas, 2002).

10. Edgerton, "Television as Historian," 6, 8.

11. Toplin, *Reel History,* 17.

12. Ibid., 8–57.

13. See, for example, John Nerone, "Does Journalism History Matter?" *American Journalism* 28.3 (2011): 7–27; Bonnie S. Brennen, *Qualitative Research Methods for Media Studies* (New York: Routledge, 2013), 93–105.

14. Joseph P. McKerns, "The Limits of Progressive Journalism History," *Journalism History* 4.3 (1977): 90–91. See also James W. Carey, "The Problem of Journalism History," *Journalism History* 1.1 (1974): 3–5, 27.

15. John Nerone, "The Problem of Teaching Journalism History," *Journalism Educator* 45.3 (1990): 16. See also Michael Schudson, "Toward a Troubleshooting Manual for Journalism History," *Journalism and Mass Communication Quarterly* 74.3 (1997): 463–76; Nerone, "Does Journalism History Matter?"

16. Bonnie Sue Brennen, "'Peasantry of the Press': A History of American Newsworkers from Novels, 1919–1938," PhD dissertation, University of Iowa, 1993, 22. In recent years press histories have routinely noted the roles of female journalists and journalists of color, but not always with a critical edge; see Nerone, "Does Journalism History Matter?" 12–13.

17. Brennen, "'Peasantry of the Press,'" 70. See also Bonnie Brennen, "Cultural Discourse of Journalists: The Material Conditions of Newsroom Labor," in *Newsworkers: Toward a History of the Rank and File,* edited by Hanno Hardt and Bonnie Brennen (Minneapolis: University of Minnesota Press, 1995), 75–109; Bonnie Brennen, "Sweat Not Melodrama: Reading the Structure of Feeling in *All the President's Men,*" *Journalism* 4.1 (2003): 115–33.

18. W. Joseph Campbell, *Getting It Wrong: Ten of the Greatest Misreported Stories in American Journalism* (Berkeley: University of California Press, 2010), 188.

19. Ibid., 2.

20. Jack Lule, *Daily News, Eternal Stories: The Mythological Role of Journalism* (New York: Guilford, 2001), 15.

21. See George Everett, "The Age of New Journalism," in *The Media in America: A History,* 3rd ed., edited by W. David Sloan and James D. Startt (Northport, Ala.: Vision, 1996), 275–304; James W. Carey, "The Communications Revolution and the Professional Communicator," in *James Carey: A Critical Reader,* edited by Eve Stryker Munson and Catherine A. Warren (Minneapolis: University of Minnesota Press, 1997), 128–43; Michael Schudson, *Discovering The News: A Social History of American Newspapers* (New York: Basic Books, 1978), 88–159; Michael Emery and Edwin Emery, *The Press and America: An Interpretive History of the Mass Media,* 7th ed. (Englewood Cliffs, N.J.: Prentice Hall, 1992), 169–299.

22. Nerone, "Problem of Teaching Journalism History," 16.

23. Ibid.; Nicholas Garnham, *Samuel Fuller* (New York: Viking, 1971), 14–15.

24. Samuel Fuller, *A Third Face: My Tale of Writing, Fighting, and Filmmaking* (New York: Knopf, 2002), 283.

25. Ibid., 280.

26. See Stephen Vaughn and Bruce Evensen, "Democracy's Guardians: Hollywood's Portrait of Reporters, 1930–1945," *Journalism Quarterly* 68.4 (1991): 829–38.

27. Howard Good, "The Image of Journalism in American Poetry," *American Journalism* 4.3 (1987): 123, 125.

28. Howard Good, *Acquainted with the Night: The Image of Journalists in American Fiction, 1890–1930* (Metuchen, N.J.: Scarecrow, 1986), 20.

29. Brennen, "Cultural Discourse of Journalists," 78, 88. See also Brennen, "'Peasantry of the Press.'"

30. Mildred Gilman, *Sob Sister* (New York: Jonathan Cape and Harrison Smith, 1931), 116–18.

31. See Simon Michael Bessie, *Jazz Journalism: The Story of the Tabloid Newspapers* (New York: Dutton, 1938).

32. Emile Gauvreau, *Hot News* (New York: Macaulay, 1931), 182. See also Emile Gauvreau, *The Scandal Monger* (New York: Macaulay, 1932).

33. William R. Hunt, *Body Love: The Amazing Career of Bernarr Macfadden* (Bowling Green, Oh.: Bowling Green University Press, 1989), 135.

34. Samuel Fuller, "News That's Fit to Film," *American Film*, October 1975, 21.

35. Maurine Watkins, *Chicago: With the* Chicago Tribune *Articles That Inspired It* (Carbondale: Southern Illinois University Press, 1997), 15.

36. Thomas H. Pauly, Introduction to Watkins, *Chicago*, x.

37. Ibid., xiii.

38. Ben Hecht, *Erik Dorn* (New York: G. P. Putnam's Sons, 1921), 82.

39. Ben Hecht and Charles MacArthur, *The Front Page* (New York: Covici-Friede, 1928), 191.

40. Ibid., 40.

41. Ibid., 49.

42. George W. Hilton, *The Front Page: From Theater to Reality* (Hanover, N.H.: Smith and Kraus, 2002), 12.

43. Hecht and MacArthur, *Front Page,* 190–91.

44. See Hilton, *Front Page.*

45. Hecht and MacArthur, *Front Page,* 31.

46. Ben Hecht, *A Child of the Century* (New York: Simon and Schuster, 1954), 191. See also Matthew C. Ehrlich, *Journalism in the Movies* (Urbana: University of Illinois Press, 2004), 20–44.

47. See Simon Callow, *Orson Welles: The Road to Xanadu* (New York: Penguin, 1997), 531; David Nasaw, *The Chief: The Life of William Randolph Hearst* (Boston: Houghton Mifflin, 2000), 564–74.

48. For more on Citizen Kane's depiction of journalism, see Ehrlich, *Journalism in the Movies,* 69–78.

49. The 1931 film of *The Front Page* retained the bite of the original play, and it was one of the movies that roused press associations to lobby for more sanitized depictions. 1940's *His Girl Friday* turned Hildy into a woman and left little doubt that she belonged with her ex-editor and ex-husband, Walter. Billy Wilder's *The Front Page* (1974) inserted profanity and sexual frankness that earlier versions had eschewed

because of censorship, whereas *Switching Channels* (1988) transported *His Girl Friday*'s plot to a contemporary TV news setting. As for *Chicago*, it was turned first into a 1927 silent film and then into the 1942 film *Roxie Hart* (which softened the original story due to the dictates of Hollywood's Production Code). That was followed by the stage and movie musical versions. The original 1975 stage production received mixed reviews, having presented a comparatively dark picture of the world shaped by the traumas of the 1970s as well as the personal demons of director Bob Fosse. The subsequent 1996 stage revival and 2002 movie fared much better in the wake of the O. J. Simpson murder trial and other Roxie Hart–like media sensations. See Vaughn and Evensen, "Democracy's Guardians"; Linda Costanzo Cahir, *Literature into Film: Theory and Practical Approaches* (Jefferson, N.C.: MacFarland, 2006), 183; Bill Condon, Foreword to Peter Kobel (text), *Chicago: The Movie and Lyrics* (New York: Newmarket, 2003), 17; Martin Gottfried, *All His Jazz: The Life and Death of Bob Fosse* (New York: Da Capo, 1998), 342.

50. See Jon Bekken, "Newsboys: The Exploitation of 'Little Merchants' by the Newspaper Industry," in *Newsworkers: Toward a History of the Rank and File*, edited by Hanno Hardt and Bonnie Brennen (Minneapolis: University of Minnesota Press, 1995), 190–225; David Nasaw, *Children of the City: At Work and At Play* (Garden City, N.Y.: Anchor/Doubleday, 1985), 167–77; Loren Ghiglione, *The American Journalist: Paradox of the Press* (Washington, D.C.: Library of Congress, 1990), 115–19.

51. Bekken, "Newsboys," 191.

52. For more on *Newsies'* depiction of journalism history and myth, see Stephen Siff, "Carrying the Banner: The Portrayal of the American Newsboy Myth in the Disney Musical *Newsies*," *IJPC Journal* 1 (2009): 12–36, http://ijpc.uscannenberg.org/journal/index.php/ijpcjournal/article/view/8/10. See also Dan Barry, "Read All About It! Kids Vex Titans!" *New York Times*, March 4, 2012, AR1.

53. Daniel C. Hallin, "The Passing of the 'High Modernism' of American Journalism Revisited," *Political Communication Report* 16.1 (2006), http://www.jour.unr.edu/pcr/1601_2005_winter/commentary_hallin.htm. See also Schudson, *Discovering the News*.

54. Daniel C. Hallin, *We Keep America on Top of the World: Television Journalism and the Public Sphere* (New York: Routledge, 1994), 172.

55. Ibid., 171.

56. Toplin, *History by Hollywood*, 201.

57. William E. Leuchtenburg, "All the President's Men," in *Past Imperfect*, edited by Mark C. Carnes (New York: Henry Holt, 1995), 291; Campbell, *Getting It Wrong*, 188; Michael Schudson, *Watergate in American Memory: How We Remember, Forget, and Reconstruct the Past* (New York: Basic Books, 1992), 126.

58. See Toplin, *History by Hollywood*, 7, 201.

59. An earlier film that portrays the hard work of investigative reporting is *Call Northside 777* (1948), which uses documentary techniques in dramatizing a real-life newspaper investigation in Chicago.

60. See Jack Hirshberg, *A Portrait of All the President's Men* (New York: Warner Books, 1976); Carl Bernstein and Bob Woodward, *All the President's Men* (New York: Pocket Books, 2005); Adrian Havill, *Deep Truth: The Lives of Bob Woodward and Carl Bernstein* (New York: Birch Lane Press, 1993); Bob Woodward, *The Secret Man: The Story of Watergate's Deep Throat* (New York: Simon and Schuster, 2005).

61. "Alan J. Pakula: Leaving Room for Life," *Films Illustrated,* June 1976, 374.

62. David Thomson, *The New Biographical Dictionary of Film* (New York: Knopf, 2002), 344.

63. Toplin, *History by Hollywood,* 7, 201.

64. The 1970s were filled with films and television programs involving sinister conspiracies. In addition to *The Parallax View,* there were 1975's *The Lives of Jenny Dolan* (in which a female reporter is almost killed in pursuit of a story), 1977's *Capricorn One* (in which a reporter uncovers an incredible conspiracy involving the space program and survives several attempts on his life as he tries to reveal the truth), 1975's *Three Days of the Condor* (in which a CIA information researcher ends up going to the *New York Times* as his only hope for survival), 1974's *The Odessa File* (in which a reporter uncovers a conspiracy involving a secret Nazi organization), a 1976 multipart episode of the TV series *City of Angels* (in which a ruthless publisher kills a Pulitzer Prize–winning writer who uncovers a conspiracy to take over the country), and 1976's *Futureworld* (in which two journalists risk their lives to uncover a monstrous conspiracy involving robots). For more on conspiracy films, see Ray Pratt, *Projecting Paranoia: Conspiratorial Visions in American Film* (Lawrence: University Press of Kansas, 2001). See also chapter 4.

65. Qtd. in Pratt, *Projecting Paranoia,* 130. *All the President's Men* also reflected the political beliefs of producer and costar Robert Redford, who had disliked Nixon since he was a youth; see Toplin, *History by Hollywood,* 181.

66. See Schudson, *Discovering the News,* 160–94.

67. Rosenstone, *Visions of the Past,* 61.

68. Schudson, *Watergate in American Memory,* 120.

69. See Michael Dillon, "Ethics in Black and White: *Good Night, and Good Luck,*" in *Journalism Ethics Goes to the Movies,* edited by Howard Good (Lanham, Md.: Rowman and Littlefield, 2008), 109–23; Gary Edgerton, "The Murrow Legend as Metaphor: The Creation, Appropriation, and Usefulness of Edward R. Murrow's Life Story," *Journal of American Culture* 15.1 (1992): 75–91. The 1986 television movie *Murrow* is similar in tone to *Good Night, and Good Luck,* although it is not quite so reverential; it shows how Murrow at times acceded to corporate interests and alienated his onetime friend and colleague William Shirer.

70. Jack Shafer, "Edward R. Movie: Good Night, and Good Luck and Bad History," *Slate,* October 5, 2005, http://www.slate.com/articles/news_and_politics/press_box/2005/10/edward_r_movie_2.single.html.

71. Thomas Doherty, *Cold War, Cool Medium: Television, McCarthyism, and American Culture* (New York: Columbia University Press, 2003), 161–62. See also Campbell, *Getting It Wrong,* 45–67.

72. David Carr, "A Ringside Seat for Murrow Versus McCarthy," *New York Times,* September 18, 2005, http://www.nytimes.com/2005/09/18/movies/18carr.html ?pagewanted=all.

73. David Auburn, *The Columnist* (New York: Faber and Faber, 2012), 10, 75.

74. Hallin, "Passing of the 'High Modernism' of American Journalism Revisited."

75. Murrey Jacobson, "Q&A: Pulitzer Prize Winner David Auburn on His New Play, 'The Columnist,'" *PBS Newshour,* April 25, 2012, http://www.pbs.org/newshour/art/blog/2012/04/qa-playwright-david-auburn-on-the-columnist.html.

76. Andrew Fleming commentary, *Dick,* DVD, Columbia Pictures, 1999.

77. John Lahr, "Peter Morgan Fills in the Gaps of History," *New Yorker,* April 30, 2007, 37.

78. James Reston Jr., "Frost, Nixon, and Me," *Smithsonian,* January 2009, 92.

79. *Frost/Nixon* press kit, Margaret Herrick Library, Academy of Motion Picture Arts and Sciences, Beverly Hills, Calif.; Peter Morgan, "I Fell for Tricky Dick," *Newsweek,* November 27, 2008, http://www.newsweek.com/i-fell-tricky-dick-84809.

80. In Britain the BBC TV series *The Hour* (2011–12) focuses on a TV news program's coverage of the 1956 Suez crisis, reflecting both the political turmoil of that time and twenty-first-century concerns regarding women in workplace positions of authority. In Australia the 1988 film *Evil Angels* (released elsewhere as *A Cry in the Dark*) depicts a true story about the media circus surrounding a woman who is accused of murdering her child, whereas *Black and White* (2002) depicts the role of the press (including a young Rupert Murdoch) in another sensational murder trial. In India movies such as *Lakshya* (2004) and *No One Killed Jessica* (2011) explore the changing roles of female journalists against the backdrop of actual events. In Germany *The Lost Honour of Katharina Blum* (1975; based on a 1974 Heinrich Böll novel), *Marianne and Juliane* (1981), and *The Baader Meinhof Complex* (2008) address the relationships between journalists and radical leftist groups of the 1970s. See Sheila Marikar, "'The Hour' Puts a Woman Ahead of the Mad Men," ABCNews.com, August 17, 2011, http://abcnews.go.com/Entertainment/hour-puts-romola-garai-ahead-mad-men/story?id=14324024; Sukhmani Khorana, "The Female Journalist in Bollywood," *Metro Magazine* 171 (2012): 102–06; Radhika Parameswaran, "Moral Dilemmas of an Immoral Nation: Gender, Sexuality and Journalism in *Page 3,*" *IJPC Journal* 1 (2009): 70–104, http://ijpc.uscannenberg.org/journal/index.php/ijpcjournal/article/view/10/12.

81. Toplin, *Reel History,* 17, 19.

82. Rosenstone, *Visions of the Past,* 56.

83. Gordon Cox, "Morgan Mines History for Drama on Stage, Screen," *Variety,* February 26, 2007, 44.

84. Francis R. Bellamy, "The Theatre," *Outlook,* August 29, 1928, 705.

85. Schudson, *Watergate in American Memory,* 124, 126.

86. Lule, *Daily News, Eternal Stories,* 15, 191.

87. Jacobson, "Q&A: Pulitzer Prize Winner David Auburn." See also Ehrlich, *Journalism in the Movies,* 132–65.

88. Edgerton, "Television as Historian," 8.

89. Orville Schell, "'We Have Been Bull-Dozed Aside.' Orville Schell Says J-Schools Have to Get More Involved," *PressThink,* July 21, 2005, http://archive.pressthink.org/2005/07/21/schl_jsc.html.

90. Bonnie Brennen and Hanno Hardt, "Introduction to Part One," in *The American Journalism History Reader,* edited by Bonnie Brennen and Hanno Hardt (New York: Routledge, 2011), 8.

91. Reston, "Frost, Nixon, and Me," 92.

Chapter 2. Professionalism

1. Daniel C. Hallin, "The Passing of the 'High Modernism' of American Journalism Revisited," *Political Communication Report* 16.1 (2006), http://www.jour.unr.edu/pcr/1601_2005_winter/commentary_hallin.htm.

2. See Michael Schudson, *Discovering the News: A Social History of American Newspapers* (New York: Basic Books, 1978); James W. Carey, "A Plea for the University Tradition," *Journalism Quarterly* 55 (1978): 846–55; Jay Rosen, *What Are Journalists For?* (New Haven, Conn.: Yale University Press, 1999); W. Lance Bennett, *News: The Politics of Illusion,* 7th ed. (New York: Pearson Longman, 2007).

3. James W. Carey, "Some Personal Notes on US Journalism Education," *Journalism* 1.1 (2000): 16.

4. Joseph Pulitzer, "The College of Journalism," *North American Review* (May 1904): 649, 651, 680.

5. Walter Lippmann, *Liberty and the News* (New York: Harcourt, Brace, and Howe, 1920), 82.

6. Clifford G. Christians, John P. Ferré, and P. Mark Fackler, *Good News: Social Ethics and the Press* (New York: Oxford University Press, 1993), 33. See also Bruce J. Evensen, "Journalism's Struggle over Ethics and Professionalism during America's Jazz Age," *Journalism History* 16.3–4 (1989): 54–63.

7. Ben Hecht and Charles MacArthur, *The Front Page* (New York: Covici-Friede, 1928), 31.

8. See Schudson, *Discovering the News,* 121–59; Dan Schiller, *Objectivity and the News: The Public and the Rise of Commercial Journalism* (Philadelphia: University of Pennsylvania Press, 1981); David T. Z. Mindich, *Just the Facts: How "Objectivity" Came to Define American Journalism* (New York: New York University Press, 1998); Richard L. Kaplan, *Politics and the American Press: The Rise of Objectivity, 1865–1920* (Cambridge: Cambridge University Press, 2002).

9. See Schudson, *Discovering the News,* 160–94.

10. Carey, "Some Personal Notes," 19.

11. See Bennett, *News: The Politics of Illusion,* 191–94.

12. See Carey, "Plea for the University Tradition"; Jay Rosen, "The People Formerly Known as the Audience," *PressThink,* June 27, 2006, http://archive.pressthink.org/2006/06/27/ppl_frmr.html.

13. Schudson, *Discovering the News*, 160.

14. Bennett, *News: The Politics of Illusion*, 186.

15. Bill Kovach and Tom Rosenstiel, *The Elements of Journalism*, revised and updated 3rd ed. (New York: Three Rivers Press, 2014), 98, 111–12.

16. Qtd. in Everette E. Dennis, "Whatever Happened to Marse Robert's Dream?: The Dilemma of American Journalism Education," *Gannett Center Journal* 2.2 (1988): 4–5. See also Carey, "Some Personal Notes."

17. Howard Good, *Acquainted with the Night: The Image of Journalists in American Fiction, 1890–1930* (Metuchen, N.J.: Scarecrow, 1986), 20.

18. Robert Greenberger and Martin Pasko, *The Essential Superman Encyclopedia* (New York: Del Rey/Ballantine, 2010), 292; emphasis in original. See also Larry Tye, *Superman: The High-Flying History of America's Most Enduring Hero* (New York: Random House, 2012), 104; *Wikipedia*, s.v. "Jimmy Olsen," last modified June 21, 2014, http://en.wikipedia.org/wiki/Jimmy_Olsen.

19. For more on the 2003 BBC miniseries, see chapter 4.

20. For more on popular culture's portrayal of blogs and new media in journalism, see the conclusion.

21. Michael Fleming and Diane Garrett, "Macdonald to Direct 'State of Play,'" *Variety*, March 19, 2007, http://www.variety.com/article/VR1117961417.

22. For examples of female investigative reporters, see chapter 3.

23. *Call Northside 777* Production/Clippings File, Margaret Herrick Library, Academy of Motion Picture Arts and Sciences, Beverly Hills, California.

24. For more on so-called documentary noir in the postwar era and its depiction of journalism, see Matthew C. Ehrlich, *Journalism in the Movies* (Urbana: University of Illinois Press, 2004), 88–93.

25. The 1992 novel written by John Grisham was made into a movie with a screenplay by Alan J. Pakula in 1993.

26. The "Amos Walker" private investigator novels date back to 1980 and are written by Loren D. Estleman. Three other series of novels center on journalists who repeatedly put themselves in danger to try to expose crime: C. C. Risenhoover's "Matt McCall" books, Jan Burke's "Irene Kelly" novels, and Julie Kramer's "Riley Spartz" books. Investigative reporters also have appeared in the comics: Jack Ryder (alias "The Creeper") was created by Steve Ditko and first appeared in *Showcase #79* comics in March 1968, whereas Melita Garner made her first appearance in *Wolverine: Weapon X #1* in June 2009.

27. TV's other investigative journalist characters have included Jeff Dillon (Anthony Franciosa) going after corporate criminals in *The Name of the Game* (1968–71), Carl Kolchak (Darren McGavin) trying to convince people that supernatural creatures exist in *Kolchak: The Night Stalker* (1974–75), Jack McGee (Jack Colvin) reporting on *The Incredible Hulk* (1977–82), J. D. Pollack (Charles Mesure) eventually getting killed on the job in *Crossing Jordan* (2001–07), and Cindy Thomas (Aubrey Dollar) teaming up with a homicide detective and an assistant district attorney to write stories

that often endanger her in *Women's Murder Club* (2007–08). Individual episodes of popular programs also have featured reporters whose investigations often have gotten them killed or saved in the nick of time by the series' heroes. See, for example, "Secrets," *NCIS: Naval Criminal Investigative Service,* originally aired February 14, 2012; "Bury the Lede," *Person of Interest,* originally aired November 1, 2012; "Deadline," *White Collar,* originally aired June 21, 2011; "Ki'ilua," *Hawaii Five-O,* originally aired November 21, 2011; "Seventeen Ain't So Sweet," *Rizzoli & Isles,* originally aired December 12, 2011.

28. Nat Hentoff, "Woodstein in the Movies," *Columbia Journalism Review* (May-June 1976): 47.

29. Carey, "Plea for the University Tradition," 850.

30. For a discussion of journalism ethics in *All the President's Men,* see Howard Good and Michael J. Dillon, *Media Ethics Goes to the Movies* (Westport, Conn.: Praeger, 2002), 39–61.

31. See the Society of Professional Journalists [SPJ] Code of Ethics, http://www.spj.org/ethicscode.asp. See also Kovach and Rosenstiel, *Elements of Journalism,* 47–68.

32. Margalit Fox, "Gregory Mcdonald, Novelist, Dies at 71," *New York Times,* September 12, 2008, A21. Such characters are common in novels; see, for example, Steve Weinberg, "Where Are the True Journalism Novels?" *Columbia Missourian,* February 22, 2008, http://www.ijpc.org/uploads/files/Weinberg%20Where%20are%20the%20True%20Journalism%20Novels.pdf.

33. The movies are *Fletch* (1985) and *Fletch Lives* (1989). In the first, Fletch assumes an outrageous series of fake identities ("Mr. Babar," "Dr. Rosenpenis," "Igor Stravinsky," "Don Corleone," and "Harry S. Truman"). He violates almost every rule of journalism, from deceiving everyone he interviews to breaking and entering so that he can photograph stolen documents. But he always gets the story.

34. The novels include Stieg Larsson, *The Girl with the Dragon Tattoo,* translated by Reg Keeland (New York: Vintage, 2008); Stieg Larsson, *The Girl Who Played with Fire,* translated by Reg Keeland (New York: Vintage, 2009); and Stieg Larsson, *The Girl Who Kicked the Hornet's Nest,* translated by Reg Keeland (New York: Knopf, 2012). Each of the three novels has been made into a Swedish-language film. In 2011 *The Girl with the Dragon Tattoo* was also made into an English-language film starring Daniel Craig as Blomkvist.

35. Larsson, *Girl Who Kicked the Hornet's Nest,* 519.

36. Larsson, *Girl with the Dragon Tattoo,* 490.

37. Ester Pollack, "The Making of Kalle Blomkvist: Crime Journalism in Postwar Sweden," in *The Girl with the Dragon Tattoo and Philosophy: Everything Is Fire,* edited by Eric Bronson (Hoboken, N.J.: Wiley, 2012), 77.

38. See the SPJ Code of Ethics, http://www.spj.org/ethicscode.asp. For a discussion of the ethics of Blomkvist's reporting, see James Edwin Mahon, "To Catch a Thief: The Ethics of Deceiving Bad People," in Bronson, *Girl with the Dragon Tattoo and Philosophy,* 198–210.

39. See Sven Ove Hansson, "The Philosopher Who Knew Stieg Larsson: A Brief Memoir," in Bronson, *Girl with the Dragon Tattoo and Philosophy,* 91–106.

40. Larsson, *Girl Who Played with Fire,* 87.

41. See Richard Campbell, *60 Minutes and the News: A Mythology for Middle America* (Urbana: University of Illinois Press, 1991); James S. Ettema and Theodore L. Glasser, *Custodians of Conscience: Investigative Journalism and Public Virtue* (New York: Columbia University Press, 1998).

42. Larsson, *Girl with the Dragon Tattoo,* 64–65.

43. See Robert W. McChesney, *The Political Economy of Media* (New York: Monthly Review Press, 2008), 47–54. See also Eric Alterman, "The Girl Who Loved Journalists: Stieg Larsson's Posthumous Gift to an Embattled Industry," *Columbia Journalism Review* (January/February 2012), http://www.cjr.org/reports/the_girl_who_loved_journalists .php?page=all.

44. The following is based upon Matthew C. Ehrlich, "Thinking about Journalism with Superman," *IJPC Journal* 4 (Fall 2012-Spring 2013): 132–63, http://ijpc.uscannenberg .org/journal/index.php/ijpcjournal/article/view/34/62.

45. Apart from the comics versions of Superman and Clark Kent, there have been a Superman radio series that aired from 1940 to 1951; an animated series of movie shorts in the early 1940s; two live-action movie serials in 1948 and 1950; the 1951 movie *Superman and the Mole Men,* which in effect served as the pilot for the George Reeves TV series that followed; a 1960s Broadway musical; four Christopher Reeve movies in the 1970s and 1980s; the 1990s TV series *Lois & Clark: The New Adventures of Superman* and the TV series *Smallville* that premiered the following decade; the 2006 movie *Superman Returns*; the 2013 movie *Man of Steel*; and assorted spinoff books, cartoons, movies, and TV series. See Greenberger and Pasko, *Essential Superman Encyclopedia*; Tye, *Superman*; Jake Rossen, *Superman vs. Hollywood* (Chicago: Chicago Review Press, 2008); Bruce Scivally, *Superman on Film, Television, Radio, and Broadway* (Jefferson, N.C.: McFarland, 2008).

46. "Wolfe vs. the Yellow Mask," *Adventures of Superman* radio series, originally aired March 22, 1940.

47. *Superman from the Thirties to the Eighties,* rev. ed., introduction by E. Nelson Bridwell (New York: Crown, 1983), 25.

48. Fred Brown and SPJ Ethics Committee, *Journalism Ethics,* 4th ed. (Portland, Ore.: Marion Street Press, 2011), 79. See also Joe Saltzman, "Deception and Undercover Journalism: *Mr. Deeds Goes to Town* and *Mr. Deeds,*" in *Journalism Ethics Goes to the Movies,* edited by Howard Good (Lanham, Md.: Rowman and Littlefield, 2008), 59–72; Kovach and Rosenstiel, *Elements of Journalism,* 119–22.

49. James W. Carey, "The Communications Revolution and the Professional Communicator," in *James Carey: A Critical Reader,* edited by Eve Stryker Munson and Catherine A. Warren (Minneapolis: University of Minnesota Press, 1997), 138. See also Gaye Tuchman, *Making News: A Study in the Construction of Reality* (New York: Free Press, 1978); Bennett, *News: The Politics of Illusion.*

50. Judith Serrin and William Serrin, Introduction to *Muckraking!: The Journalism that Changed America,* edited by Judith Serrin and William Serrin (New York: New Press, 2002), xxi.

51. A similar popular culture character is Peter Parker, the young photojournalist whose alter ego is Spider-Man.

52. See "Clan of the Fiery Cross," parts 1 through 16, *Adventures of Superman* radio series, originally aired June 10–July 1, 1946; Tye, *Superman,* 81–86.

53. Philip Skerry with Chris Lambert, "From Panel to Panavision," in *Superman at Fifty!,* edited by Dennis Dooley and Gary Engle (Cleveland: Octavia, 1987), 71. The lynch mob incident was first seen in the 1951 movie *Superman and the Mole Men,* starring George Reeves; it later was broadcast in 1953 as part of Reeves's *Adventures of Superman* TV series under the episode title "The Unknown People."

54. Dennis O'Neil, "The Man of Steel and Me," in Dooley and Engle, *Superman at Fifty!,* 57–58.

55. "Wall of Sound," *Lois & Clark: The New Adventures of Superman,* originally aired September 25, 1994.

56. In 2012 Clark Kent left the *Daily Planet* altogether after complaining that journalism was giving way to entertainment. A Superman writer said that Kent likely would take his journalistic talents to the Internet. See Brian Truitt, "Clark Kent Makes a Major Life Change in New 'Superman,'" *USA Today,* October 23, 2012, http://www.usatoday.com/story/life/2012/10/22/clark-kent-superman-comic-book-series/1648921.

57. Kovach and Rosenstiel, *Elements of Journalism,* 129–30; Bennett, *News: The Politics of Illusion,* 210.

58. In particular, Greeley showed up in many novels and short stories, including *Eben Holden* (1900) by Irving Bacheller and *The Welding* (1907) by Emily Lafayette McLaws.

59. James Fenimore Cooper was the most severe of any nineteenth-century novelist in his criticism of the press, and his arguments were often filled with fury and personal rancor. Other nineteenth-century examples of editor characters included Charles Dickens's scurrilous Colonel Diver in *The Life and Adventures of Martin Chuzzlewit,* from the 1840s; a villainous editor-publisher in William Thackeray's *The Adventures of Philip* (1862); the honest and conscientious Mr. Clarendon in Bayard Taylor's *John Godfrey's Fortunes* (1864); and various editor characters in Mark Twain and Charles Dudley Warner's *The Gilded Age* (1873). Booth Tarkington's *The Gentleman from Indiana* was made into a 1915 film. It showed an editor coming under attack for trying to expose a crooked politician running for Congress. As in the novel, the town rallies behind the editor to bring the crooks to justice.

60. George Murray, *The Madhouse on Madison Street* (Chicago: Follett, 1965), 180. See also George W. Hilton, *The Front Page: From Theater to Reality* (Hanover, N.H.: Smith and Kraus, 2002), 52.

61. Hecht and MacArthur, *Front Page,* 32, 38, 129, 138, 155, 189.

62. Apart from appearing in the comics version of Spider-Man, Jameson also has

been featured in three Tobey Maguire Spider-Man movies, multiple Spider-Man TV series and animated cartoons, and the Broadway musical *Spider-Man: Turn Off the Dark*.

63. *Wikipedia*, s.v. "J. Jonah Jameson," last modified June 20, 2014, http://en.wikipedia.org/wiki/Jonah_Jameson. *Wikipedia* also notes that in some versions of Jameson in the comics, he has been more of a "caring boss" capable of "great bravery and integrity."

64. Greenberger and Pasko, *Essential Superman Encyclopedia*, 471. A less attractive version of White did appear in the *Smallville* TV series, in which he was "a television hack and a drunk"; see Tye, *Superman*, 278.

65. Douglass K. Daniel, *Lou Grant: The Making of TV's Top Newspaper Drama* (Syracuse, N.Y.: Syracuse University Press, 1996), 74, 104. See also "Cophouse," *Lou Grant*, originally aired September 20, 1977.

66. Daniel, *Lou Grant*, 154.

67. An earlier example of a crusading editor was Steve Wilson, who was the hero of the *Big Town* classic radio series that also was adopted for novels, movies, and television.

68. Small-town editors appear in a number of novels, including R. F. Delderfield's *All over the Town* (1947), Robert Inman's *Home Fires Burning* (1987), John Blanchard's *Without Fear or Favor* (2005), and Dan Marsh's *Klandestined* (2005). For more on such characters, see Loren Ghiglione, *The American Journalist: Paradox of the Press* (Washington, D.C.: Library of Congress, 1990), 135–41; Good, *Acquainted with the Night*, 71–85. See also *Wikipedia*, s.v. "William Allen White," last modified July 3, 2014, http://en.wikipedia.org/wiki/William_Allen_White.

69. Crime-busting female editors have appeared in Karen Hawkins's *Lois Lane Tells All* (2010), Janet Boling's *Deadly Sources* (2002) and *Breaking News* (2007), and a series of books by Janet Evanovich and Charlotte Hughes that feature the exploits of editor Jamie Swift at the *Beaumont Gazette*.

70. Larsson, *Girl Who Kicked the Hornet's Nest*, 152, 190.

71. For detailed case studies of popular culture's treatments of journalism ethics, see Good and Dillon, *Media Ethics Goes to the Movies*; Howard Good, ed., *Journalism Ethics Goes to the Movies* (Lanham, Md.: Rowman and Littlefield, 2008).

72. See Good and Dillon, *Media Ethics Goes to the Movies*, 77–87; Sandra L. Borden, "Responsible Journalistic Inquiry: *The Paper*," in Good, *Journalism Ethics Goes to the Movies*, 9–18.

73. See Good and Dillon, *Media Ethics Goes to the Movies*, 1–20.

74. "Lions Gate Films Presents *Shattered Glass*," unpublished publicity materials, Margaret Herrick Library, Academy of Motion Picture Arts and Sciences, Beverly Hills, Calif. See also Matthew C. Ehrlich, "Fabrication in Journalism: *Shattered Glass*," in Good, *Journalism Ethics Goes to the Movies*, 19–33.

75. "City Editor Augustus 'Gus' Haynes Character Bio," HBO.com, http://www.hbo.com/the-wire/cast-and-crew#/the-wire/cast-and-crew/augustus-gus-haynes/index.html.

76. See Lawrence Lanahan, "Secrets of the City: What *The Wire* Reveals about Urban Journalism," *Columbia Journalism Review* (January-February 2008): 22–31.

77. Ibid., 24, 31; David Simon, "Does the News Matter to Anyone Anymore?" *Washington Post*, January 20, 2008, B1; "The Wire Final Season," *Slate*, January 8, 2008, http://www.slate.com/articles/arts/tv_club/features/2008/the_wire_final_season/david_simon_responds.html. Simon has said that the Scott Templeton character was based on an actual *Baltimore Sun* reporter who made up stories and whose fabrications were ignored by the editors; see "The Wire Final Season."

78. Simon, "Does the News Matter to Anyone Anymore?" See also "-30-," *The Wire*, originally aired March 9, 2008; Linda Steiner, Jing Guo, Raymond McCaffrey, and Paul Hills, "*The Wire* and Repair of the Journalistic Paradigm," *Journalism* 14.6 (2012): 703–20.

79. George Gordon Battle, "Stage Profanity again under Fire," *New York Times*, September 9, 1928, sec. 10, 2.

80. John E. Drewry, "Presidential Address: The Journalist's Inferiority Complex," *Journalism Quarterly* 8 (1931): 14; Frank Parker Stockbridge, "Public Gets False Picture of Journalism," *American Press*, November 1931, 2.

81. See, for example, Pamela J. Shoemaker and Stephen D. Reese, *Mediating the Message: Theories of Influences on Mass Media Content*, 2nd ed. (White Plains, N.Y.: Longman, 1996), 92–95; Everette E. Dennis and John C. Merrill, *Media Debates: Issues in Mass Communication*, 2nd ed. (White Plains, N.Y.: Longman, 1996), 207–16.

82. See Robert B. Ray, *A Certain Tendency of the Hollywood Cinema, 1930–1980* (Princeton, N.J.: Princeton University Press, 1980), 58–63.

83. Carey, "Plea for the University Tradition," 849.

84. Jack Lule, *Daily News, Eternal Stories: The Mythological Role of Journalism* (New York: Guilford, 2001), 23.

85. See, for example, W. Lance Bennett, Lynne A. Gressett, and William Haltom, "Repairing the News: A Case Study of the News Paradigm," *Journal of Communication* 35.2 (1985): 50–68; Dan Berkowitz, "Doing Double Duty: Paradigm Repair and the Princess Diana What-a-Story," *Journalism* 1.2 (2000): 125–43; Matthew Cecil, "Bad Apples: Paradigm Overhaul and the CNN/Time 'Tailwind' Story," *Journal of Communication Inquiry* 26.1 (2002): 46–58; Steiner et al., "*The Wire* and Repair."

86. James W. Carey, "Mirror of the Times," *Nation*, June 16, 2003, 5. See also David L. Eason, "On Journalistic Authority: The Janet Cooke Scandal," *Critical Studies in Mass Communication* 3 (1986): 429–47.

87. Michael Schudson, *The Power of News* (Cambridge, Mass.: Harvard University Press, 1995), 17.

Chapter 3. Difference

1. Jay Rosen, "Look, You're Right, Okay? But You're Also Wrong," *PressThink*, February 2, 2013, http://pressthink.org/2013/02/look-youre-right-okay-but-youre-also-wrong.

2. Roland Joffé, Director's Commentary, *The Killing Fields,* DVD, Warner Brothers, 2001.

3. Qtd. in Eric Newton, ed., *Crusaders, Scoundrels, Journalists: The Newseum's Most Intriguing Newspeople* (New York: Times Books, 1999), 304.

4. Ben Hecht, *A Child of the Century* (New York: Simon and Schuster, 1954), 178.

5. Jerome Lawrence and Robert E. Lee, *Inherit the Wind* (1955; reprint, Toronto: Bantam, 1985), 112–13. The 1955 stage play was turned into a 1960 movie with Spencer Tracy as Drummond and Gene Kelly as Hornbeck. Later versions were produced for American television in 1965 (with Melvyn Douglas as Drummond and Murray Hamilton as Hornbeck), 1988 (with Jason Robards as Drummond and Darren McGavin as Hornbeck), and 1999 (with Jack Lemmon as Drummond and Beau Bridges as Hornbeck). The play was revived on Broadway in 1996 and 2007.

6. William Chaloupka, *Everybody Knows: Cynicism in America* (Minneapolis: University of Minnesota Press, 1999), xv.

7. Journalists, with their avowed commitment to verifiable fact, often have had problems in covering faith and religion; see, for example, Paul Marshall, Lela Gilbert, and Roberta Green Ahmanson, eds., *Blind Spot: When Journalists Don't Get Religion* (New York: Oxford University Press, 2009). One movie that does take religious difference seriously is *Gentleman's Agreement* (1947), which was based upon a Laura Z. Hobson novel of the same name and which focuses on a journalist's investigation of anti-Semitism.

8. Hunter S. Thompson, *Songs of the Doomed* (New York: Summit Books, 1990), 46; Hunter S. Thompson, *Fear and Loathing in Las Vegas* (1971; reprint, New York: Vintage, 1998), 200. See also William McKeen, *Outlaw Journalist: The Life and Times of Hunter S. Thompson* (New York: Norton, 2008).

9. Frank Rich, "Gonzo Gone, Rather Going, Watergate Still Here," *New York Times,* March 6, 2005, sec. 2, 1.

10. *Wikipedia,* s.v. "Uncle Duke," last modified May 8, 2014, http://en.wikipedia.org/wiki/Uncle_Duke.

11. For more on popular culture's depictions of Hunter Thompson, see Brian McNair, "Johnny Be Gonzo," *Journalism Practice* 6.4 (2012): 581–83.

12. Alex Barris, *Stop the Presses!: The Newspaperman in American Films* (South Brunswick, N.J.: A. S. Barnes, 1976), 135. Charles Ruggles appeared as a comically inebriated reporter in several movies, including *The Friends of Mr. Sweeney* (1934).

13. Howard Good, *The Drunken Journalist: The Biography of a Film Stereotype* (Lanham, Md.: Scarecrow, 2000), 151.

14. Tracy Everbach, "Family-Friendly?: A Study of Work-Life Balance in Journalism," *Media Report to Women* 37.2 (2009): 18.

15. The following discussion is partly based upon Joe Saltzman, "Sob Sisters: The Image of the Female Journalist in Popular Culture," *Image of the Journalist in Popular Culture,* 2003, http://www.ijpc.org/uploads/files/sobsessay.pdf.

16. Donna Born, "The Image of the Woman Journalist in American Popular Fiction: 1890 to the Present," paper presented to the Association for Education in Journalism, August 1981, 24–25, http://www.ijpc.org/uploads/files/Donna%20Born%20

-%20The%20Image%20of%20the%20Woman%20Journalist%20in%20American
%20Popular%20Fiction.pdf.

17. Qtd. in Mary P. Ryan, *Womanhood in America: From Colonial Times to the Present* (New York: New Viewpoints, 1975), 108–09.

18. Maurine H. Beasley and Sheila J. Gibbons, *Taking Their Place: A Documentary History of Women and Journalism* (Washington, D.C.: American University Press, 1993), 87. See also Deborah Chambers, Linda Steiner, and Carole Fleming, *Women and Journalism* (London: Routledge, 2004), 16.

19. In 2012 the popular TV period drama *Downton Abbey* featured another young woman (the character of Lady Edith Crawley) who came from a comparatively privileged background and whose interest in women's rights led to a journalism career.

20. Jean Marie Lutes, *Front-Page Girls: Women Journalists in American Culture and Fiction, 1880–1930* (Ithaca, N.Y.: Cornell University Press, 2006), 94, 97. One early study identified thirteen American novels between 1871 and 1900 that featured women journalists; see James G. Harrison, "Nineteenth-Century American Novels on American Journalism: I," *Journalism Quarterly* 22.3 (1945): 217.

21. Lutes, *Front-*Page Girls, 97.

22. Deborah Chambers and Linda Steiner, "The Changing Status of Women Journalists," in *The Routledge Companion to News and Journalism*, edited by Stuart Allan (London: Routledge, 2010), 50; emphasis in original.

23. Ishbel Ross, *Ladies of the Press* (New York: Harper and Brothers, 1936), 65. Ross observed that the "sob sister" label dated from the 1907 trial of millionaire Harry K. Shaw, who was accused of murdering his wife's lover. Male journalists believed the four women reporters covering the trial were there just to generate sympathy for the adulterous wife and derisively nicknamed them "sob sisters." See also Howard Good, *Girl Reporter: Gender, Journalism, and the Movies* (Lanham, Md.: Scarecrow, 1998), 50; Phyllis Leslie Abramson, *Sob Sister Journalism* (New York: Greenwood, 1990).

24. Born, "Image of the Woman Journalist," 7; Lutes, *Front-Page Girls,* 102.

25. Bonnie Brennen, "Cultural Discourse of Journalists: The Material Conditions of Newsroom Labor," in *Newsworkers: Toward a History of the Rank and File,* edited by Hanno Hardt and Bonnie Brennen (Minneapolis: University of Minnesota Press, 1995), 85–87.

26. Mildred Gilman, *Sob Sister* (New York: Jonathan Cape and Harrison Smith, 1931), 176. See also Lutes, *Front-Page Girls,* 105.

27. For more on silent films with female journalists, see Saltzman, "Sob Sisters," 2, 9n10.

28. Good, *Girl Reporter,* 7.

29. *Mr. Deeds Goes to Town* was remade into the 2002 Adam Sandler film, *Mr. Deeds,* with Winona Ryder playing the reporter. See Joe Saltzman, "Deception and Undercover Journalism: *Mr. Deeds Goes to Town* and *Mr. Deeds*," in *Journalism Ethics Goes to the Movies,* edited by Howard Good (Lanham, Md.: Rowman and Littlefield, 2008), 59–72.

30. See ibid., 40–41; Joe Saltzman, *Frank Capra and the Image of the Journalist in American Film* (Los Angeles: Image of the Journalist in Popular Culture, 2002), 53–82; Matthew C. Ehrlich, *Journalism in the Movies* (Urbana: University of Illinois Press, 2004), 55–65.

31. Hildy Johnson and Tess Harding were said to have been based respectively on journalists Adela Rogers St. Johns and Dorothy Thompson. See Pauline Kael, "Raising Kane," in *The Citizen Kane Book,* by Pauline Kael, Herman J. Mankiewicz, and Orson Welles (New York: Limelight, 1984), 48; Peter Kurth, *American Cassandra: The Life of Dorothy Thompson* (Boston: Little, Brown, 1990).

32. See, for example, Robin Wood, *Howard Hawks* (Garden City, N.Y.: Doubleday, 1968), 77; Andrew Britton, *Katharine Hepburn: Star as Feminist* (New York: Continuum, 1995), 203. In the similarly themed *June Bride* (1948), Bette Davis plays a strong and independent magazine editor who hires her ex-fiancé against her better judgment. After he quits the magazine, she tearfully pursues him. At the end of the film, she picks up his suitcases and follows him out the door, suggesting her willingness to subordinate her career to his.

33. Molly Haskell, *Holding My Own in No Man's Land* (New York: Oxford University Press, 1997), 115. See also Ehrlich, *Journalism in the Movies,* 50–55; Good, *Girl Reporter,* 41–47.

34. Les Daniels, *Superman: The Complete History* (San Francisco: Chronicle, 1998), 20.

35. Bruce Scivally, *Superman on Film, Television, Radio, and Broadway* (Jefferson, N.C.: McFarland, 2008), 49. Phyllis Coates would be succeeded by Noel Neill in playing Lane in the 1950s TV series; Neill's characterization was not so tough as Coates's.

36. J. P. Williams, "All's Fair in Love and Journalism: Female Rivalry in *Superman,*" *Journal of Popular Culture* 24.2 (1990): 109. The image of Lane as simultaneously tough and flighty carried over to Margot Kidder's portrayal of her in the Christopher Reeve Superman films. In *Superman II* (1980) Lane pursues nuclear-armed terrorists to the top of the Eiffel Tower. Then she pursues Superman and shares his bed in his Fortress of Solitude, only to have her memory of the event erased via a kiss from the superhero.

37. "Jane Arden" was written by Monte Barrett and drawn by Frank Ellis for the Register and Tribune Syndicate. The strip, which was especially popular in Canada and Australia, was adapted into a 1939 film. See *Wikipedia,* s.v. "Jane Arden (comics)," last modified June 23, 2014, http://en.wikipedia.org/wiki/Jane_Arden_%28comics%29.

38. Jackie Leger, "Dale Messick: A Comic Strip Life," *Animation World Magazine,* July 2000, http://www.awn.com/mag/issue5.04/5.04pages/legermessick.php3.

39. Barbara Taylor Bradford, *Remember* (New York: Random House, 1991), 5–6, 16–17, 94–95. The book was turned into a 1993 TV movie.

40. Jackie Collins, *Hollywood Kids* (New York: Simon and Schuster, 1994), 22, 117, 514.

41. Danielle Steel, *Passion's Promise* (1976; reprint, Detroit: Thorndike, 2010), back cover.

42. Danielle Steel, *Message from Nam* (New York: Dell, 1991), 393, 395. *Message from Nam* was turned into a 1993 TV movie.

43. Loren Ghiglione, *The American Journalist: Paradox of the Press* (Washington, D.C.: Library of Congress, 1990), 126.

44. Examples from TV include sports reporter Noelle Saris (Michaela McManus), who helps a source by planting a story after she spends a night with him (*Necessary Roughness,* 2012); reporter Christine Hill (Courtney Ford), who sleeps with a policeman to get the inside information on a serial killer (*Dexter,* 2009); and tabloid editor Lucy Spiller (Courteney Cox), who sleeps with anyone who can give her exclusive gossip on celebrities (*Dirt,* 2007–08). Similarly, in Patricia Potter's novel *Tempting the Devil* (2006), reporter Robin Stuart sleeps with an FBI agent, and in the movie musical *Rock of Ages* (2012), *Rolling Stone* journalist Constance Sack (Malin Åkerman) has a comically kinky encounter with a musician (Tom Cruise) she is interviewing to the strains of the power ballad "I Want to Know What Love Is." Female reporters in popular culture also regularly enter into liaisons with government officials; see chapter 4. It should be noted that male reporters are not immune from sexual relationships with their sources. In just two TV examples, journalist Jeff Flender (Dermot Mulroney) of the *Los Angeles Times* sleeps with the whistleblower who is working with him on a story of corporate corruption in *Enlightened* (2013), and reporter Sam Miller (Troy Garity) sleeps with a political aide who is feeding him information in *Boss* (2011–12).

45. See Saltzman, "Sob Sisters," 5, 12–13nn36–38. See also chapter 5.

46. Practically every major television journalist appeared on *Murphy Brown* during its run and interacted with Brown as though she were an actual peer. When in 1992 Vice President Dan Quayle entered into a national debate over single mothers with the Brown character as an example (a debate that Brown then addressed in the TV series), reality and fiction seemingly became inseparable.

47. Bonnie J. Dow, *Prime-Time Feminism: Television, Media Culture, and the Women's Movement since 1970* (Philadelphia: University of Pennsylvania Press, 1996), 34, 146, 160; Bonnie J. Dow, "Hegemony, Feminist Criticism, and *The Mary Tyler Moore Show,*" *Critical Studies in Mass Communication* 7.3 (1990): 264, 271.

48. Brian McNair, *Journalists in Film* (Edinburgh: Edinburgh University Press, 2010), 53.

49. Chambers and Steiner, "Changing Status of Women Journalists," 56. One example is the movie *Veronica Guerin* (2003), about a real-life Irish journalist (played by Cate Blanchett) who was murdered for her reporting on the drug trade. The film shows her courageous reporting creating conflicts in her family life prior to her murder.

50. Stacy L. Spaulding and Maurine H. Beasley, "Crime, Romance, and Sex: Washington Women Journalists in Recent Popular Fiction," *Media Report to Women* 32.4 (2004): 11. See also Maurine H. Beasley, *Women of the Washington Press: Politics, Prejudice, and Persistence* (Evanston, Ill.: Northwestern University Press, 2012). Out-

side Washington, contemporary novels often center on a savvy female reporter or columnist who captures a murderer and who stars in her own series of mysteries. Other women journalists include newspaper publishers and owners; investigative and crime reporters from Toronto, London, Georgia, Oregon, Los Angeles, New York, and Washington, D.C.; TV and radio reporters; gossip and food columnists; documentarians and journalism teachers; sportswriters; and even a writer for *Dog's Life*. See Saltzman, "Sob Sisters," 5, 11n34.

51. *The Devil Wears Prada* is based on the 2003 novel of the same name by Lauren Weisberger. The book was said to have been based on the author's experiences as an assistant to *Vogue* editor Anna Wintour. Earlier movies had featured powerful editors of women's magazines, including *June Bride* (1948) with Bette Davis and *Funny Face* (1957) with Kay Thompson playing the editor.

52. McNair, *Journalists in Film*, 110–11. One study argues that fashion and lifestyle news represents a "post-feminist" journalism that "arguably celebrates popular culture at the expense of hard-hitting investigative journalism on gendered issues"; see Chambers and Steiner, "Changing Status of Women Journalists," 57.

53. Daniels, *Superman: The Complete History*, 160.

54. McNair, *Journalists in Film*, 238.

55. In the TV series *Lois & Clark: The New Adventures of Superman* (1993–97), Lane and Clark Kent have an antagonistic relationship, including an argument over whose byline should appear first. In that series, at least, the two manage to set aside their differences long enough to marry. For more on Lois Lane, see Nadine Farghaly, ed., *Examining Lois Lane: The Scoop on Superman's Sweetheart* (Lanham, Md.: Scarecrow, 2013).

56. Juan González and Joseph Torres, *News for All the People: The Epic Story of Race and the American Media* (London: Verso, 2011), 8.

57. Donald Bogle, *Toms, Coons, Mulattoes, Mammies, and Bucks: An Interpretive History of Blacks in American Films*, new 3rd ed. (New York: Continuum, 1994).

58. A similar film featuring African American journalists is *Murder with Music*, aka *Mistaken Identity* (1941).

59. González and Torres, *News for All the People*, 2.

60. See David Caute, *Joseph Losey: A Revenge on Life* (New York: Oxford University Press, 1994). *The Lawless* was also released as *The Dividing Line*.

61. "Cliché Odyssey," *Newsweek*, May 25, 1964, 110.

62. Bogle, *Toms, Coons, Mulattoes*, 206.

63. United States: National Advisory Commission on Civil Disorders, *Report of the National Advisory Commission on Civil Disorders* (Washington, D.C.: U.S. Government Printing Office, 1968), 203.

64. See Bogle, *Toms, Coons, Mulattoes*, 366.

65. Qtd. in *Wikipedia*, s.v. "List of *Family Guy* Characters: Quahog Channel 5 News," last modified July 7, 2014, http://en.wikipedia.org/wiki/List_of_Family_Guy _characters#Quahog_Channel_5_News.

66. Thanks to University of Illinois journalism student Erika Strebel for observations on *The Year of the Dragon*. See also Thomas K. Nakayama, "Framing Asian-Americans," in *Images of Color, Images of Crime,* 3rd ed., edited by Coramae Richey Mann, Marjorie S. Zatz, and Nancy Rodriguez (Los Angeles: Roxbury, 2006), 102–10. The animated TV series *Superman* (1996–2000) featured the Asian American reporter "Angela Chen." The "star gossip columnist" for the *Daily Planet,* Chen is willing to "use her looks and charm" and "'stretch' the truth in order to come up with a sensational story." See "Superman Bios: Angela Chen," Worldsfinestonline.com, http://www.worldsfinestonline.com/WF/superman/bios/heroes/chen.

67. They include Yolanda Joe's "Georgia Barnett" mysteries, Susan Moody's "Penny Wannawake" mysteries, Mike Phillips's "Sam Dean" mysteries, Jim Butcher's "Dresden Files" science fiction books, and Isaac Adamson's "Billy Chaka" adventures. Gwendolyn Zepeda's novel *Lone Star Legend* features a journalist who works for the website *¡LatinoNow!*; for more on that book, see the conclusion to the present text.

68. For more on *The Wire,* see chapter 2.

69. See, for example, Joe Dziemianowicz, "Off-Broadway Play 'CQ/CX' Dramatizes Jayson Blair Scandal at the New York Times," *New York Daily News,* February 15, 2012, http://www.nydailynews.com/entertainment/music-arts/off-broadway-play -cq-cx-dramatizes-jayson-blair-scandal-new-york-times-article-1.1022920; Jennifer Farrar, "One Man's Fraud Taints Famed Newspaper in 'CQ/CX,'" *Yahoo! News,* February 15, 2012, http://news.yahoo.com/one-mans-fraud-taints-famed-newspaper-cq-qx -034251375.html. For more on the Jayson Blair scandal, see Seth Mnookin, *Hard News: The Scandals at the* New York Times *and Their Meaning for American Media* (New York: Random House, 2004).

70. See Tracey Scott Wilson, *The Story* (New York: Dramatists Play Service, 2004).

71. Three years after *Livin' Large!* African American writer-actor Damon Wayans cowrote the film *Blankman* (1994), in which Wayans plays a shy nerd named Darryl Walker who becomes a crime fighter. The film includes typically heroic images of the journalist: Darryl's brother Kevin Walker (David Alan Grier), who works for the tabloid TV show *Hard Edition,* and TV reporter Kimberly Jonz (Robin Givens), who works for a respectable news program and hires Kevin as her videographer. Kevin is a serious reporter who tries to expose the mayor's mob ties, but his white boss (Jason Alexander) is not interested—he assigns stories by throwing darts at a board listing clichéd tabloid subjects.

72. Mat Johnson and Warren Pleece, *Incognegro* (New York: Vertigo/DC Comics, 2008), 4. See also Kenneth Robert Janken, *White: The Biography of Walter White, Mr. NAACP* (New York: New Press, 2003), 29–55.

73. Christopher John Farley, *My Favorite War* (New York: Farrar, Straus, and Giroux, 1996), 102–03, 226.

74. Chris Benson, *Special Interest* (New York: One World Books/Ballantine, 2003), 6, 276.

75. Qtd. in Talia Whyte, "For McLarin, Path to Hub TVs Anything but 'Basic,'" *Boston Banner,* January 10, 2008, 2–3.

76. Kim McLarin, *Taming It Down* (New York: Morrow, 1998), 109, 119, 208. McLarin's 2001 novel, *Meeting of the Waters,* also features an African American female journalist who enters into a complex romantic relationship with a white male journalist.

77. McLarin, *Taming It Down,* 49; Amanda Rossie, "Looking to the Margins: The 'Outsider Within' Journalistic Fiction," *IJPC Journal* 1 (2009): 105–37, http://ijpc .uscannenberg.org/journal/index.php/ijpcjournal/article/view/11/13. See also Patricia Hills Collins, "Learning from the Outsider Within: The Sociological Significance of Black Feminist Thought," *Social Problems* 33.6 (1986): S14-S32.

78. See, for example, Jill Nelson, *Volunteer Slavery: My Authentic Negro Experience* (Chicago: Noble Press, 1993); Pamela Newkirk, *Within the Veil: Black Journalists, White Media* (New York: New York University Press, 2000).

79. Sukhmani Khorana, "The Female Journalist in Bollywood," *Metro Magazine* 171 (2011): 102, 105.

80. Radhika Parameswaran, "Moral Dilemmas of an Immoral Nation: Gender, Sexuality, and Journalism in *Page 3,*" *IJPC Journal* 1 (2009): 71–72, http://ijpc.uscannenberg .org/journal/index.php/ijpcjournal/article/view/10/12.

81. Nonwhite journalists appear regularly in the pop culture of other countries besides India. They are featured in many Spanish-language publications and videos as well as in numerous imports from Japan, China, and Hong Kong.

82. See "Bibliography: The Image of the Gay Journalist in Popular Culture," *Image of the Journalist in Popular Culture,* 2010, http://www.ijpc.org/page/Gay_Journalist _Annotated_Bibliography.htm; "The Image of the Gay Journalist in Movies and Television," *Image of the Journalist in Popular Culture,* 2009, http://www.ijpc.org/ page/ijpc_the_image_of_the_gay_journalist.htm.

83. Vito Russo, *The Celluloid Closet: Homosexuality in the Movies,* rev. ed. (New York: Harper and Row, 1987), 26, 31.

84. Ibid., 45, 94.

85. Dixon T. Gaines, "The Gay Steppin' Fetchits of *He's Just Not That Into You,*" *Queerty,* February 5, 2009, http://www.queerty.com/the-gay-steppin-fetchits-of-hes -just-not-that-into-you-20090205. Sacha Baron Cohen wickedly parodies the most outrageous stereotypes of the gay journalist (and gay men generally) in the movie *Brüno* (2009). All of the stereotypes associated with gays and with journalists also can be found in hard-core and soft-core pornography; see *IJPC,* "Bibliography: The Image of the Gay Journalist in Popular Culture."

86. Examples of such films targeted at LGBT audiences include *The Living End* (1992), *Thin Ice* (1995), and *The Trip* (2002). Examples of films made outside the United States include the French Canadian *À corps perdu* (1988), *Chaos and Desire* (*La turbulence des fluides,* 2002), and *The Far Side of the Moon* (*La face cachée de la lune,* 2003); Italy's *A Special Day* (*Una giornata particolare,* 1977) and *Tenebre* (1982); Poland's *Without Love* (*Bez milosci,* 1980); Hungary's *Another Way* (*Egymásra nézve,* 1982); Egypt's *The Yacoubian Building* (*Omaret yakobean,* 2006); Germany's *Virgin Machine* (*Die Jungfrauenmaschine,* 1988), *Aimée & Jaguar* (1999), and *Whispering*

Moon (*Das Flüstern des Mondes,* 2006); Japan's *Hong Kong Night Club* (*Hon Kon daiyasokai: Tatchi and Magi,* 1997) and *Boys Love* (2006); Hong Kong's *The Map of Sex and Love* (*Qingse ditu,* 2001); and Britain's *He Kills Coppers* (2008). In contrast, India's stereotypes of gay journalists seem to be a Bollywood staple; see, for example, *Kis Kis Ki Kismat* (2004) and *Dostana* (2008).

87. McNair, *Journalists in Film,* 195.

88. For specific examples, see the appendix to the present text and *IJPC,* "Bibliography: The Image of the Gay Journalist in Popular Culture."

89. Fiction series with LGBT journalist protagonists include Elizabeth Sims's "Lillian Byrd" detective novels, Jon P. Bloch's "Rick Domino" mysteries, Carlene Miller's "Lexy Hyatt" mysteries, John Morgan Wilson's "Benjamin Justice" novels, French writer Maud Tabachnik's "Sandra Khan" books, R. D. Zimmerman's "Todd Mills" novels, Claudia McKay's "Lynn Evans" books, Val McDermid's "Lindsay Gordon" novels, and Joseph Hansen's "Dave Brandstetter" books. The latter feature a young gay African American news writer-reporter who has a long-term relationship with Brandstetter, an insurance claims investigator and sleuth.

90. Judith A. Markowitz, *The Gay Detective Novel: Lesbian and Gay Main Characters and Themes in Mystery Fiction* (Jefferson, N.C.: McFarland, 2004), 6, 112–21.

91. Qtd. in ibid., 10.

92. Vicki P. McConnell, *The Burnton Widows* (Tallahassee: Naiad, 1984), 181; emphasis in original.

93. Sally Munt, *Murder by the Book?: Feminism and the Crime Novel* (London: Routledge, 1994), 128.

94. Markowitz, *Gay Detective Novel,* 119.

95. Penny Mickelbury, *Keeping Secrets* (Tallahassee: Naiad, 1994), 47; Penny Mickelbury, *Night Songs* (Tallahassee: Naiad, 1995), 209. See also Markowitz, *Gay Detective Novel,* 221–23.

96. Lisa Haddock, *Edited Out* (Tallahassee: Naiad, 1994), 12, 59.

97. Rossie, "Looking to the Margins," 117. See also Lisa Haddock, *Final Cut* (Tallahassee: Naiad, 1995).

98. Qtd. in Markowitz, *Gay Detective Novel,* 133. In the TV series *The Bridge* (2013–), a young Latina reporter who works for the El Paso newspaper angers her family when she comes out as a lesbian.

99. Ibid., 126–27; Jared S. Anderson, "Author Interview: Michael Craft," *JSAScribes,* July 11, 2012, http://jsascribes.wordpress.com/2012/07/11/author-interview-michael-craft; Michael Craft, *Bitch Slap* (New York: St. Martin's Minotaur, 2005), 45, 241.

100. Chambers and Steiner, "Changing Status of Women Journalists," 49.

101. Arlene Notoro Morgan, Alice Irene Fifer, and Keith Woods, eds., *The Authentic Voice: The Best Reporting on Race and Ethnicity* (New York: Columbia University Press, 2006), xv.

102. Marguerite Moritz, "Getting It Straight: Gay News Narratives and Changing Cultural Values," in Allan, *Routledge Companion to News and Journalism,* 321.

103. Ross, *Ladies of the Press,* 13; Chambers, Steiner, and Fleming, *Women and Journalism,* 1.

104. United States, *Report of the National Advisory Commission,* 203; Sally Lehrman, *News in a New America* (Miami: John S. and James L. Knight Foundation, 2005), 14, 19.

105. Rodney Benson, "American Journalism and the Politics of Diversity," *Media, Culture, and Society* 27.1 (2005): 17. See also González and Torres, *News for All the People.*

106. Linda Steiner, "Gender in the Newsroom," in *The Handbook of Journalism Studies,* edited by Karin Wahl-Jorgensen and Thomas Hanitzsch (New York: Routledge, 2009), 127.

107. Moritz, "Getting It Straight," 329. See also Lehrman, *News in a New America.*

108. Rosen, "Look, You're Right, Okay?"

109. Rossie, "Looking to the Margins," 130.

Chapter 4. Power

1. Society of Professional Journalists Code of Ethics, SPJ.org, http://www.spj.org/ethicscode.asp; Bill Kovach and Tom Rosenstiel, *The Elements of Journalism,* revised and updated 3rd ed. (New York: Three Rivers Press, 2014), 171.

2. Robert W. McChesney, *The Political Economy of Media: Enduring Issues, Emerging Dilemmas* (New York: Monthly Review Press, 2008), 25.

3. Jay Black, Bob Steele, and Ralph Barney, *Doing Ethics in Journalism,* 3rd ed. (Boston: Allyn and Bacon, 1999), 40.

4. See Theodore Peterson, "The Social Responsibility Theory," in *Four Theories of the Press,* by Fred S. Siebert, Theodore Peterson, and Wilbur Schramm (Urbana: University of Illinois Press, 1956), 73–103; Stephen J. A. Ward, "Journalism Ethics," in *The Handbook of Journalism Studies,* ed. Karin Wahl-Jorgensen and Thomas Hanitzsch (New York: Routledge, 2009), 295–309.

5. In the case of *All the President's Men,* some ethicists have questioned Woodward and Bernstein's handling of sources, regardless of the greater good their reporting may have served. See Howard Good and Michael J. Dillon, *Media Ethics Goes to the Movies* (Westport, Conn.: Praeger, 2002), 39–61; Sissela Bok, *Lying: Moral Choice in Public and Private Life* (New York: Vintage, 1999), 107, 120–21.

6. The film *Philomena* (2013) is another mostly positive portrayal of the journalist helping people—in this case, a British reporter (Steve Coogan) who assists a woman (Judi Dench) in discovering what happened to the son she had given up for adoption decades earlier, although the truth turns out to be painful. The movie is based on a real investigation by journalist Martin Sixsmith.

7. To be sure, there were older depictions that also showed anonymous journalists wreaking havoc, directly or indirectly. In *King Kong* (1933) a pack of reporters and photographers frightens the great ape into breaking his bonds and going on the

Manhattan rampage that culminates in his fatal trek to the top of the Empire State Building.

8. See Loren Ghiglione, *CBS's Don Hollenbeck: An Honest Reporter in the Age of McCarthyism* (New York: Columbia University Press, 2008). O'Brian and his column are frequently referred to in *Good Night, and Good Luck.*

9. *Blessed Event,* original theatrical trailer, Warner Brothers, 1932, available on YouTube, http://www.youtube.com/watch?v=hsQ3KviXERw.

10. Apart from inspiring columnist characters in the movies and in novels (notably Emile Gauvreau's 1932 book, *The Scandal Monger*), Winchell appeared as himself in films such as *Wake Up and Live* and *Love and Hisses,* both from 1937. He was referred to on radio and in poems and animated cartoons, and he was mentioned in the song "Shuffle Off to Buffalo" as well as in tunes by Cole Porter ("Let's Fly Away") and Rodgers and Hart ("The Lady Is a Tramp").

11. Neal Gabler, *Winchell: Gossip, Power, and the Culture of Celebrity* (New York: Vintage, 1995), 552.

12. See Ernest Lehman, Introduction to *Sweet Smell of Success,* by Clifford Odets and Ernest Lehman (London: Faber and Faber, 1998), vii-viii.

13. John Lithgow played Hunsecker in a Tony Award–winning performance in the 2002 musical. Similarly villainous New York columnists appear in the movies *Laura* (1944) and *All About Eve* (1950). In *Laura* Clifton Webb plays Waldo Lydecker, who commits murder. In *All About Eve* George Sanders plays Addison DeWitt, who recognizes the malevolence in rising star Eve Harrington before almost anyone else and uses it to blackmail her into giving him complete control over her life and career.

14. Like Winchell, Parsons and Hopper appeared as themselves in several movies, including *Hollywood Hotel* (1937), *That's Right—You're Wrong* (1939), *Without Reservations* (1946), and *Sunset Boulevard* (1950), as well as on popular radio and TV programs such as *The George Burns and Gracie Allen Show* and *I Love Lucy.* Hopper also played a gossip columnist much like herself in the 1939 movie *The Women.*

15. Parsons also was a character in the 1985 TV movie *The Hearst and Davies Affair.* A tipsy Parsons-and-Hopper-type gossip columnist was featured in the 1999–2001 TV series *The Lot,* about the golden age of Hollywood.

16. "Rita Skeeter," *Harry Potter Wiki,* http://harrypotter.wikia.com/wiki/Rita_Skeeter.

17. Daxton R. Stewart, "Harry Potter and the Exploitative Jackals: Media Framing and Credibility Attitudes in Young Readers," *IJPC Journal* 2 (2010): 1, 7–10, http://ijpc.uscannenberg.org/journal/index.php/ijpcjournal/article/view/18/26; Project for Excellence in Journalism, *The State of the News Media 2007: An Annual Report on American Journalism,* http://stateofthemedia.org/2007/overview/public-attitudes.

18. Gabler, *Winchell,* 552. Vicious gossip columnists have regularly appeared in popular culture. Film examples include the characters of Patty Benedict in *The Big Knife* (1955) and Molly Luther in *The Legend of Lylah Clare* (1968). Douglas Carter Beane's play *Mr. and Mrs. Fitch* (2010) tells of married celebrity journalists who fabricate a fictional celebrity to try to resuscitate their careers. Novels have featured

the evil Porter Wren in Colin Harrison's *Manhattan Nocturne* (1996) and loathsome political writer Brandon Sladder in Jeffrey Frank's *The Columnist* (2002), as well as gossip columnists Kate Simon, Tim Mack, and Blake Bradley in Deborah Schoeneman's *4% Famous* (2006). Lindsey Davis's book *Scandal Takes a Holiday* (2004) includes a gossip columnist who uses the pen name "Infamia" for the official government newspaper of ancient Rome. Over the years there also have been many positive depictions of columnists who dispense advice and put the interests of others ahead of their own; they range from the 1934 film *Hi, Nellie!* to TV series such as *Eight Is Enough* (1977–81) and *Charmed* (1998–2006). Columnists also appear in mystery series by Nancy G. West (the "Aggie Mundeen" novels), Persia Walker (the "Lanie Price" novels), Glen Albert Ebisch (the "Laura Magee" novels), Morgan St. James and Phyllice Bradner (the "Godiva Olivia DuBois" novels), Roberta Isleib (the "Rebecca Butterman" novels), Stephen F. Wilcox (the "Elias Hackshaw" novels), Nancy Fairbanks (the "Carolyn Blue" novels), Bill Kent (the "Andrea Cosicki" novels), Sheryl J. Anderson (the "Molly Forrester" novels), and Jo Bannister (the "Rosie Holland" novels). On stage, David Auburn's play *The Columnist* (2012) tells of the life and career of Joseph Alsop (see chapter 1), and Nora Ephron's *Lucky Guy* (2013) relates the story of New York columnist Mike McAlary, who won a Pulitzer Prize for exposing police brutality.

19. Hoffman's reporter character is egged on by an egomaniacal TV network anchor played by Alan Alda.

20. See, for example, Michael Schudson, *Watergate in American Memory* (New York: Basic Books, 1992), 120.

21. See David Barsamian, *Stenographers to Power* (Monroe, Me.: Common Courage, 1992). See also chapter 2.

22. Other examples of reporters (both male and female) who fall in love with sources close to government power include *Born Yesterday,* which premiered on Broadway in 1946 and then was made into movies in 1950 and 1993. It features a journalist who becomes romantically entangled with the girlfriend of an uncouth businessman who is attempting to bribe members of Congress. In Rachel Bailey's 2013 romance novel *No Stranger to Scandal,* a young reporter enters into a romantic relationship with a congressional investigator who is targeting her media mogul stepfather for alleged criminal misdeeds.

23. For more on female (and male) reporters sleeping with sources, see chapter 3.

24. "Chapter 9," *House of Cards* (U.S. version), originally released February 1, 2013.

25. The incestuousness of the reporter-politician relationship is also underlined by the American version of *House of Cards*, in which the "I couldn't possibly comment!" line appears as well. The original British *House of Cards* was inspired by a novel of the same name, which was written by onetime journalist Michael Dobbs, who later became chief of staff for the Conservative Party.

26. Joseph McBride, *Frank Capra: The Catastrophe of Success* (New York: Simon and Schuster, 1992), 411–15, 418.

27. Some professional journalism organizations protested *Mr. Smith Goes to Washington,* saying that one man could not muzzle the press of an entire state. For more on the movie's portrayal of journalism, see Joe Saltzman, *Frank Capra and the Image of the Journalist in American Film* (Los Angeles: Image of the Journalist in Popular Culture, 2002), 27–36; Matthew C. Ehrlich, *Journalism in the Movies* (Urbana: University of Illinois Press, 2004), 59–61.

28. See Ray Pratt, *Projecting Paranoia: Conspiratorial Visions in American Film* (Lawrence: University Press of Kansas, 2001). See also chapter 1.

29. In the similarly themed *Bob Roberts* (1992), an investigative reporter for *Troubled Times* correctly guesses that a right-wing conspiracy is behind a U.S. Senate campaign. The campaign attempts to frame the reporter for attempted assassination; when that does not work, the reporter is murdered.

30. For example, when a journalist learns new information about the 9/11 attack on America, the FBI pressures him and his editor to reveal their sources and drop the story in *The Reflecting Pool* (2008). Journalist Simon Ross (Paddy Considine) finds out too much about CIA assassins and is "neutralized" in *The Bourne Ultimatum* (2007).

31. In *Boss* (2011–12) a mayor finally gets rid of his journalistic nemesis by flexing his political muscle and getting the publisher to fire him. In *The Andromeda Strain* (2008) a reporter gets too close to exposing a deadly disease of extraterrestrial origin, and the government targets him for assassination.

32. Examples have included "The Question," a comic book series that debuted in 1967 and featured an investigative TV reporter who created a secret identity to expose government corruption, and "Kolchak," which debuted as a TV series in 1974 and then spun off into graphic novels and comic books.

33. In the 2009–11 TV series *V,* a television journalist is chased by aliens and the government. That followed a 1980s television version of *V,* in which the news media were silenced and killed by alien reptiles.

34. For example, in David Hagberg's *The Cabal* (2010) a *Washington Post* investigative reporter is about to expose a shadowy group of high-ranking government officials when he and his family are killed. In Allan McLeod's *The Money Washers* (2008) a journalist exposes an international money-laundering scheme that members of the CIA, the Pentagon, and the White House want to continue even at the cost of the journalist's life. In Kathleen Lamarche's *The Plot* (2003), when a reporter discovers that a conspiracy to control the world's resources extends to the highest levels of government and the news media, those in power kill and discredit everyone around her to stop her from publishing the story. In Michael D. O'Brien's *Plague Journal: Children of the Last Days* (1999) an editor and his family are hunted down by a police state seeking to crush all freedoms. In John Robert Marlow's *Nano* (2004) government agents are dispatched to kill a reporter who is investigating a new nanotechnology that could create a world without hunger, disease, or death.

35. Berrin A. Beasley, "Political Manipulation of the Media: *Wag the Dog,*" in *Journalism Ethics Goes to the Movies,* edited by Howard Good (Lanham, Md.: Rowman

and Littlefield, 2008), 45. There is a long history of popular culture depictions of the public relations profession, including many of principled and virtuous practitioners. For overviews, see Joe Saltzman, "The Image of the Public Relations Practitioner in Movies and Television 1901–2011," *IJPC Journal* 3 (Fall 2011-Spring 2012): 1–50, http://ijpc.uscannenberg.org/journal/index.php/ijpcjournal/article/view/25/50; Karen S. Miller, "Public Relations in Film and Fiction: 1930 to 1995," *Journal of Public Relations Research* 11.1 (1999): 3–28; Carol Ames, "PR Goes to the Movies: The Image of Public Relations Improves from 1996 to 2008," *Public Relations Review* 36.2 (2010): 164–70.

36. Examples include *Cannon*; *Owen Marshall: Counselor at Law*; *Eight Is Enough*; *Mrs. Columbo*; *Mork and Mindy*; *Goodnight, Beantown*; *Anything but Love*; *Perfect Strangers*; *Major Dad*; *Murphy Brown*; *Evening Shade*; *The Naked Truth*; *Law and Order*; *Pepper Dennis*; *The Defenders*; *Covert Affairs*; and *Bones*. See the appendix for information about the specific episodes of those series that depict journalists going to jail to protect sources.

37. Examples of such novels include Arthur Lyons's *The Dead Are Discreet* (1974), Les Whitten's *Conflict of Interest* (1976), Patricia Potter's *Tempting the Devil* (2006), and Mike Lawson's *House Justice* (2010).

38. See Matt Carlson, *On the Condition of Anonymity: Unnamed Sources and the Battle for Journalism* (Urbana: University of Illinois Press, 2011), 35–39; "'Nothing but the Truth'' Valerie Plame Game Now a Work of Friction," *New York Daily News,* November 16, 2008, http://www.nydailynews.com/entertainment/gossip/truth-valerie-plame-game-work-friction-article-1.339050.

39. Carlson, *On the Condition of Anonymity,* 12.

40. In the movie *Street Smart* (1987) a reporter refuses to name his source for good reason: he fabricated his story. He has no choice but to go to jail rather than reveal a fictitious source. The reporter finally is released, but he still faces perjury charges.

41. "Will Mary Richards Go to Jail?" *The Mary Tyler Moore Show,* September 14, 1974. Richards subsequently agrees to go to jail, but not before tearfully telling Grant, "I don't want to go to jail. . . . I never even had to stay after school!"

42. The words were taken from the actual Murrow broadcast from 1954.

43. Stieg Larsson, *The Girl Who Kicked the Hornet's Nest,* translated by Reg Keeland (New York: Knopf, 2012), 311.

44. Judith Serrin and William Serrin, Introduction to *Muckraking!: The Journalism That Changed America,* edited by Judith Serrin and William Serrin (New York: New Press, 2002), xxii. Pop culture's celebrations of freedom of the press are not always so reverential; the movie *The People vs. Larry Flynt* (1996) relates the real-life story of a pornographer who went all the way to the U.S. Supreme Court in successfully defending his right to publish scabrous parodies of public figures.

45. W. Lance Bennett, *News: The Politics of Illusion,* 7th ed. (New York: Pearson/Longman, 2007), 269.

46. Robert W. McChesney and Ben Scott, Introduction to *Our Unfree Press,* edited by Robert W. McChesney and Ben Scott (New York: New Press, 2004), 1–2.

47. W. Lance Bennett and William Serrin, "The Watchdog Role," in *The Press*, edited by Geneva Overholser and Kathleen Hall Jamieson (New York: Oxford University Press, 2005), 169.

48. Ibid., 187.

49. McChesney and Scott, Introduction, 2. See also Robert W. McChesney and John Nichols, *The Death and Life of American Journalism* (Philadelphia: Nation Books, 2010); Leonard Downie Jr. and Michael Schudson, "The Reconstruction of American Journalism," *Columbia Journalism Review*, October 19, 2009, http://www.cjr.org/reconstruction/the_reconstruction_of_american.php?page=all.

50. For a cold war–era summary of this argument, see Wilbur Schramm, "The Soviet Communist Theory," in *Four Theories of the Press*, by Fred S. Siebert, Theodore Peterson, and Wilbur Schramm (Urbana: University of Illinois Press, 1956), 105–46. Bill Kovach and Tom Rosenstiel contrast Polish state control of the media during the 1981 crackdown against the Solidarity movement with the concurrent rise of a free underground media in Poland; see Kovach and Rosenstiel, *Elements of Journalism*, 13–15.

51. The first season of the British TV series *The Hour* (2011) is far less apocalyptic than *V for Vendetta*, but it also raises questions about state control of the media: the government pressures a BBC news program to neuter its coverage of the 1956 Suez crisis. For more on speculative fiction's dystopian portrayals of state coercion of the press, see the conclusion of the present text.

52. "About the Story," *V for Vendetta* Production Notes, 2006, http://wwws.warnerbros.co.uk/vforvendetta/cmp/prod_notes_ch_02.html; *Wikipedia*, s.v. "*V for Vendetta* (film)," last modified July 4, 2014, http://en.wikipedia.org/wiki/V_for_Vendetta_%28film%29. The comic book series similarly drew an explicit connection between the state and big business in forming the totalitarian state: "It was all the fascist groups, the right-wingers. They'd all got together with some of the big corporations." See Alan Moore and David Lloyd, *V for Vendetta* (New York: DC Comics, 2005), 28.

53. Loren Ghiglione, *The American Journalist: Paradox of the Press* (Washington, D.C.: Library of Congress, 1990), 157–58. For more on depictions of small-town editor-publishers, see ibid., 135–41; Howard Good, *Acquainted with the Night: The Image of Journalists in American Fiction, 1890–1930* (Metuchen, N.J.: Scarecrow, 1986), 71–85. See also chapter 2 of the present text.

54. Robert B. Ray, *A Certain Tendency of the Hollywood Cinema, 1930–1980* (Princeton, N.J.: Princeton University Press, 1985), 57. See also Ehrlich, *Journalism in the Movies*, 69–78.

55. Sarah Street, "*Citizen Kane*," in *The Movies as History*, edited by David W. Ellwood (Stroud, England: Sutton, 2000), 100.

56. David Thomson, *The New Biographical Dictionary of Film* (New York: Knopf, 2002), 925.

57. William Dean Howells, *Their Silver Wedding Journey* (New York: Harper and Brothers, 1899), 248. See also Ghiglione, *American Journalist*, 157.

58. Bernard Hinchecliffe likely was based at least in part on Bernarr Macfadden, publisher of the notorious *New York Graphic* tabloid newspaper of the 1920s. *Five Star Final* playwright Louis Weitzenkorn had been the *Graphic*'s managing editor.

59. For more on *Meet John Doe*'s portrayal of Norton, see Saltzman, *Frank Capra and the Image of the Journalist in American Film*, 117–23. Capra portrayed another ruthless newspaper publisher in *State of the Union* (1948), with Angela Lansbury playing the vicious Kay Thorndyke, who seeks power by installing her husband as president of the United States. The movie was based on a Broadway play of the same name by Howard Lindsay and Russel Crouse. See Saltzman, *Frank Capra*, 124–28.

60. Lester Roebuck, "The Good, the Bad, and the Oedipal," in *Superman at Fifty!*, edited by Dennis Dooley and Gary Engle (Cleveland: Octavia, 1987), 145. Later incarnations of the Superman franchise also highlighted concerns over media ownership. In the movie *Superman IV: The Quest for Peace* (1987), a sleazy publisher seizes control of the *Daily Planet* and fires editor Perry White while imposing tabloid values on the paper. In the episode "Gemini" from the TV series *Smallville* (aired December 13, 2007), Lex Luthor buys the *Planet* and kills an exposé that Lois Lane is writing about him. "You want to bury the truth? Buy the media!" an editor bitterly observes.

61. One movie example is *The China Syndrome* (1979), in which a local TV news reporter and photographer try to report the story of falsified records and a near meltdown at a nuclear power plant. They are thwarted (at least until the climax of the film) by station management, which refuses to air their story in seeming deference to villainous plant officials and state regulators.

62. Ghiglione, *American Journalist*, 159; David Aaron, *Agent of Influence* (1989; reprint, New York: Avon, 1990), 413.

63. According to *Tomorrow Never Dies*'s screenwriter, Bruce Feirstein, the "role model" for Elliot Carver was British press magnate Robert Maxwell, who after his death was found to have committed fraud. See Bruce Feirstein, "The Tao of Bond-Film Naming," *Vanity Fair Daily*, January 29, 2008, http://www.vanityfair.com/online/daily/2008/01/bruce-feirste-2.

64. See Ehrlich, *Journalism in the Movies*, 120–28.

65. Wallace and Hewitt were incensed at how *The Insider* portrayed them, with both saying that the film distorted what actually had happened. See Mary Murphy, "Mighty Mike," *TV Guide*, September 18–24, 1999, 32; Don Hewitt, *Tell Me a Story* (New York: Public Affairs, 2001), 199.

66. "Louder Than Words," *Boss*, originally aired August 17, 2012; "The Blackout Part I: Tragedy Porn," *The Newsroom*, originally aired August 12, 2012. In *The Newsroom* the news staff is able to stop the mogul by threatening to reveal that her son has been hacking into the phones of news sources to get inside information and scoops for the company's tabloid. That had clear parallels to Rupert Murdoch's News International, which had engaged in similar hacking in Britain; see *Wikipedia*, s.v. "News International Phone Hacking Scandal," last modified July 3, 2014, http://en.wikipedia.org/wiki/News_International_phone_hacking_scandal.

67. Ghiglione, *American Journalist*, 157.

68. Peterson, "Social Responsibility Theory of the Press," 78–79.

69. John Nerone, "The Historical Roots of the Normative Model of Journalism," *Journalism* 14.4 (2013): 453, 455.

70. Bennett, *News: The Politics of Illusion,* 269–70.

71. McChesney and Scott, Introduction, 1.

72. Ghiglione, *American Journalist,* 157.

73. See Jack Lule, *Daily News, Eternal Stories: The Mythological Role of Journalism* (New York: Guilford, 2001); Matthew C. Ehrlich, "*Shattered Glass,* Movies, and the Free Press Myth," *Journal of Communication Inquiry* 29.2 (2005): 103–18. See also chapter 2 for a discussion of the casting out of journalists who violate professional values.

74. For a historical summary of competing perspectives on the effects of mass media, see Jennings Bryant and Susan Thompson, *Fundamentals of Media Effects* (Boston: McGraw-Hill, 2002), 21–64.

75. Examples from recent novels include Jim Hipps's *Tenacious Bulldogs* (2012), Larry Matthews's *Brass Knuckles* (2012), and Douglas Fetterly's *Breach of Justice* (2012).

76. See "Kidnap," *Lou Grant,* originally aired November 26, 1979.

77. Todd Gitlin, "Down the Tubes," in *Seeing through Movies,* edited by Mark Crispin Miller (New York: Pantheon, 1990), 39.

78. Christy Lemire, "Review: 'State of Play' a Slick Political Thriller,'" Fox News. com, April 14, 2009, http://www.foxnews.com/printer_friendly_wires/2009Apr14/0,4675,FilmReviewStateofPlay,00.html.

79. Mark Deuze, "Journalism and Convergence Culture," in *The Routledge Companion to News and Journalism,* ed. Stuart Allan (London: Routledge, 2010), 275.

80. David L. Eason, "On Journalistic Authority: The Janet Cooke Scandal," in *Media, Myths, and Narratives,* edited by James W. Carey (Newbury Park, Calif.: Sage, 1988), 222–23.

81. Stephen B. Shepard, *Deadlines and Disruption* (New York: McGraw-Hill, 2013), 9.

82. Downie and Schudson, "Reconstruction of American Journalism."

83. Bennett, *News: The Politics of Illusion,* 269.

84. John Nichols and Robert W. McChesney, "The Death and Life of Great American Newspapers," *Nation,* April 6, 2009, http://www.thenation.com/article/death-and-life-great-american-newspapers?page=full.

Chapter 5. Image

1. Kiku Adatto, *Picture Perfect: Life in the Age of the Photo Op,* new ed. (Princeton, N.J.: Princeton University Press, 2008), 120.

2. Bonnie Brennen, "Photojournalism: Historical Dimensions to Contemporary Debates," in *The Routledge Companion to News and Journalism,* edited by Stuart Allan (London: Routledge, 2010), 75.

3. Daya Kishan Thussu, "Television News in the Era of Global Infotainment," in Allan, *Routledge Companion to News and Journalism*, 362–63, 370.

4. Robert Hariman and John Louis Lucaites, *No Caption Needed: Iconic Photographs, Public Culture, and Liberal Democracy* (Chicago: University of Chicago Press, 2007), 295.

5. Barbie Zelizer, *About to Die: How News Images Move the Public* (New York: Oxford University Press, 2010), 326.

6. Claude Cookman, *American Photojournalism: Motivations and Meanings* (Evanston, Ill.: Northwestern University Press, 2009), 265.

7. Al Tompkins, *Aim for the Heart: Write, Shoot, Report, and Produce for TV and Multimedia,* 2nd ed. (Washington, D.C.: CQ Press, 2012), 2, 321.

8. For a historical overview of photojournalism's development, see Cookman, *American Photojournalism,* 61–98.

9. See Brennen, "Photojournalism"; Cookman, *American Photojournalism,* 67–69, 89–94; Earle Bridger, "From the Ridiculous to the Sublime: Stereotypes of Photojournalists in the Movies," *Visual Communication Quarterly* 4.1 (1997): 4.

10. See Raymond Fielding, *The American Newsreel, 1911–1967* (Norman: University of Oklahoma Press, 1972).

11. Bonnie S. Brennen, "From *Headline Shooter* to *Picture Snatcher*: The Construction of Photojournalists in American Film," *Journalism* 5.4 (2004): 428, 429–30. The image of the newsreel cameraperson was so prevalent by the late 1920s that Buster Keaton parodies the genre in *The Cameraman* (1928) as a man who becomes a newsreel photographer to try to win a woman's love and respect. Other movie depictions of newsreel photographers from this era include *Hot News* (1928), *Above the Clouds* (1933), *Headline Shooter* (1933), *Burn 'Em Up Barnes* (1934), *Ladies Crave Excitement* (1935), *Anything for a Thrill* (1937), *I Cover the War* (1937), and *Chasing Danger* (1939). The films frequently enhanced the drama by splicing in footage of actual disasters. Fiction also featured newsreel shooters; for example, a pair of 1940 juvenile novels celebrated the exploits of sixteen-year-old Jimmy "Flash" Evans.

12. Qtd. in "Too Hot to Handle," DearMrGable.com, http://dearmrgable.com/?page_id=3837.

13. Brennen, "From *Headline Shooter* to *Picture Snatcher*," 431.

14. Bridger, "From the Ridiculous to the Sublime," 5.

15. See ibid., 5–6; Brennen, "From *Headline Shooter* to *Picture Snatcher*," 432–33. Other early film examples of photojournalists include *The Final Edition* (1932), *Page Miss Glory* (1935), *Too Tough to Kill* (1935), *A Face in the Fog* (1936), *Murder with Pictures* (1936), *Bank Alarm* (1937), *They Wanted to Marry* (1937), *Here's Flash Casey* (1938), and *Time Out for Murder* (1938).

16. Cookman, *American Photojournalism,* 193–94.

17. Bridger, "From the Ridiculous to the Sublime," 8.

18. John Belton, "Introduction: Spectacle and Narrative," in *Alfred Hitchcock's* Rear Window, edited by John Belton (Cambridge: Cambridge University Press, 2000), 7.

19. Norman K. Denzin, *The Cinematic Society: The Voyeur's Gaze* (London: Sage, 1995), 118. It should be noted that Jefferies's spying has its upside: it helps him catch a killer.

20. Loudon Wainwright, *The Great American Magazine: An Inside History of* Life (New York: Knopf, 1986), 150–51, 153; emphasis in original.

21. See Belton, "Introduction," 5–7.

22. For example, "Steve Roper" was an intrepid photojournalist (as well as investigative reporter, editor, and television anchor) in the comics from 1940 to 2004. He was said to be as "good with his fists as with his cameras and typewriter." See *Wikipedia*, s.v. "Steve Roper and Mike Nomad," last modified April 14, 2014, http://en.wikipedia.org/wiki/Steve_Roper_and_Mike_Nomad.

23. In the series *Man with a Camera* (1958–60), Charles Bronson played a globetrotting journalist who saw the world through his camera while solving one mystery after another. The British *Man of the World* (1962–63) also focused on a peripatetic photojournalist. More recently, an episode of *The West Wing* ("Gaza," originally aired May 12, 2004) depicted a female presidential aide becoming romantically involved with a handsome Irish photojournalist who helps her see the difficulties experienced by Gaza residents.

24. Recent examples include Ally Blake's *Falling for the Rebel Heir* (2008), Roxanne Rustand's *Wildfire* (2008), Jill Monroe's *Primal Instincts* (2008), Helen Brenna's *First Come Twins* (2009), Diana Kingham's *The Road to Imphal* (2009), Adriana Kraft's *Return to Purgatory Point* (2009), JoAnn Ross's *One Summer* (2011), and Teri Wilson's *Alaskan Hearts* (2012). Another example of a globetrotting photojournalist having his head turned by love is *National Geographic*'s Robert Kincaid in Robert James Waller's novel *The Bridges of Madison County* (1992) and Clint Eastwood's movie of the same name (1995).

25. Barbara Taylor Bradford, *Remember* (New York: Random House, 1991), 22, 88.

26. Promotional copy for Ruth Langan's *Retribution* (2004), Amazon.com, http://www.amazon.com/Retribution-Silhouette-Intimate-Moments-Devils/dp/0373273738; promotional copy for Gary B. Hudson's *Brief* (2010), Amazon.com, http://www.amazon.com/Brief-Gary-B-Hudson/dp/1432759108; promotional copy for JoAnn Ross's *Fair Haven* (2000), Amazon.com, http://www.amazon.com/Fair-Haven-JoAnn-Ross/dp/0671786113.

27. Promotional copy for Tom Davis's *Scared: A Novel on the Edge of the World* (2009), Amazon.com, www.amazon.com/Scared-Novel-World-Tom-Davis/dp/1589191021. Daniels's character was inspired by photojournalist Kevin Carter; see "Character Spotlight: Tom Davis' Stuart Daniels & Katya with Giveaway," RelzReviewz.com, June 14, 2010, http://relzreviewz.com/character-spotlight-tom-davis-stuart-daniels-katya-with-giveaway. For more about Carter, see the discussion of *The Bang Bang Club* later in this chapter.

28. Ward Just, *Exiles in the Garden* (Boston: Houghton Mifflin Harcourt, 2009), 231, 259. Before writing fiction, Just had been a *Washington Post* Vietnam correspon-

dent during the 1960s and had been badly wounded; see Ward S. Just, *To What End: Report from Vietnam* (Boston: Houghton Mifflin, 1968).

29. Richard Boyle was an actual photojournalist who coauthored *Salvador*'s script. *The Killing Fields* (1984) shows a similarly disheveled photojournalist based on a real person (Al Rockoff, played in the film by John Malkovich). Linda Hunt won an Oscar for playing photojournalist Billy Kwan, who sacrifices his life for the good of his country, in *The Year of Living Dangerously* (1982). In Francis Ford Coppola's *Apocalypse Now* (1979), Dennis Hopper is a coked-out news photographer who offers rambling, incoherent commentaries about the madness of the Vietnam War. Other psychologically damaged photojournalists appear in *Somebody Has to Shoot the Picture* (1990), *Deadly Exposure* (1993), and *Road to Perdition* (2002). *Harrison's Flowers* (2000) shows a photojournalist vanishing in Yugoslavia and his wife searching for him with the help of other journalists.

30. The movie quotes from Carter's actual 1994 suicide note. Marinovich was seriously wounded in the same 1994 war zone shooting that killed Oosterbroek. Marinovich and fellow photojournalist João Silva then coauthored a book on which the movie was based. See Greg Marinovich and João Silva, *The Bang-Bang Club: Snapshots from a Hidden War* (New York: Basic Books, 2000); Bill Keller, "'To Be on the Edge of History,'" NYTimes.com, May 5, 2011, http://lens.blogs.nytimes.com/2011/05/05/the-inner-lives-of-wartime-photographers/?ref=magazine.

31. Ron Dorfman, "Journalists Under Fire," *The Quill*, October 1983, 13. See also Stephen Badsey, "The Depiction of War Reporters in Hollywood Feature Films from the Vietnam War to the Present," *Film History* 14.3/4 (2002): 250–51.

32. Bridger, "From the Ridiculous to the Sublime," 10.

33. Judith Matloff, "Bang Bang Off Target," *Columbia Journalism Review*, July 5, 2011, http://www.cjr.org/review/bang_bang_off_target.php?page=all.

34. Pauline Kael, "Image Makers," *New Yorker*, October 31, 1983, 122. For a discussion of the ethical choices in *Under Fire*, see Howard Good and Michael J. Dillon, *Media Ethics Goes to the Movies* (Westport, Conn.: Praeger, 2002), 63–76.

35. Cookman, *American Photojournalism*, 204.

36. Once more, it is novels that most often depict female photojournalists, including those who have witnessed terrible things on the job and who subsequently try to rebuild their lives. Some recent examples are Kristin Hannah's *Winter Garden* (2010), Tatjana Soli's *The Lotus Eaters* (2010), Jan Neuharth's *The Kill* (2010), Kimberly Kaye Terry's *Hot to Touch* (2010), BethAnn Buehler's *Broken Together* (2010), Louis Hillary Park's *Wolf's Run* (2010), Patricia Spencer's *Day Three* (2011), Dawn Atkins's *The Baby Connection* (2011), Dawn Reno's *Foxglove* (2011), Carol L. Johnston's *A Lifetime of Tomorrows* (2012), Joshua Graham's *Darkroom* (2012), and Donna Hill's *Everything Is You* (2012).

37. Danielle Steel, *Bittersweet* (New York: Delacorte, 1999), 239.

38. Suzanne Arruda, *Treasure of the Golden Cheetah* (New York: New American Library, 2009), 3.

39. "Mark of the Lion: A Jade del Cameron Mystery" (book review), Publishers Weekly.com, October 24, 2005, http://www.publishersweekly.com/978-0-451-21748-6.

40. Kyle Ross McDaniel, "Reviewing the Image of the Photojournalist in Film: How Ethical Dilemmas Shape Stereotypes of the On-Screen Press Photographer in Motion Pictures from 1954 to 2006," MA thesis, University of Missouri, 2007, 111, http://ijpc.org/uploads/files/Photojournalist%20Thesis.pdf. According to McDaniel, movie examples of flawed female photographers include *Friday Foster* (1975), *Eyes of Laura Mars* (1978), *Kalifornia* (1993), *High Art* (1998), *The Weight of Water* (2000), *Closer* (2004), *November* (2004), and *Blood Diamond* (2006). Not all of those films show the photographer relying on male companionship (for example, in *High Art* she is a lesbian), but they do suggest that the photographer is frequently troubled and ethically compromised. See ibid., 97–111.

41. Qtd. in Douglass K. Daniel, *Lou Grant: The Making of TV's Top Newspaper Drama* (Syracuse, N.Y.: Syracuse University Press, 1996), 83.

42. The chief shutterbug in this film set in the 1940s is Leon Bernstein (Joe Pesci), a character loosely based on New York photojournalist Arthur "Weegee" Fellig. Bernstein aspires to a more noble career through his photography but finds it difficult to overcome his tabloid roots and sense of alienation.

43. Paparazzi also have been immortalized—rarely flatteringly—in popular song (Lady Gaga's 2008 song "Paparazzi"); music videos (Britney Spears's "Piece of Me" from 2007 and "I Wanna Go" from 2011); and a slew of commercials for companies including Target, Pepsi, Heineken, Verizon, Macy's, American Express, AT&T, Pizza Hut, Nike, Yahoo, and International House of Pancakes.

44. For more on anonymous journalists, see chapter 4.

45. Some other radio journalist films include *Professional Sweetheart* (1933), *Here Comes Carter* (1936), *Love Is on the Air* (1937, starring Ronald Reagan), *Sued for Libel* (1939), *Assignment: Paris* (1952), and *The Great Man* (1956). See Richard Ness, "From *A Voice in the Night* to *A Face in the Crowd*: The Rise and Fall of the Radio Film," paper presented to the Association for Education in Journalism and Mass Communication, San Francisco, Calif., 2006, http://ijpc.org/uploads/files/Rise%20and%20Fall %20of%20the%20Radio%20Film%20-%20Richard%20Ness.pdf.

46. See ibid., 4. Although radio reporters largely disappeared from films by the end of the 1950s, two decades later the hapless Les Nessman (Richard Sanders) was a prominent character on the TV series *WKRP in Cincinnati* (1978–82). His signature moment (from the episode "Turkeys Away") came during his live Thanksgiving broadcast when he was describing a disastrous turkey drop from a helicopter: "Oh, the humanity!" Another comedic TV take on radio news was *NewsRadio* (1995–99).

47. Loren Ghiglione, *The American Journalist: Paradox of the Press* (Washington, D.C.: Library of Congress, 1990), 149.

48. For more on *Medium Cool,* see chapter 1.

49. "You Sometimes Hurt the One You Hate," The *Mary Tyler Moore Show,* September 28, 1974.

50. Episode 0710, *Sesame Street,* January 3, 1975. The "Hickory Dickory Dock" excerpt is available on YouTube: https://www.youtube.com/watch?v=0KkkowQVf38. A scholarly analysis of *Sesame Street*'s comic portrayal of journalism notes that it is markedly less harsh than has been seen in some adult-oriented programming: "Kermit ultimately embodies a positive image of a reporter, if for nothing else than his loveable ambition and dedication." See Ashley Ragovin, "N is for News: The Image of the Journalist on *Sesame Street*," *IJPC Journal* 2 (2010): 58, http://ijpc.uscannenberg.org/journal/index.php/ijpcjournal/article/view/19/27.

51. Promotional copy for Bonnie Tucker's *Stay Tuned: Wedding at 11:00* (1998), Amazon.com, http://www.amazon.com/Stay-Tuned-Wedding-Love-Laughter/dp/0373440529.

52. Promotional copy for Montana Mills's *Need* (2011), Amazon.com, http://www.amazon.com/Need-erotica-ebook/dp/B005234NDA.

53. Venise Berry, *All of Me: A Voluptuous Tale* (New York: Dutton, 2000), 82, 228. Williamson's attitude is rather more healthy than that of television anchor Sally McCormick (Suzanne Somers) in the TV movie *Devil's Food* (1996), in which the anchor is so desperate to lose weight and stay on the air that she sells her soul to the devil. Another novel that tells of a female TV journalist struggling with her weight is Kathryn Lilley's *Makeovers Can Be Murder* (2009).

54. Liz French video interview with Julie Kramer, RT Book Reviews.com, June 22, 2010, http://www.rtbookreviews.com/rt-daily-blog/video-interview-mystery-author-julie-kramer.

55. Ironically or not, *Network* was written by Paddy Chayefsky and directed by Sidney Lumet, both of whom had first made their names in television. See Matthew C. Ehrlich, *Journalism in the Movies* (Urbana: University of Illinois Press, 2004), 121–28.

56. For more on *Good Night, and Good Luck* and *The Insider,* see chapters 1 and 4.

57. "The 112th Congress," *The Newsroom,* originally aired July 8, 2012.

58. See Rosalind Wright, "The Temptress Bride," *Ladies' Home Journal,* July 1991, 93–95, 152–55.

59. Other 1990s movies that explored TV's impact on impressionable young women included *Hero* (1992), in which Geena Davis plays a reporter who is easily duped by a handsome homeless man falsely claiming to have rescued people from a plane crash, and *Mad City* (1997), in which a newsroom intern parlays coverage of a hostage crisis into a full-fledged reporting job.

60. *American Cinema: Romantic Comedy,* film documentary, writer-producer-director Molly Ornati, Fox Video, 1995. Before writing and directing *Broadcast News,* James L. Brooks had cocreated *The Mary Tyler Moore Show* with its TV news backdrop.

61. For more on *The Mary Tyler Moore Show* and *Murphy Brown,* see chapter 3. See also Jennifer Keishin Armstrong, *Mary and Lou and Rhoda and Ted: And All the Brilliant Minds Who Made* The Mary Tyler Moore Show *a Classic* (New York: Simon

and Schuster, 2013); Robert S. Alley and Irby B. Brown, Murphy Brown: *Anatomy of a Sitcom* (New York: Delta, 1990).

62. "We Just Decided To," *The Newsroom*, originally aired June 24, 2012. Television journalists have continued to be omnipresent characters on television series and specials, ranging from anchor Robin Scherbatsky (Cobie Smulders) on the long-running show *How I Met Your Mother* (2005–14) to bickering male and female coanchors in a 2005 BBC reimagining of *Much Ado about Nothing* (part of the *ShakespeaRe-Told* series).

63. For more on the making of *Up Close & Personal*, see John Gregory Dunne, *Monster: Living Off the Big Screen* (New York: Random House, 1997). For more on Jessica Savitch, see Gwenda Blair, *Almost Golden: Jessica Savitch and the Selling of Television News* (New York: Avon, 1989); Alanna Nash, *Golden Girl: The Story of Jessica Savitch* (New York: Harper Paperbacks, 1996).

64. "Prime Suspect," *NCIS*, originally aired March 5, 2013.

65. Adatto, *Picture Perfect*, 19, 122.

66. See chapter 2 for more on the *Lou Grant* TV series. One 1990 study suggested that in some instances television journalists actually have been portrayed more positively than newspaper journalists; see Gerald Stone and John Lee, "Portrayal of Journalists on Prime Time Television," *Journalism Quarterly* 67.4 (1990): 697–707.

67. Adatto, *Picture Perfect*, 23–24.

68. Hanno Hardt, *In the Company of Media: Cultural Constructions of Communication, 1920s-1930s* (Boulder, Colo.: Westview, 2000), 63. See also Kevin G. Barnhurst and John Nerone, *The Form of News: A History* (New York: Guilford, 2001), 111–39.

69. Susan Sontag, *On Photography* (New York: Farrar, Straus, and Giroux, 1977), 178. See also John Tagg, *The Burden of Representation: Essays on Photographies and Histories* (Amherst: University of Massachusetts Press, 1988); Michel Foucault, *Discipline and Punish: The Birth of the Prison,* translated by Alan Sheridan (New York: Pantheon, 1977).

70. John Hartley, "Documenting Kate Moss: Fashion Photography and the Persistence of Photojournalism," *Journalism Studies* 8.4 (2007): 561. See also Adatto, *Picture Perfect*, 36.

71. Zelizer, *About to Die*, 313, 322.

72. Susan Sontag, *Regarding the Pain of Others* (New York: Farrar, Straus, and Giroux, 2003), 117.

73. Cookman, *American Photojournalism*, 265.

74. Vicky Ball, "The 'Feminization' of British Television and the Re-Traditionalization of Gender," *Feminist Media Studies* 12.2 (2012): 248. The 1982 Don Henley song "Dirty Laundry" reflects such attitudes with its reference to silly blonde anchorwomen delivering televised news of tragedy and scandal.

75. Ghiglione, *American Journalist*, 152.

76. Linda A. Detman, "Negotiating the Woman of *Broadcast News*," *Studies in Symbolic Interaction* 15 (1993): 5; emphasis in original.

77. Ibid., 10. See also Denzin, *Cinematic Society,* 68–73.

78. Neil Postman, *Amusing Ourselves to Death: Public Discourse in the Age of Show Business* (New York: Viking, 1985).

79. Pierre Bourdieu, *On Television,* translated by Priscilla Parkhurst Ferguson (New York: New Press, 1998), 36–37.

80. Todd Gitlin, "Down the Tubes," in *Seeing through Movies,* edited by Mark Crispin Miller (New York: Pantheon, 1990), 33.

81. "We Just Decided To," *The Newsroom,* originally aired June 24, 2012.

82. Emily Nussbaum, "Broken News: The Artificial Intelligence of *The Newsroom,*" *New Yorker,* June 25, 2012, http://www.newyorker.com/arts/critics/television/2012/06/25/120625crte_television_nussbaum?currentPage=all.

83. Jack Shafer, "Edward R. Movie: *Good Night, and Good Luck* and Bad History," *Slate,* October 5, 2005, http://www.slate.com/articles/news_and_politics/press_box/2005/10/edward_r_movie_2.single.html.

84. Gitlin, "Down the Tubes," 40.

85. Dunne, *Monster,* 105, 201–03.

86. *Up Close & Personal* also perpetuated the myth of the experienced TV journalist mentor who plays Professor Henry Higgins to his Eliza Doolittle, and who cares so much about doing good journalism and bringing the news to the public at all costs that he is killed in the process.

87. For more on the mythology surrounding Murrow, see chapter 1.

88. Tompkins, *Aim for the Heart,* 1; Edward R. Murrow, *In Search of Light: The Broadcasts of Edward R. Murrow, 1938–1961* (New York: Knopf, 1967), 364.

Chapter 6. War

1. Qtd. in Bill Keller, "'To Be on the Edge of History,'" NYTimes.com, May 5, 2011, http://lens.blogs.nytimes.com/2011/05/05/the-inner-lives-of-wartime-photographers/?ref=magazine. See also Anne Wilkes Tucker and Will Michels with Natalie Zelt, *War/Photography: Images of Armed Conflict and Its Aftermath* (Houston: Museum of Fine Arts, 2012); Howard Tumber, "Journalists and War Crimes," in *The Routledge Companion to News and Journalism,* edited by Stuart Allan (London: Routledge, 2010), 536–41. For more on the film *The Bang Bang Club,* see chapter 5.

2. Roy Gutman, Foreword to *The Military and the Press: An Uneasy Truce* by Michael S. Sweeney (Evanston, Ill.: Northwestern University Press, 2006), ix; Howard Tumber, "Covering War and Peace," in *The Handbook of Journalism Studies,* edited by Karin Wahl-Jorgensen and Thomas Hanitzsch (New York: Routledge, 2009), 387; Raluca Cozma and John Maxwell Hamilton, "Film Portrayals of Foreign Correspondents," *Journalism Studies* 10.4 (2009): 490.

3. Stuart Allan and Barbie Zelizer, "Rules of Engagement: Journalism and War," in *Reporting War: Journalism in Wartime,* edited by Stuart Allan and Barbie Zelizer (London: Routledge, 2004), 3.

4. Anthony DiMaggio, *When Media Goes to War: Hegemonic Discourse, Public Opinion, and the Limits of Dissent* (New York: Monthly Review Press, 2009), 13. See also Edward S. Herman and Noam Chomsky, *Manufacturing Consent: The Political Economy of the Mass Media* (New York: Pantheon, 2002). Journalists can feel pressure to put patriotism before professional ethics and suppress information that might be detrimental to the war effort.

5. Allan and Zelizer, "Rules of Engagement," 5.

6. See Daniel C. Hallin, "The Media and War," in *International Media Research: A Critical Survey,* edited by John Corner, Philip Schlesinger, and Roger Silverstone (London: Routledge, 1997), 209–11; Daniel C. Hallin, *The "Uncensored War": The Media and Vietnam* (New York: Oxford University Press, 1986).

7. Characters who bear some resemblance to modern-day war correspondents have existed in popular storytelling from ancient times. The focus here (as in the rest of this book) is from roughly 1890 to the present.

8. Howard Good, "The Image of War Correspondents in Anglo-American Fiction," *Journalism Monographs,* no. 97 (July 1986): 6; Loren Ghiglione, *The American Journalist: Paradox of the Press* (Washington, D.C.: Library of Congress, 1990), 143.

9. Rudyard Kipling, *The Light That Failed* (1890; reprint, New York: R. F. Fenno, 1899), 340. Kipling's novel would be adapted multiple times for the stage, movies, and television, most notably in a 1939 film starring Ronald Colman.

10. Examples of that fiction include Crane's novel *Active Service* (1899) and Davis's short story "A Derelict" (1902). For a discussion of those works, see Good, "Image of War Correspondents," 7–9. Davis also wrote the short story "Gallegher" (1890), which likewise focused on a journalist and became widely popular after it appeared in novel form in 1907. "Gallegher" then was made into multiple silent films (including 1928's *Let 'Er Go, Gallegher*) before becoming the focus of a popular 1960s Disney TV series. (War correspondents had been characters in several silent films dating back to 1898.)

11. Raymond A. Schroth, "The Journalist as Autobiographer," Worldview, September 1980, http://worldview.carnegiecouncil.org/archive/worldview/1980/09/3436.html/_res/id=sa_File1/v23_i009_a004.pdf. See also "Richard Harding Davis," *Newspaper Heroes on the Air,* http://jheroes.com/real-life-reporters/richard-harding-davis; "Richard Harding Davis," The Literature Network, http://www.online-literature.com/richard-davis.

12. See Phillip Knightley, *The First Casualty: From the Crimea to Vietnam: The War Correspondent as Hero, Propagandist, and Myth Maker* (New York: Harvest, 1975), 124–26; *Wikipedia,* s.v. "Floyd Gibbons," last modified March 30, 2014, http://en.wikipedia.org/wiki/Floyd_Gibbons.

13. Other examples of popular culture celebrating Gibbons include a 1949 comic book called *King of Reporters: Floyd Gibbons* and the 1962 TV episode "The Floyd Gibbons Story" that appeared as part of the series *The Untouchables*.

14. Good, "Image of War Correspondents," 9–14.

15. In 1938 *Clear All Wires* was adapted into the stage musical *Leave It to Me!* It is chiefly remembered today for representing the Broadway debut of Mary Martin, who introduced the Cole Porter song "My Heart Belongs to Daddy" in the show. Samuel and Bella Spewack wrote the book for the musical and also directed it. Later they authored the screenplay for *Week-End at the Waldorf* (1945), which costarred Walter Pidgeon as a burned-out war correspondent.

16. John Maxwell Hamilton, *Journalism's Roving Eye: A History of American Foreign Reporting* (Baton Rouge: Louisiana State University Press, 2009), 418.

17. Good, "Image of War Correspondents," 11.

18. See Michael B. Salwen, "Evelyn Waugh's *Scoop*: The Facts behind the Fiction," *Journalism and Mass Communication Quarterly* 78.1 (2001): 150–71. See also Evelyn Waugh, *Waugh in Abyssinia* (1936; reprint, London: Penguin, 2000); Hamilton, *Journalism's Roving Eye*, 423–24.

19. Evelyn Waugh, *Scoop* (Boston: Little, Brown, 1938), 26, 92–93; emphasis in original. *Scoop* would be adapted for British television in 1972 and 1987 and for BBC Radio in 2009.

20. Hamilton, *Journalism's Roving Eye*, 2.

21. Cozma and Hamilton, "Film Portrayals of Foreign Correspondents," 496–97.

22. Hamilton, *Journalism's Roving Eye*, 205–06. See also Vincent Sheean, *Personal History* (1935; reprint, Boston: Houghton Mifflin, 1969); Donald Spoto, *The Dark Side of Genius: The Life of Alfred Hitchcock* (Boston: Little, Brown, 1983), 221–35.

23. See Jeanine Basinger, *The World War II Combat Film: Anatomy of a Genre* (New York: Columbia University Press, 1986), 73–75.

24. James Tobin, *Ernie Pyle's War: America's Eyewitness to World War II* (New York: Free Press, 1997), 219.

25. A similar scene occurs in the TV movie *Margaret Bourke-White* (1989) as Bourke-White (played by Farrah Fawcett) photographs the death camps. The Dachau-Auschwitz scene in *Hemingway & Gellhorn* appalled at least one critic, who wrote that combining Kidman with documentary images of corpses constituted "a shockingly maudlin, melodramatic moment, one that would be deeply questionable in the best of films." See Maureen Ryan, "'Hemingway and Gellhorn' on HBO Review: Nicole Kidman and Clive Owen's Crime against TV," *Huffington Post*, May 25, 2012, http://www.huffingtonpost.com/maureen-ryan/hemingway-and-gellhorn-hbo-review_b_1540274.html.

26. During the Spanish Civil War, Ernest Hemingway wrote a play that then was rewritten by Benjamin Glazer and produced on Broadway in 1940. The play, *The Fifth Column*, includes a romance between a counterespionage agent who works undercover as a foreign correspondent and a female journalist who bears similarities to Gellhorn. See Verna Kale, "Review: *The Fifth Column*," *Hemingway Review* 27.2 (2008): 131–34. *Arise, My Love*'s female correspondent also was said to have been based on Gellhorn; see Maurice Zolotow, *Billy Wilder in Hollywood* (1977; reprint, New York: Limelight, 1996), 87.

27. One exception was *Sabre Jet* (1953), which told of a female journalist reporting on Korean War pilots and their wives on station with them. In *Love Is a Many-Splendored Thing* (1955) a correspondent (William Holden) is killed in Korea. That film, though, concentrates on the doomed romance between the reporter and a Eurasian doctor (Jennifer Jones) as opposed to the war itself.

28. "The Interview," *M*A*S*H,* originally aired February 24, 1976.

29. *M*A*S*H*'s antiwar stance also appeared in the episode "Blood and Guts" (originally aired January 18, 1982), in which surgeon Hawkeye Pierce (Alan Alda) challenges a correspondent to stop spreading flag-waving falsehoods through his dispatches: "You make this sound like some glorious escapade—something every American boy should aspire to. In case you haven't noticed, this is ugly. It is not exciting!" After the correspondent is seriously injured through his own foolish bravado, he confesses in his column that he "finally got it through his thick head how tragic and inhumane war can be."

30. Qtd. in Martin F. Nolan, "Graham Greene's Unquiet Novel; On Film and in Print, 'The Quiet American' Still Fascinates," *New York Times,* January 30, 2003, http:// www.nytimes.com/2003/01/30/movies/graham-greene-s-unquiet-novel-film-print -quiet-american-still-fascinates.html?pagewanted=all&src=pm.

31. Graham Greene, *The Quiet American* (New York: Penguin, 1955), 94, 152.

32. Ibid., 18, 28, 96.

33. Ibid., 167–68, 183.

34. See, for example, David Craig Hutton, "'I'll Still Be Reporting, Whoever Wins': Journalism and Media in Graham Greene's *Stamboul Train, It's a Battlefield,* and *The Quiet American,*" MA thesis, University of Saskatchewan, 2007, 61–80, http://ijpc.org/ uploads/files/Graham%20Greene%20Use%20of%20Journalists%20in%20His%20 Novels.pdf.

35. Greene, *Quiet American,* 20.

36. Good, "Image of War Correspondents," 18.

37. Graham Greene, *The Graham Greene Film Reader: Reviews, Essays, Interviews, and Film Stories,* edited by David Parkinson (New York: Applause Books, 1995), 443.

38. A 1968 movie that actually did focus on World War II was *Anzio,* with Robert Mitchum playing a war correspondent.

39. Qtd. in Lawrence H. Suid, *Guts and Glory: Great American War Movies* (Reading, Mass: Addison-Wesley, 1978), 227–28. See also Howard Good, *Outcasts: The Image of Journalists in Contemporary Film* (Metuchen, N.J.: Scarecrow, 1989), 39–43; Stephen Badsey, "The Depiction of War Reporters in Hollywood Feature Films from the Vietnam War to the Present," *Film History* 14.3/4 (2002): 246–47.

40. Hallin, "Media and War," 210.

41. For a discussion of movie depictions of anti-press sentiment in connection with Vietnam, see Badsey, "Depiction of War Reporters," 249–50.

42. Good, "Image of War Correspondents," 16.

43. "How to Stay Alive in Vietnam," parts 1 and 2, *China Beach,* originally aired on November 29 and December 6, 1989.

44. David Auburn, *The Columnist* (New York: Faber and Faber, 2012), 73. For more on *The Columnist,* see chapter 1. Amlin Gray's 1979 play, *How I Got That Story,* depicts a correspondent covering a war in a Vietnam-like country and losing his sanity.

45. Marti Leimbach, *The Man from Saigon* (New York: Nan A. Talese/Doubleday, 2009), 299; emphasis in original. In Danielle Steel's *Message from Nam* (1990) a female journalist in Vietnam loses multiple men she loves to the war; see chapter 3. *The American Blues* (1984) was written by Ward Just, a former war reporter who was wounded in Vietnam; his novel details the struggles of a onetime Vietnam correspondent in coming to grips with the war's legacy. For a discussion of that book, see Good, "Image of War Correspondents."

46. Badsey, "Depiction of War Reporters," 257.

47. See Harold G. Moore and Joseph L. Galloway, *We Were Soldiers Once—and Young: Ia Drang, The Battle That Changed the War in Vietnam* (New York: Random House, 1992). The frontline Vietnam combat correspondent also has been depicted in Don Lomax's comic series *Vietnam Journal* (1987–91). Dennis Hopper's drug-addled photojournalist in the film *Apocalypse Now* (1979) undercuts noble depictions of such correspondents.

48. Brian McNair, "Journalists at War," *Journalism Practice* 5.4 (2011): 492.

49. Badsey, "Depiction of War Reporters," 251.

50. Cozma and Hamilton, "Film Portrayals of Foreign Correspondents," 500.

51. *Salvador* contrasts the newly idealistic Boyle with a cynical and arrogant TV correspondent to whom Boyle's friend slips LSD. It reduces her to a giggling, incoherent mess on the air.

52. The murder of Price's journalist friend was loosely based on the killing of ABC journalist Bill Stewart in Nicaragua in 1979, an incident that was captured on film. For more on *Under Fire* and *Salvador,* see chapter 5.

53. See Sydney H. Schanberg, *The Death and Life of Dith Pran* (New York: Penguin, 1985).

54. *The Year of Living Dangerously* was based on a 1978 novel of the same name by Christopher Koch.

55. See Michael Nicholson, *Welcome to Sarajevo* (New York: Miramax, 1997; originally published 1993). See also Howard Good, "Journalism and the Victims of War: *Welcome to Sarajevo,*" in *Journalism Ethics Goes to the Movies,* edited by Howard Good (Lanham, Md.: Rowman and Littlefield, 2008), 149–62.

56. Michael Ignatieff, *Charlie Johnson in the Flames* (New York: Grove, 2003), 107.

57. Sexual harassment of women war correspondents is common, and assaults against them do occur, as evidenced by the 2011 attack on Lara Logan in Egypt. See Brian Stelter, "CBS Reporter Recounts a 'Merciless' Assault," *New York Times,* April 29, 2011, A13; Anthony Feinstein, *Journalists Under Fire: The Psychological Hazards of Covering War* (Baltimore: Johns Hopkins University Press, 2006), 115–35; Deborah Chambers, Linda Steiner, and Carole Fleming, *Women and Journalism* (London: Routledge, 2004), 196–215.

58. In the Serbian film *Pretty Village, Pretty Flame* (1996), a CBC-TV correspondent is trapped in a tunnel along with Serbian soldiers after she has sneaked aboard a medical truck. She alternates between begging for her life and quarreling with the soldiers, who strike her unconscious to quiet her. They remark that she can make them look bad through her coverage. Eventually she is shot dead in a firefight, an event recorded by her own camera.

59. Daniel C. Hallin and Todd Gitlin, "The Gulf War as Popular Culture and Television Drama," in *Taken by Storm: The Media, Public Opinion, and U.S. Foreign Policy in the Gulf War,* edited by W. Lance Bennett and David L. Paletz (Chicago: University of Chicago Press, 1994), 161.

60. See Robert Wiener, *Live from Baghdad: Making Journalism History behind the Lines* (New York: St. Martin's Griffin, 2002).

61. Hallin and Gitlin, "Gulf War as Popular Culture," 150.

62. For more on *Wag the Dog,* see chapter 4.

63. See, for example, W. Lance Bennett, Regina G. Lawrence, and Steven Livingston, *When the Press Fails: Political Power and the News Media from Iraq to Katrina* (Chicago: University of Chicago Press, 2007).

64. See William Prochnau, "The Military and the Media," in *The Press,* edited by Geneva Overholser and Kathleen Hall Jamieson (New York: Oxford University Press, 2005), 325–27; Tumber, "Covering War and Peace," 392–94.

65. W. Lance Bennett, *News: The Politics of Illusion,* 7th ed. (New York: Pearson Longman, 2007), 148.

66. For a critique of Jessica Lynch coverage, see W. Joseph Campbell, *Getting It Wrong: Ten of the Greatest Misreported Stories in American Journalism* (Berkeley: University of California Press, 2010), 144–62. *Embedded* was videotaped and presented in that form as *Embedded Live!* (2005).

67. The *Law and Order* TV episode "Embedded" originally aired on November 19, 2003.

68. The reporter in *Over There* is eventually kidnapped and beheaded by jihadists, which was the same fate that had befallen *Wall Street Journal* reporter Daniel Pearl in Pakistan in 2002. The story of his kidnapping and its aftermath is told in the movie *A Mighty Heart* (2007), with Pearl played by Dan Futterman and Pearl's wife and fellow journalist, Mariane, played by Angelina Jolie.

69. Anthony Lappé and Dan Goldman, *Shooting War* (New York: Grand Central, 2007), 129–31, 136, 187. In the book the president who decides not to run for reelection is John McCain. In reality, of course, McCain lost the 2008 presidential election to Barack Obama.

70. "Evan Wright on *Generation Kill,*" c. 2008, http://www.youtube.com/watch?v=WnadK7ye5sg.

71. Ibid. See also Evan Wright, *Generation Kill: Devil Dogs, Iceman, Captain America, and the New Face of American War* (New York: G. P. Putnam's Sons, 2004).

72. Chris Hedges, Foreword to Feinstein, *Journalists Under Fire,* ix. A Peabody

Award–winning video documentary, *Under Fire: Journalists in Combat* (2011), is based on Feinstein's book and describes the toll that war takes on journalists.

73. For more on war photographers, see chapter 5.

74. Anna Blundy, *Vodka Neat* (New York: Thomas Dunne/St. Martin's Minotaur, 2008), front jacket, 13, 65–66. *Vodka Neat* also has been published under the title *Neat Vodka*. Author Anna Blundy is a British journalist, and her father, David Blundy, was a war correspondent who was killed in 1989 by a sniper in El Salvador.

75. Kira Salak, *The White Mary* (New York: Henry Holt, 2008), 71. Salak is another journalist who has visited war zones as part of her work.

76. The novel reveals that Lewis was tortured by Indonesian soldiers during the war in East Timor. The Australian film *Balibo* (2009) tells of five Australian reporters whom the film indicates were killed by Indonesian soldiers during the same conflict. See McNair, "Journalists at War," 493–94.

77. Salak, *White Mary*, 330–31, 347; emphasis in original.

78. Tumber, "Covering War and Peace," 386.

79. Susan L. Carruthers, *The Media at War*, 2nd ed. (New York: Palgrave Macmillan, 2011), 253.

80. Cozma and Hamilton, "Film Portrayals of Foreign Correspondents," 499.

81. Knightley, *First Casualty*, vii.

82. Carruthers, *Media at War*, 9.

83. Lilie Chouliaraki, "Journalism and the Visual Politics of War and Conflict," in Allan, *Routledge Companion to News and Journalism*, 527.

84. Hamilton, *Journalism's Roving Eye*, 460; emphasis in original.

85. Anna Blundy, *The Bad News Bible* (2004; reprint, New York: Felony and Mayhem Press, 2008), 32.

86. Howard Tumber, "Prisoners of News Values?: Journalism, Professionalism, and Identification in Times of War," in Allan and Zelizer, *Reporting War*, 201.

87. Michael S. Sweeney, *The Military and the Press: An Uneasy Truce* (Evanston, Ill.: Northwestern University Press, 2006), 221.

88. Jake Lynch, "Peace Journalism," in Allan, *Routledge Companion to News and Journalism*, 547.

89. Nicholson, *Welcome to Sarajevo*, xiv.

90. Susan Sontag, *Regarding the Pain of Others* (New York: Farrar, Straus and Giroux, 2003), 115.

Conclusion

1. Paolo Mancini, "Media Fragmentation, Party System, and Democracy," *International Journal of Press/Politics* 18.1 (2013): 43–44.

2. Bregtje van der Haak, Michael Parks, and Manuel Castells, "The Future of Journalism: Networked Journalism," *International Journal of Communication* 6 (2012): 2923, 2926, 2935.

3. Loren Ghiglione, "Does Science Fiction—Yes, Science Fiction—Suggest Futures for News?" *Daedalus* 139.2 (2010): 144, 147. Ghiglione notes that popular culture depictions of the future of journalism date back to the nineteenth century. French writers such as Émile Souvestre, Albert Robida, and Jules and Michel Verne foresaw a world with round-the-clock news (including news that readers could get for free) as well as things approximating radio, interactive television, and smartphones.

4. For more on popular culture's takes on journalism history, see chapter 1.

5. Qtd. in Tony Perez, "Cory Doctorow: Radical Presentism," *Tin House,* October 6, 2009, http://www.tinhouse.com/blog/4410/cory-doctorow-radical-presentism.html.

6. David Seed, *American Science Fiction and the Cold War: Literature and Film* (Edinburgh: Edinburgh University Press, 1999), 2.

7. Loren Ghiglione, *The American Journalist: Paradox of the Press* (Washington, D.C.: Library of Congress, 1990), 166.

8. Isaac Asimov, *Nightfall and Other Stories* (Garden City, N.Y.: Doubleday, 1969), 3. More recently Rita Skeeter has carried on the cynical columnist archetype in J. K. Rowling's Harry Potter fantasy books; for more on Skeeter, see chapter 4. More positive depictions of columnists have appeared in speculative fiction works such as 2009's *Northland: A City within a Nation* by John Barth (not the same John Barth who has won the National Book Award and other major honors).

9. Alex Aagaard, "4 Hollywood Films from the 1950s and Their Cold War Perspectives," WhatCulture!, April 19, 2013, http://whatculture.com/film/4-hollywood-sci-fi -films-from-the-1950s-and-their-cold-warc-perspectives.php/3. See also M. Keith Booker, *Monsters, Mushroom Clouds, and the Cold War: American Science Fiction and the Roots of Postmodernism, 1946–1964* (Westport, Conn.: Greenwood, 2001). Reporters in 1950s cinema confronted no shortage of scary "others" or other odd phenomena in such films as *The Day the Earth Stood Still* (1951), *The Man from Planet X* (1951), *Red Planet Mars* (1952), *Tarantula* (1955), *The Gamma People* (1956), *Godzilla, King of the Monsters!* (1956), *The Deadly Mantis* (1957), *The Land Unknown* (1957), *War of the Colossal Beast* (1958), and *Island of Lost Women* (1959). In *Francis Covers the Big Town* (1953), the "other" is a friendly talking mule who turns out to be a more conscientious and knowledgeable journalist than most of his human counterparts.

10. Reporter Tom Crane (James Hazeldine) starred in the BBC TV series *The Omega Factor* (1979).

11. Reporter Gregory McAllister is a character in Jack McDevitt's novel *Deepsix* (2001).

12. Reporter Cameron "Buck" Williams is featured in Tim LaHaye and Jerry B. Jenkins's "Left Behind" book series (1995–2007) and the associated graphic novels and TV movies. The works express a dispensationalist reading of the Bible. See *Wikipedia,* s.v. "*Left Behind,*" last modified June 28, 2014, http://en.wikipedia.org/wiki/ Left_behind.

13. Promotional copy for Don Chase's *Cindy Jones and the Secret of Craycroft* (2013), Amazon.com, www.amazon.com/Cindy-Secret-Craycroft-Adventures-ebook/dp/ B00BZZS9EI.

14. *Wikipedia*, s.v. Sarah Jane Smith," last modified May 20, 2014, http://en.wikipedia.org/wiki/Sarah_Jane_Smith; Kevin Wicks, "Interview: Toby Whithouse on Cast Changes for 'Being Human,' 'Doctor Who,'" BBCAmerica.com, February 24, 2012, http://www.bbcamerica.com/anglophenia/2012/02/interview-toby-whithouse-on-cast-changes-for-being-human-doctor-who/2. *Doctor Who* debuted in 1963 with the Smith character first appearing in 1973; *The Sarah Jane Adventures* aired from 2007 to 2011.

15. Promotional copy for James Dobson and Kurt Bruner's *Childless* (2013), Amazon.com, http://www.amazon.com/Childless-Novel-James-Dobson/dp/1455513156.

16. Promotional copy for Laura Knots's *Brandi Bloom Galactic Reporter Enslaved* (2013), Amazon.com, http://www.amazon.com/Brandi-Galactic-Reporter-Enslaved-ebook/dp/B00CXAE39Y.

17. Ghiglione, *American Journalist,* 168.

18. For example, Bradbury's story "The Veldt" (1950) depicts petulant children harnessing television's magic to conjure up lions that eat their parents, and Dick's novel *The Penultimate Truth* (1964) portrays a dystopian world kept in submission by fraudulent TV news coverage.

19. In the original *RoboCop* movie from 1987, TV anchors Mario Machado and Leeza Gibbons poke fun at their profession by playing the fake anchor team of "Casey Wong" and "Jesse Perkins." A more positive depiction of the TV journalist appeared in the series *V* (1984–85), with reporter-videographer Mike Donovan (Marc Singer) investigating an alien takeover of Earth. The series added credibility to the futuristic premise with actual TV journalists Howard K. Smith and Clete Roberts. Before that, *War of the Colossal Beast* (1958) had featured the real TV reporter Stan Chambers, and *The Day the Earth Stood Still* (1951) had included the journalist Drew Pearson, famous both for his newspaper column and his radio program.

20. Kage Baker, "Welcome to Olympus, Mr. Hearst," in *Gods and Pawns: Stories of The Company* (New York: Tom Doherty Associates, 2007), 250, 291. Hearst also appears in Baker's novel *The Sons of Heaven* (2007).

21. Dan Abnett, *Embedded* (Nottingham, England: Angry Robot, 2011), 11. Embedment of a different kind occurs in Leroy Smith's aptly named tale *Constant Jay: Embedded Reporter in Hell* (2012), in which a journalist discovers firsthand that Satan is a glutton for media attention.

22. See Ghiglione, "Does Science Fiction," 141–42.

23. "The Blood from the Stones," *Bones*, originally aired March 25, 2013.

24. See "Film-maker Demonstrates Bionic Eye," BBC News, September 19, 2011, http://www.bbc.co.uk/news/health-14915281. See also Van der Haak, Parks, and Castells, "Future of Journalism," 2932. John Varley's novel *Steel Beach* (1992) had anticipated the use of such a device; it depicts reporter Hildy Johnson (the name borrowed from that of the protagonist of *The Front Page*) producing moving images from an eye "holocam." Even before that, D. G. Compton's novel *The Continuous Katherine Mortenhoe* (1974) and the 1980 movie based on Compton's book (*Death Watch*) had featured a miniature camera implanted into a reporter's brain. See Ghiglione, "Does Science Fiction," 144–45; Ghiglione, *American Journalist,* 168.

25. See, for example, Professional Society of Drone Journalists, http://www.drone journalism.org; Drone Journalism Lab, http://www.dronejournalismlab.org; and *Wikipedia,* s.v. "Drone Journalism," last modified June 23, 2014, http://en.wikipedia.org/wiki/Drone_journalism.

26. See Van der Haak, Parks, and Castells, "Future of Journalism," 2929–30.

27. See, for example, Narrative Science, http://narrativescience.com; Steven Levy, "Can an Algorithm Write a Better News Story Than a Human Reporter?" *Wired,* April 24, 2012, http://www.wired.com/gadgetlab/2012/04/can-an-algorithm-write-a-better -news-story-than-a-human-reporter.

28. Van der Haak, Parks, and Castells, "Future of Journalism," 2923.

29. See *Wikipedia,* s.v. "Metallo," last modified June 1, 2014, http://en.wikipedia.org/wiki/Metallo.

30. For example, in the film *Futureworld* (1976) reporters investigating a robot-run theme park are horrified to be confronted by automaton clones of themselves, and in the TV movie *Annihilator* (1986) a reporter is replaced by a killer android.

31. For example, in Barbara Paul's short story "Who What When Where Why" (1991), a reporter uses a male simulacrum (i.e., a robot replica of a person) and a female simulacrum to help her conduct her more dangerous investigations. All goes well until the female simulacrum is found dead and the male is charged with her murder.

32. See Ghiglione, *American Journalist,* 168–70; Ghiglione, "Does Science Fiction," 143. Not all journalist-robots have been evil. The animated children's series *Cyberchase* (which debuted in 2002) features robotic reporter Sam Vander Rom (voiced by network TV weather reporter Al Roker). The *Transformers* comics and toys franchise include beneficent "autobots" Raindance and Grand Slam, who create an audio and video record of the many battles they have experienced. One of the incarnations of Isaac Asimov's robot character R. Daneel Olivaw ("R" for "Robot") appears as reporter Chetter Hummin in Asimov's novel *Prelude to Foundation* (1988).

33. Van der Haak, Parks, and Castells, "Future of Journalism," 2929.

34. See, for example, Jay Rosen, "The Twisted Psychology of Bloggers vs. Journalists: My Talk at South by Southwest," *PressThink,* March 12, 2011, http://pressthink.org/2011/03/the-psychology-of-bloggers-vs-journalists-my-talk-at-south-by-southwest. The distinction between bloggers and journalists often remains relevant in terms of who qualifies for state "shield" protection when courts seek information concerning confidential sources; see, for example, Nicole Lozare, "Bloggers Fight for Status as Journalists," *News Media and the Law* (Spring 2013): 6–8. Popular culture has addressed that controversy in the "Whitten v. Fenlee" episode of the TV series *The Defenders* (aired November 17, 2010). A blogger who reveals the secret behind an illusionist's trick claims journalistic privilege when a court orders him to reveal his sources. The court says that as a blogger he has no such protection.

35. Ghiglione, *American Journalist,* 170–71.

36. A trio of hacker-journalists also appear in the *X-Files* TV series (1993–2002) and one of its spinoff series *The Lone Gunmen* (2001). The three men publish *The*

Lone Gunman newsletter and dedicate their hacking skills to uncovering government conspiracies.

37. For more on the film *State of Play,* see chapter 2.

38. "Agent of Change," *Enlightened,* originally aired March 3, 2013.

39. "But You Don't Do That Anymore," *Damages,* originally aired September 12, 2012. See also "Exclusive Interview: Ryan Phillippe," DirectTV.com, May 7, 2012, http://news.directv.com/2012/05/07/exclusive-interview-ryan-phillippe. The 2013 movie *The Fifth Estate* focuses directly on Assange (played by Benedict Cumberbatch) and WikiLeaks. The film presents a cautionary tale, depicting the good accomplished by WikiLeaks's exposés (published in cooperation with established newspapers such as *The Guardian* and the *New York Times*) while also suggesting that Assange is reckless.

40. In the "Stealing Secrets" episode of *King & Maxwell* (aired July 15, 2013), a tabloid gossip blogger dealing in politics hides under the pen name "Madame Beltway" to protect herself. She turns out to be journalist Angela Miller (Stephanie Bennett), who is killed before revealing her source.

41. "Chapter 5," *House of Cards,* released February 1, 2013. For more on the U.S. version of *House of Cards,* see chapter 4.

42. Promotional copy for Gwendolyn Zepeda's *Lone Star Legend* (2010), Gwendolyn Zepeda.com, http://gwendolynzepeda.com/books.

43. Margaret Wheeler Johnson, "Jessica Grose, 'Sad Desk Salad' Author, Talks Blogging, Scandal and 'Work MuuMuus,'" *Huffington Post,* October 5, 2012, http://www.huffingtonpost.com/2012/10/02/jessica-grose-sad-desk-salad_n_1932519.html.

44. Qtd. in Rosen, "Twisted Psychology of Bloggers vs. Journalists."

45. "The Inside Man," *NCIS,* originally aired October 6, 2009.

46. Nick Laird, *Glover's Mistake* (New York: Viking, 2009), 29, 81, 239; emphasis in original.

47. A caustic food critic is kidnapped by the chef he has criticized in the film *Bitter Feast* (2010). A happier depiction of an online food expert appears in the movie *Julie & Julia* (2009), starring Meryl Streep and Amy Adams. The film is based upon the blog and subsequent book of Julie Powell, who documented her attempts to cook every recipe in Julia Child's cookbook.

48. A Washington, D.C., sex blog is the focus of Jessica Cutler's novel *The Washingtonienne.* Cutler based the novel on her own experiences as a Capitol Hill aide whose pseudonymous blog triggered a scandal. See Jessica Cutler, *The Washingtonienne* (New York: Hyperion, 2005).

49. The finale of the TV show reveals that "Gossip Girl" is actually male and that he launched the blog to help him feel that he belonged in elite circles. See "New York, I Love You XOXO," *Gossip Girl,* originally aired December 17, 2012.

50. "Queen of Snark," *Harry's Law,* originally aired October 12, 2011.

51. See, for example, Lizette Alvarez, "Girl's Suicide Points to Rise in Apps Used by Cyberbullies," *New York Times,* September 13, 2013, http://www.nytimes.com/2013/09/14/us/suicide-of-girl-after-bullying-raises-worries-on-web-sites.html.

52. Seth Schiesel, "Supreme Court Has Ruled; Now Games Have a Duty," *New York Times,* June 28, 2011, http://www.nytimes.com/2011/06/29/arts/video-games/what-supreme-court-ruling-on-video-games-means.html.

53. See "Scarlet Lake," GiantBomb.com, http://www.giantbomb.com/scarlet-lake/3005–15567.

54. "Terror Is Reality," GiantBomb.com, http://www.giantbomb.com/terror-is-reality/3015-6138/. See also Jake Gaskill, "Heroes at the Push of a Button: The Image of the Photojournalist in Videogames," *Image of the Journalist in Popular Culture,* n.d., http://ijpc.org/uploads/files/IJPC%20Student%20Journal%20-%20Jake%20Gaskill.pdf; "Dead Rising 2," GiantBomb.com, http://www.giantbomb.com/dead-rising-2/3030-25187/.

55. Journalists in fact have been characters in a wide range of video games, some violent and some not. Examples include the long-running *Castlevania* series that debuted in 1986; *The Colonel's Bequest* (1989) and *The Dagger of Amon Ra* (1992), both starring aspiring journalist Laura Bow; *Who Killed Taylor French?* (1994); *Full Throttle* (1995); *Ripper* (1996); *Grim Fandango* (1998); *Broken Sword* (1996) and *Broken Sword II* (1997); *Donald Duck Goin' Quackers* (2000); *Eternal Darkness: Sanity's Requiem* (2002); *Beyond Good & Evil* (2003); *Resident Evil: Outbreak* (2003) and *Resident Evil: Outbreak—File #2* (2004); the *Uncharted* games with journalist Elena Fisher (2007–11); and multiple *Spider-Man* video games featuring photojournalist Peter Parker.

56. Sisi Wei, "Creating Games for Journalism," *ProPublica Nerd Blog,* July 11, 2013, http://www.propublica.org/nerds/item/creating-games-for-journalism. See also Ian Bogost, Simon Ferrari, and Bobby Schweizer, *Newsgames: Journalism at Play* (Cambridge: MIT Press, 2010). A similarly educational computer game is *Global Conflicts: Palestine* (2007), which was developed by Serious Games Interactive and invites players to assume the role of a journalist covering the Israeli-Palestinian conflict.

57. See, for example, Mark Glaser, "Reuters Closes Second Life Bureau, but (Virtual) Life Goes On," PBS.org, February 19, 2009, http://www.pbs.org/mediashift/2009/02/reuters-closes-second-life-bureau-but-virtual-life-goes-on050.

58. "About," *Alphaville Herald,* http://alphavilleherald.com/about. See also *Second Life,* http://secondlife.com.

59. Bonnie Brennen and Erika dela Cerna, "Journalism in Second Life," *Journalism Studies* 11.4 (2010): 553.

60. Promotional copy for *Imagine: Reporter* (2010), Amazon.com, www.amazon.com/Imagine-Reporter-Nintendo-DS/dp/B002SMVMSC. The earlier computer game *Curious George Reads, Writes, and Spells* (2000) starred Curious George as a newspaper reporter and was aimed at teaching children basic skills.

61. "Rebecca Chang," GiantBomb.com, http://www.giantbomb.com/rebecca-chang/3005-16693. To a degree, Chang also can be seen as reproducing the stereotypes of sexualized Asian women; see, for example, the discussion of the film *The Year of the Dragon* in chapter 3.

62. Gaskill, "Heroes at the Push of a Button," 25.

63. For one example of a study that links the research area of journalistic "paradigm repair" to a 1958 Israeli play about the press (*Zrok oto la-klavim*, or *Throw Him to the Dogs*), see Oren Meyers, "Expanding the Scope of Paradigmatic Research in Journalism Studies: The Case of Early Mainstream Israeli Journalism and Its Discontents," *Journalism* 12.3 (2011): 261–78. See also chapter 3's discussion of popular culture depictions of female journalists in India.

64. See, for example, Thomas Hanitzsch, "Comparative Journalism Studies," in *The Handbook of Journalism Studies*, edited by Karin Wahl-Jorgensen and Thomas Hanitzsch (New York: Routledge, 2009), 413–27; Herman Wasserman and Arnold S. de Beer, "Towards De-Westernizing Journalism Studies," in Wahl-Jorgensen and Hanitzsch, *Handbook of Journalism Studies*, 428–38; Rodney Benson, "Comparative News Media Systems: New Directions in Research," in *The Routledge Companion to News and Journalism*, edited by Stuart Allan (London: Routledge, 2010), 614–26.

65. For overviews of cultivation research as it relates to the effects of exposure to television, see George Gerbner, Larry Gross, Michael Morgan, and Nancy Signorielli, "Living with Television: The Dynamics of the Cultivation Process," in *Perspectives on Media Effects*, edited by Jennings Bryant and Dolf Zillmann (Hillsdale, N.J.: Lawrence Erlbaum Associates, 1986), 17–40; Michael Morgan and James Shanahan, "The State of Cultivation," *Journal of Broadcasting and Electronic Media* 54.2 (2010): 337–55.

66. See, for example, Ghiglione, *American Journalist*, 8–9.

67. For one example of a study that links popular culture framing of journalists to perceptions of journalistic credibility among the young, see Daxton R. Stewart, "Harry Potter and the Exploitative Jackals: Media Framing and Credibility Attitudes in Young Readers," *IJPC Journal* 2 (2010): 1–33, http://ijpc.uscannenberg.org/journal/index.php/ijpcjournal/article/view/18/26.

68. James W. Carey, "Editor's Introduction: Taking Culture Seriously," in *Media, Myths, and Narratives: Television and the Press*, edited by James W. Carey (Newbury Park, Calif.: Sage, 1988), 16.

69. See, for example, Dave Stafford, "Professor Outlines How Technology Is Changing the Practice of Law," Indiana Lawyer.com, September 11, 2013, http://www.theindianalawyer.com/professor-outlines-how-technology-is-changing-the-practice-of-law/PARAMS/article/32320.

70. See, for example, Pauline Chen, "The Gulf between Doctors and Nurse Practitioners," *New York Times*, June 27, 2013, http://well.blogs.nytimes.com/2013/06/27/the-gulf-between-doctors-and-nurse-practitioners.

71. Qtd. in Ethan Bronner, "Law School Applications Fall as Costs Rise and Jobs Are Cut," *New York Times*, January 30, 2013, http://www.nytimes.com/2013/01/31/education/law-schools-applications-fall-as-costs-rise-and-jobs-are-cut.html. See also Pauline W. Chen, "Should Medical School Last Just 3 Years?" *New York Times*, October 24, 2013, http://well.blogs.nytimes.com/2013/10/24/should-medical-school-last-just-3-years.

72. Michael Schudson, "The Trouble with Experts—and Why Democracies Need Them," *Theory and Society* 35 (2006): 493.

73. See, for example, Joseph Turow, *Playing Doctor: Television, Storytelling, and Medical Power* (New York: Oxford University Press, 1989); Michael Asimow, "Bad Lawyers in the Movies," *Nova Law Review* 24.2 (2000): 531–91.

74. John J. Pauly, "The Professional Communicator as a Symbolic Figure," *American Journalism* 2.1 (1985): 89.

75. Ibid., 79.

76. See Matthew C. Ehrlich, *Journalism in the Movies* (Urbana: University of Illinois Press, 2004), 166–82.

77. Roger Ebert, "*State of Play*," RogerEbert.com, April 15, 2009, http://www.roger ebert.com/reviews/state-of-play-2009.

78. Ben Hecht and Charles MacArthur, *The Front Page* (New York: Covici-Friede, 1928), 178–80.

Index

Note: Page numbers in *italics* indicate illustrations

MATTHEW C. EHRLICH is a professor of journalism at the University of Illinois at Urbana-Champaign and the author of *Journalism in the Movies*.

JOE SALTZMAN directs the Image of the Journalist in Popular Culture, a project of the Norman Lear Center at the Annenberg School for Communication and Journalism at the University of Southern California. He is a professor at USC Annenberg and author of *Frank Capra and the Image of the Journalist in American Film*.

DATE DUE